Integrated Library Systems

Integrated Library Systems: Planning, Selecting, and Implementing

Desiree Webber and Andrew Peters

LIBRARIES UNLIMITED

AN IMPRINT OF ABC-CLIO, LLC
Santa Barbara, California • Denver, Colorado • Oxford, England

Library of Congress Cataloging-in-Publication Data

Webber, Desiree, 1956-
  Integrated library systems : planning, selecting, and implementing /
Desiree Webber and Andrew Peters.
      p. cm.
    Includes bibliographical references and index.
    ISBN 978-1-59158-897-9 (acid-free paper) — ISBN 978-1-59884-734-5 (ebook)
  1. Integrated library systems (Computer systems) I. Peters, Andrew, 1951- II. Title.
    Z678.93.I57W43 2010
    025.00285—dc22   2010014410

ISBN: 978-1-59158-897-9
EISBN: 978-1-59884-734-5

14 13 12 11 10   1 2 3 4 5

This book is also available on the World Wide Web as an eBook.
Visit http://www.abc-clio.com for details.

Libraries Unlimited
An Imprint of ABC-CLIO, LLC

ABC-CLIO, LLC
130 Cremona Drive, P.O. Box 1911
Santa Barbara, California 93116-1911

This book is printed on acid-free paper ∞

Manufactured in the United States of America

To all the individuals, organizations, and government entities who support libraries so that every individual has the opportunity to enjoy and benefit from libraries.
I want to especially thank the following people for making a difference:
Carolyn Klepper, Vicki Mohr, Sandra Keig, and David Cockrell.—dlw

Contents

Introduction

Selecting an integrated library system is the most important and crucial purchase one can make for the library. The integrated library system (ILS) affects every aspect of the library's daily operations—from circulation and cataloging to the library's ability to deliver resources and services via its Web site and public-access catalog.

When you are responsible for recommending or approving the expenditure of the institution's funds, it becomes necessary for you to learn about ILS software, hardware, and its impact on staff and network resources. This book will help you gain an overall knowledge about selecting and implementing ILSs whether or not you purchase and install the software and hardware yourself or hire an outside consultant to assist with the project.

Integrated Library Systems: Planning, Selecting, and Implementing walks the reader through the process from start to finish. The first chapter begins with an explanation of the types of ILSs available: turnkey, stand-alone, hosted, software-as-a-service/cloud computing, and open-source. Chapter 1 also covers how to evaluate your facility and use a cost-benefit analysis for the different types of integrated library systems. This will assist the reader in analyzing the best choice for his or her institution. Chapter 2 discusses researching and evaluating ILS software and includes a comparison of features grid for modules and services offered by vendors. Chapter 3 covers the basics of the hardware needed for both the ILS and peripheral devices. This discussion also covers backup options and network security. Chapter 4 provides information about add-on modules such as acquisitions and serials, plus third-party products such as RFID (radio-frequency identification), print management, computer reservation software, and e-commerce.

The authors of *Integrated Library Systems: Planning, Selecting, and Implementing* have many years of hands-on experience with automation systems. This book covers the process of working with sales consultants in Chapter 5 and has sections about the seven stages of this relationship: Introduction, Questions and Answers, Demonstration of ILS, the Request for Proposal Process, the Contract, the Invoice, and After the Sale.

Chapter 5 provides helpful insights into the demonstration process and includes a product demonstration form for staff to use.

Project planning is covered in Chapter 6. A quick-scan timeline illustrates the implementation of the ILS from start to finish. There is also a detailed implementation time line providing explanations for each step.

"Planning Creates Success" is the title of Chapter 7; the focus is on writing a strategic plan that will bring stakeholders/administration on board for purchasing an integrated library system. Chapter 7 also covers the technology plan that details all the necessary software, hardware, other equipment, and costs for the installation of the ILS. Chapter 8 discusses constructing the budget and writing a justification statement. A vendor price-comparison grid is included in Chapter 8 to assist the reader in comparing price quotes from vendors on a product-by-product and service-by-service basis. The justification statement is a necessary component of the budget. It explains the facts behind the budget numbers to those who are not familiar with the benefits of an ILS and how it can improve services in your institution. The justification statement is written for the benefit of the board or the administration that approves the budget. A sample justification statement is included in Chapter 8.

Chapter 9 provides detailed insights into constructing a request for proposal that will best serve your institution and create the basis for the contract with the vendor. Chapter 9 also provides a sample RFP evaluation tool and gives important coverage to the contract process.

Chapter 10 discusses the installation of the ILS, from network considerations to retrospective conversion to implementation meetings with staff to "going live" and ending with information regarding the final payment to the vendor. The appendices include an ILS vendors and features comparison grid, a sample strategic plan, a sample technology plan, and a sample request for proposal.

Integrated Library Systems: Planning, Selecting, and Implementing helps librarians and system administrators who do not have the time and expertise to know all the steps involved with purchasing an ILS. This book strives to make the reader knowledgeable and successful in his/her endeavors.

The authors of this book have many years of direct, hands-on experience in researching, planning, implementing, and installing integrated library systems in public library settings. The information herein may be utilized by all types of libraries. It is the intention and aspiration of the authors that this manual provides solid instruction in guiding librarians through this process.

1 Getting Started

- Researching Integrated Library Systems
- Types of Integrated Library Systems
- Open-Source ILS Software
- Evaluating Library Facility and Staffing
- Cost-Benefit Analysis Worksheet

Reading through the chapters of this book will give readers an overall scope of planning, selecting, and implementing an integrated library system, from the first steps through the last. This book is designed for librarians or information-technology staff members who find themselves involved with migrating to or purchasing for the first time an integrated library system (ILS). Selecting an ILS is a major undertaking whether you are affiliated with a small, medium, or large library system. It is all relative. No matter whether your library is small or large, or what type of library you are with, purchasing an ILS is a substantial investment of an institution's funds and staff time.

"Any savvy consumer knows the importance of researching major purchases before investing. This is doubly important when you are dealing with your institution's somewhat larger budget and recommending and approving the purchase of software, products and services on which your staff and users must rely. . . ." (Gordon, Rachel Singer. *The Accidental Systems Librarian*, 2002, p. 96). When you are the one responsible for recommending or approving the expenditure of the institution's funds, it becomes necessary for you to learn about the ILS software and hardware along with the impact on staff and network resources.

Educating yourself about ILSs will enable you to understand and speak the jargon when you interact with vendor representatives, speak with IT staff, read the literature, or confer with colleagues. You must be able to think, speak, and interpret information about ILSs in order to intelligently assess your facility against what is available in the ILS arena.

This first chapter will discuss the types of integrated library systems available—the software/hardware architecture platforms—along with evaluating your institution so that you can determine the best type of system for your requirements and budget.

1

The first terms to discuss are "integrated library system" and "automation system." You will read both terms in the literature and when speaking with vendor representatives.

The two phrases are interchangeable and mean the same thing. An automation system and integrated library system (ILS) are terms used to describe the software that operates the circulation, cataloging, public-access catalog, reports, and other modules that do the work of typical library operations. When libraries moved from a card-based system (card catalog, shelf list, etc.), staff would state that they had "automated" their circulation and catalog processes, hence the term "automation system." Their books had bar codes instead of book pockets with book cards, and their customers searched for materials using a computer screen and keyboard instead of perusing polished wooden drawers full of three-by-five catalog cards.

Over time, more and more functions of the library are being automated, and the software is continually improving. Libraries currently have automation systems that manage their serials, track and process their interlibrary loan requests, acquire materials from vendors, and provide patron authentication for remote access to the electronic databases on their Web sites. Most vendors use the term "integrated media library system" instead of "automation system." The former better describes that the computerized functions or modules are interconnected and dependent on one another. For example, staff can use the circulation module to search the catalog, add items to a bibliographic record, and even catalog materials "on the fly." Another example is the electronic databases to which many libraries subscribe and make available on their Web sites. Remote access to a library's online databases uses the patron database within the ILS software to "authenticate" that the person is a library customer before allowing entry into the database.

Every library needs an integrated library system. The software utilizes the patron and bibliographic records to perform a host of efficient functions due to the processing speed and power of computers. Just as an automobile depends on an engine to engage the axle and turn the wheels in order to drive, a library needs an integrated library system to move forward in its daily operations. And, just as there are different types of car engines—gas, diesel, and electric—there are different types of ILSs.

It is important to find the system that will fit both the institution's needs and its budget. So the first steps are (1) to educate oneself about the field of integrated library systems, and (2) to evaluate the needs of your facility. These steps are necessary whether you are purchasing an integrated library system for the first time or migrating to another system. Researching information about integrated library systems and evaluating your facility is a two-pronged approach toward selecting the best ILS for your library.

There are differing opinions as to which step to take first: evaluating the library's collection, staffing, customer base, technology needs, access to technical support, and budget, or researching integrated library systems and what is available. Those who follow trends in technology and the ever-changing field of integrated library systems will be able to assess their institution and write a request for proposal (RFP), view demonstrations, and make a purchasing decision. Those who are new to selecting and implementing an ILS, or have not delved into this area for several years, will want to first research what is available.

Researching Integrated Library Systems

Dania Bilal writes in her book *Automating Media Centers and Small Libraries*, "Staff who engage in an automation project must possess adequate knowledge about a wide range of topics including evaluating, selecting and implementing an automated system. . . . Learning about automation is vital for the success of the automation project" (Bilal, Dania. *Automating Media Centers and Small Libraries*, 2002, pp. 9, 10).

Even if you were involved with the installation of the library's current automation system and are migrating to a new integrated library system, it is important to learn what has changed in the industry since the library last acquired its ILS. For example, does one stay with the traditional hardware-based system with an on-site server or does one select an Internet-based model in which the software is located on an off-site server? Which system(s) will best serve your customers? Which system offers the best cost-effective decision for your institution? Which companies are financially stable but are also researching technological innovations for the future?

Some might contend that it is necessary only to evaluate the needs and requirements of the library before writing an RFP to purchase an integrated library system. After the RFP is issued, vendors selling integrated library systems will respond to the RFP and demonstrate their product to staff. However, it is hard to write an effective RFP if one is not aware of the types of systems available (turnkey, software-as-a-service, hosted, and/or open-source) along with the array of modules, features, and services from which to choose. Unless you closely monitor the ILS software industry, it is difficult to just simply evaluate your library, write the RFP, and then view demonstrations. A lot of valuable staff time will be mishandled if the process is not narrowed by first researching the types of systems and companies that will best serve the facility. Why spend valuable and limited time sitting through demonstrations of integrated library systems that do not provide the features you need, will not work well for your staff or customers, and are beyond your budgetary constraints?

The field of library automation is rapidly evolving and increasingly complex due to technological innovations in software, delivery of services, mergers, and competition. Marshall Breeding, Director for Innovative Technologies and Research for the Jean and Alexander Heard Library at Vanderbilt University, writes extensively on integrated library systems and future trends in this arena. Each April, Breeding covers the automation marketplace in *Library Journal*. This annual coverage discusses industry trends along with company profiles and contact information. Sometimes the company profiles will discuss whether its customer base is public, school, academic, or special and whether or not its focus is on small- to medium-sized libraries or large libraries. *Computers in Libraries* provides an annual Buyer's Guide in its July/August issue that covers library automation with company listings, product reviews, and company contact information.

Directory of Library Automation Software, Systems, and Services, edited and compiled by Pamela R. Cibbarelli, also lists vendors, automation consultants, a bibliography of books and serials, and related products and services such as retrospective conversion. A helpful feature of this directory is the details it provides for each integrated library system:

● Gives hardware requirements for servers and clients along with the operating systems and recommended Web browsers.

● Lists what modules and applications are available (circulation, cataloging, online public-access catalog [OPAC], Z39.50, acquisitions, serials, etc.).

● Gives details on MARC formats and interfaces, such as whether or not the software can import or export full MARC, has a graphical user interface for the OPAC, etc.

● States the type of libraries for which the ILS is recommended: corporate and government, public, school, and university libraries.

● Provides initial installation date, total number of installed sites, and a sampling of current customers.

- Lists system and component prices (along with the caveat that prices are subject to change).
- Supplier comments are given at the end of each description.

Directory of Library Automation Software, Systems, and Services is published every two years, so some of the information will change, but it is a solid reference tool that every library should own. You can review the ILS companies listed in the directory to gather information on vendors you may want to visit at an upcoming conference or to contact for further information.

When reviewing information about integrated library system vendors, you may note terminology about the type of software or "architecture" of the system the company delivers. The terms to be familiar with are "stand-alone," "client/server," "hosted," "software-as-a-service (SaaS)," "open-source," and "cloud computing." The system architecture describes how the ILS software works between servers and workstations and is utilized by the library. For example, client-server architecture means that the ILS software is stored on the library's on-site server and interfaces with the library's client workstations located at the circulation desk, reference desk, public-access catalog, or self-checkout stations.

Following is a list of the basic types of integrated library systems currently available at this writing. It is important to be knowledgeable about the different types of architecture available so that you can select the right system for your library and narrow the choice of vendors offering the type of system you want. It is also vital to understand that technology is never static. Vendors will blend terminologies such as "hosted" and "software-as-a-service." The following definitions will help you communicate with vendors when discussing and researching their products.

Types of Integrated Library Systems

Turnkey: A turnkey implementation refers to purchasing from a single vendor an integrated library system that includes both the software and the hardware. The server(s) may arrive preinstalled with the software or the vendor's staff will install the software on-site. In addition, the vendor will install the server(s) for the library and connect to the network. It is a hardware-based system referred to as a client-server architecture. The ILS software and the patron and bibliographic data are stored on the server and communicate via the network with the client workstations located within the library at the circulation desk, reference desk, public-access catalogs, and so forth. This option requires that the library house the server(s) on-site and manage the client workstations and network.

In a turnkey arrangement, the vendor's technical support staff can act in the capacity of a system administrator for the library, if needed. The vendor's staff can access the server(s) remotely, troubleshoot software problems, and install software upgrades. If the server fails, it is the vendor who handles the service calls to the hardware manufacturer.

One or more library staff members are trained by the vendor to perform minor duties such as ensuring that the backup of data is performed each night. Designated library staff will also provide on-site assistance for the vendor's technical support, who will occasionally need physical hands and eyes to help them. No special expertise is required of the library staff, who most likely have other responsibilities besides managing the ILS, but the staff member interfacing with technical support needs to be familiar with computers and the operating system (Windows, Mac, or Linux).

One of the benefits of turnkey systems is that small libraries are able to purchase powerful, complex integrated library systems without the necessity of having a system administrator on staff. Libraries will pay more in hardware costs when purchasing servers from the vendor, but that is the tradeoff of having the company fill the role of system administrator.

It is important to note that a network administrator is still needed to operate the network for the library (cabling, router, firewall, DMZ, switches, security, troubleshooting, etc.). If the library has Internet access for its staff and public workstations, then it has a network in place. The network administrator, whether a contact or on staff, will work with the ILS vendor in the installation of the ILS server(s) to the existing network.

Stand-alone installation: Stand-alone installations describe systems in which the hardware and software are purchased separately and the system administrator or library staff installs the client-server software him/herself. Stand-alone implementations occur in all types and sizes of libraries. At this writing, the majority of installations implemented are stand-alone and turnkey installations. Stand-alone installations can be on a single computer workstation in a very small library or on a local area network (LAN)/wide area network (WAN) in a client-server architecture.

Hardware may or may not be purchased from the vendor. The system administrator/staff member installs the ILS software onto the server(s) and/or workstation(s). The ILS vendor provides technical support when called upon, but the system administrator maintains day-to-day operations, troubleshoots problems, installs software upgrades, and may customize features to suit the library. One benefit of the stand-alone installation is that the library has an in-house expert to oversee the network, hardware, and ILS software, allowing other library staff members to focus on their primary duties. In a small library, the downside to a stand-alone installation is that the library has one person, usually the library director or media specialist, to oversee the network, hardware, and ILS software along with the myriad of other responsibilities he or she must perform. Managing a stand-along ILS requires attention to issues as varied as:

- Regular backups of patron and bibliographic data.
- Maintaining the ILS server and database.
- Creating and running reports.
- Technical support for ILS users.
- Customizing the display of the public-access catalog.
- Managing access to and setting up security for staff modules.
- Installing client software on staff workstations.
- Serving as the liaison between the library and the ILS vendor.
- Keeping current with new versions and features and coordinating any needed software upgrades.
- Testing connections between the ILS and any linked external databases.
- Setting up policies in conjunction with other library staff.
- Implementing new or additional modules.

Hosted system: In this type of integrated library system, the vendor hosts the library's ILS software, bibliographic records, patron records, and sometimes the library's Web site on its server farms. Sometimes vendors will use the term "hosted" when they mean software-as-a-service (SaaS), which is described in detail in the next section. If the vendor describes a "subscription price," then the vendor is describing SaaS. If the library purchases the software but the vendor hosts the software on its servers, then the vendor is describing a hosted system.

Hosted systems are cost-effective choices for libraries that do not want to invest in server hardware or that do not have adequate space to house a server. It can also be a good choice for libraries that want or require minimal interaction with software issues. The vendor's technical-support department troubleshoots any software problems and installs all updates at its location. A dependable, high-speed Internet connection is required so that the staff workstations and public-access catalogs can communicate with the vendor's servers.

Depending upon the ILS product, there may be client software that needs to be installed on the library's staff workstations and public-access catalogs in order to communicate with the vendor's server. This software may be installed remotely but staff interaction may be required in assisting technical support with this process. Sometimes the workstations access the ILS software simply through a Web browser, and often there is a mixture of both PC-based and Web-based modules. For example, the circulation module may be PC-based with client software loaded onto the workstations at the circulation desk, but the reports module is Web-based and is accessed by typing in a URL, such as http://www.your libraryreports.com. The latter is password-protected so only library staff can access the module.

One benefit of a hosted system is that libraries can purchase robust integrated library system software and save on the cost of purchasing a server. It also saves staff time because the vendor is responsible for troubleshooting all problems related to the software and the server hardware. The library will still have to troubleshoot, maintain, and repair any problems with the network and Internet connection (router, cabling, switches, firewall, and an Internet service provider). The downside to hosted systems is response time in conducting transactions and searches due to the Internet service provider, bandwidth, workstation hardware, or server capacity. Poor response time is frustrating for circulation staff who are checking materials in and out, and for library customers who are searching for materials on the online catalog. Check with other libraries that have purchased hosted systems. (This is covered at the end of Chapter 2.)

It is important to clarify in the vendor contract whether or not the hosting service involves a dedicated server or a virtual server. There should be details stating that the applications will work during peak utilization times as this affects the speed and dependability in the delivery of software and data (Breeding, Marshall. "The Advance of Computing From the Ground to the Cloud." *Computers in Libraries*, November/December 2009, p. 23).

Other considerations include the security of the library's data, how the ILS software and library's data is stored on the vendor's servers, and who owns the library's data. If the library migrates to another system in the future, will it retain ownership of its data?

Software-as-a-service (SaaS): SaaS refers to a subscription service for Web-based software. Unlike a hosted system, the library does not purchase the ILS software. Instead, it pays an initial fee for the ILS software along with an annual or monthly subscription fee to the vendor. The vendor uses the Internet to deliver software functionality instead of installing software on the library's hardware. Staff access the modules—circulation, reports, cataloging, and the like—via a Web browser. The bibliographic and patron data are stored on the vendor's servers.

A specialized form of SaaS is "cloud computing." (Many times, the two terms are used interchangeably.) Technically, cloud computing refers to the way the vendor structures services. In a SaaS environment, the vendor installs a separate instance of the software for each library subscriber. In a cloud-computing environment, the vendor runs a single instance of the software for all libraries and manages the separation of all the data by configuration within the software itself. As of this writing, the Online Computer

Library Center (OCLC) is testing this architecture with several libraries. It is a form that may be very competitive and appealing in the future because the vendor may be able to offer services much less expensively and with greater ease of operation while also offering the advantages of sharing information among libraries and library consortia. Marshall Breeding writes, "The days of client/server systems are waning. We're now in an age of web-based cloud computing" (Breeding, Marshall. "Moving Forward Through Tech Cycles." *Computers in Libraries*, May 2009, p. 20).

Some SaaS vendors provide a Web site for the library, and some offer to host the library's Web site for a fee. The vendor performs all software upgrades and maintenance duties at its site. The vendor also has responsibility for the security of the library's data, including sufficient backups. Bandwidth can be the biggest concern for the libraries choosing SaaS or cloud-based integrated library systems. The cost of increased bandwidth should be considered in figuring the total cost of these systems in comparison with other architectures. Some vendors state that they are utilizing or will utilize browser-based technology, remote desktop, and thin clients to minimize the amount of bandwidth needed to operate their systems. In any case, libraries must possess sufficient bandwidth for fast and effective transactions during peak times of usage.

One of the benefits of SaaS is the ability to purchase ILS software and save on the cost of purchasing and maintaining a server, not to mention the savings in staff time dedicated to troubleshooting server and software issues. Points to consider when working with a vendor offering SaaS/cloud computing: (1) Does the library have the ability to migrate to another system in the future? (2) Does the library own the data and have the ability to retrieve its data at no charge? One should also the weigh the annual subscription fees of a SaaS system against a system in which one purchases the software up front and pays annual licensing and technical support fees.

Open-source software systems: Open-source software (OSS) is software in which a program's source code is available for individuals to use, copy, modify, and redistribute. This is opposed to closed software in which the program's source code is not publicly available. Most integrated library system software is closed. Examples of well-known open-source software are the Firefox Web browser, Linux operating system, Koha, and Evergreen integrated library systems.

Open-Source ILS Software

Open-source ILS software is software that has either been developed by communities of libraries, such as Evergreen, or is a product in which its source code can be accessed and adapted by others. In all instances, the open-source ILS software is free for libraries to download, use, and modify. OPALS is an example of an OSS in which the library does not pay for the software but pays an annual subscription fee to use it.

Open-source software is available in the architectures listed before under "Types of Integrated Library Systems;" that is, stand-alone, hosted, and software-as-a-service. Some of the more well-known OSS integrated library systems are Koha, Evergreen, and OPALS (Open-Source Automated Library System). If you go to Evergreen's Web site at http://www.evergreen-ils.org, there is a link to download the ILS software for both the server and the client. If you go to the Web site for Koha at http://koha.org, there is a link to download software to the server. OPALS, at http://www.opals-na.org/, however, is an Internet-based system. There is no software to download. Instead, there is a set-up and annual subscription fee to use the software.

Open-source software is being developed specifically for research and academic libraries in the open library environment (OLE) project (http://oleproject.org). "A \$2.38 million grant from The Andrew W. Mellon Foundation to Indiana University will be used to develop software created specifically for the management of print and electronic collections for academic and research libraries around the world. IU will lead the Kuali OLE (Open Library Environment) project, a partnership of research libraries dedicated to managing increasingly digital resources and collections" (http://oleproject.org/2010/01/11/mellon-foundation-awards-2-3-million-for-ole-development). Academic library staff can visit the Web site to seek more information or to become involved in a regional design group.

Some OSS ventures have a community of users. One can join the OSS community to share modifications to the software, share information, and keep abreast of changes and new features. While open-source communities are supportive, it is vital for stand-alone systems to have staff with sufficient expertise to perform the installation and migration plus deal with ongoing troubleshooting and maintenance.

If a library wants to use OSS and does not have the knowledgeable staff to install, migrate the data, provide training, download software upgrades, and troubleshoot the ILS, then a library can contract with companies to perform these functions at a cost. The software is free, but if your library needs assistance managing the system, then you will need to contract with a commercial vendor to manage the product.

Eric Lease Morgan writes, "People often advocate open source software because it is free. While you will not pay for the source code directly, open source software is only as free as a free kitten. . . . First you buy a collar. Then you buy food and a food bowl. Next you take it to the veterinarian and they charge you a fee for shots. Alas, the kitten starts to cost money" (Morgan, Eric Lease, December 12, 2004, http://infomotions. com/musings/biblioacid/).

OSS is a growing field and one reason is that there are commercial companies that market and support ILS software. "Although in theory any library can implement an open source ILS completely on its own, the vast majority of libraries choose to work with commercial companies" (Breeding, Marshall. "The Viability of Open Source ILS." *Bulletin of the American Society for Information Science and Technology*, December 2008/January 2009, Vol. 35, No. 2, p. 21). This relationship also includes the development of features or modules by libraries paying commercial vendors for the software development ("sponsored development contract"), and then the feature or module becomes available at no charge to other libraries using the same software.

One of the benefits of open-source software is the cost savings. One is not paying for software developers because the developers are employed by libraries that share their knowledge and expertise within the library OSS community at large. On the other hand, if something goes awry, there is no one to contact unless, of course, you are paying a company to manage your OSS integrated library system. Check to see what features are available within the different modules and explore what companies sell add-ons that interface with the open-source software that you are considering. Open Source Systems for Libraries, at http://www.oss4lib.org, maintains a listing of free software and systems designed for libraries and tracks product updates.

Evaluating Library Facility and Staffing

After reading the section entitled "Types of Integrated Library Systems," the next step is to evaluate you library and determine which system(s) will work best for your facility. This evaluation process will be twofold: (1) overview of facility, staff, and collection; and (2) cost-benefit analysis.

In the overview of your facility, consider the following questions:

- Do you already manage a server and a network for the library? If so:
  ○ Is this a burden on your existing staff members?
  ○ Does an on-site technical support staff member handle the network, server, computer hardware, and existing integrated library system?
  ○ Does a contract IT company handle the network and computer repair? Is it a reliable or unreliable company?
- Is the library operating a LAN that is part of a larger network, such as a campus-wide WAN? If so, do you need to work with the WAN system administrator in selecting the type of ILS?
- What is the composition of your staff? If you were to select a turnkey system, do you have someone with the skill sets and knowledge to work with the ILS vendor's technical support staff?
- Do you have reliable, high-speed Internet access? This would be necessary to access software-as-a-service Web-based modules or to connect with the vendor's server with a hosted system.
- What is your comfort level in not having the ILS software located on your institution's server?
- What is your comfort level in not purchasing the ILS software, but instead paying a subscription fee each year or each month?
- In addition to staffing considerations in managing a turnkey or stand-alone system, would your institution realize substantial cost benefits in not having on-site servers? The cost benefits could include a savings in utility charges for not only running servers, but also cooling the room in which they are housed.
- What are the opportunities in your area to form or join a consortium with other similar-type libraries, or even multi-type (school, public, academic, and special) libraries in which the costs for a software, hardware, wide-area network, and system administration personnel are shared?
- What is the composition of your collection? Do you have serials, journals, online resources, special collections, artwork, or titles in multiple formats?
- What modules will you need and what modules can you disregard? For example, if you have a small number of serial and journal titles in the collection, you may opt not to purchase a serials module. (For more information, refer to Chapter 4.)
- Who are your customers, and what are their needs in accessing information? One of the challenges of purchasing an ILS is meeting customer demand for services. "Today patrons may wonder why, in addition to knowing that a library owns a particular item, a library system cannot suggest other titles of interest based on their previous borrowing habits and the title they are searching at the moment" (Dougherty, William C. "Integrated Library Systems: Where Are They Going? Where Are We Going?" *The Journal of Academic Librarianship*, September 2009, Vol. 35, No. 5, p. 482). Amazon provides suggested titles based on previous viewing and buying habits, but libraries struggle with privacy issues. "If the library cannot match what users have access to on the outside, users will and do move on" (Bertot, John Carlo. "Public Access Technologies in Public Libraries: Effects and Implications." *Information Technology and Libraries*. June 2009, p. 84). It is especially important to have a Web site and online public-access catalog that offers features that library customers want.

Cost Benefit Analysis Worksheet

Type of ILS	Costs	Benefits	Considerations
TURNKEY			
Domain controller server	(insert cost of server)	Manages e-mail, network printing and other software that is utilized within the library's network.	Adequate space for housing equipment. Equipment room needs to be kept cool to prevent equipment degredation. At least one designated staff member needs to manage the LAN or interface with the contract network administrator.
Data server	(insert cost of server)	Data server manages ILS software, patron and bibliographic data.	Libraries can sometimes combine the domain controller server, data server and Webserver. Speak with ILS vendors regarding recommendations.
Web server	(insert cost of server)	Web server manages the library's Web site.	At least one staff member needs to interact with ILS vendor to troubleshoot software and hardware issues.
Client hardware	(insert cost of staff workstations, public access catalogs)	Client software, such as the Circulation module, can operate if server is down.	Client software updates are managed by vendor.
ILS software	(insert cost of software)	ILS software is managed by vendor.	Vendor installs software updates and manages problems remotely.
TOTAL START-P COSTS Annual software mainte-nance and licensing.	(insert cost of software plus 3% increase per year)		

With a turnkey system, the hardware and ILS software are on-site. Libraries are able to purchase robust integrated library systems without the need of a full-time system administrator.

STAND-LONE		
Domain controller server	(insert cost of server)	Manages e-mail, network printing and other software that is utilized within the library's network.	Adequate space for housing equipment. Equipment room needs to be kept cool to prevent equipment degredation. At least one designated staff member needs to manage the LAN or interface with the contract network administrator. Depending upon the size of the institution, may need a full-time systems administrator to manage the ILS software, hardware, and network.
Data server	(insert cost of server)	Data server manages ILS software, patron, and bibliographic data.	Libraries can sometimes combine the domain controller server, data server, and Web server Speak with ILS vendors regarding recommendations.
Web server	(insert cost of server)	Web server manages the library's Web site.	
Client hardware	(insert cost of staff workstations, public access catalogs)	Client software, such as the Circulation module, can operate if server is down.	
Technology personnel	(insert salary, benefits, continuing education costs)	May need in-house technical expertise to administer the library's network, hardware and software.	Automation systems for small libraries will not require a technology person on staff. Designate a library staff member to interact with vendor on troubleshooting software issues.
ILS software	(insert cost of software)	ILS software is on-site.	
TOTAL START-P COSTS Annual software mainte-nance and licensing.	(insert cost of software plus 3% increase per year)		

Cost Benefit Analysis Worksheet (Continued)

HOSTED SYSTEM Client hardware	(insert cost of staff workstations, public access catalogs)	Client software is loaded on library's workstations. Client software communicates with ILS software on vendor's servers.	Client software updates are managed by vendor.
ILS software	(insert cost of software)	ILS software is managed by vendor.	Vendor installs software updates and manages problems remotely.
TOTAL START UP COSTS Annual software maintenance and licensing.	(insert cost of software plus 3% increase per year)		

With a hosted system, ILS vendor hosts the library's software, patron, and bibliographic data on their servers. Libraries are able to purchase robust integrated library systems without the need of a full-time system administrator.

SOFTWARE-SERVICE/ CLOUD COMPUTING Library workstations	(insert cost of staff workstations, public access catalogs)	Software is delivered via the Internet.
Software initial start-up fee.	(insert cost of initial start-up fee.)	
TOTAL START-P COSTS Software annual subscription fee.	(insert cost of annual subscription fee.)	

With SaaS, library pays subscription fee for software. ILS vendor hosts the library's patron and bibliographic data on their servers. Some vendors also host library's Web site for a fee.

After casting a critical eye over your library's operations, staffing, and collection, the next step is to consider the costs involved with each type of integrated library system. By this reading, you probably have an idea of which type of system or systems would work best for your institution now and in the future. The following cost-benefit analysis worksheet will provide assistance in inserting costs for hardware, software, and personnel. The worksheet is a template for you to plug in your own information, quotes for hardware, and personnel salary. Benefits of the software will also need to be inserted, as this will vary among libraries. What is seen as a benefit by one institution may be of no interest to another institution.

Cost-Benefit Analysis Worksheet

Update the cost-benefit analysis worksheet as you evaluate the ILS software, which is covered in the following chapter. For example, a SaaS open-source system may be less costly but it may not offer the modules that your institution needs. It is important that you select software that will benefit your facility even if it requires additional funds.

Investing in an integrated library system is a time-intensive project that requires careful inquiry, study, and critical analysis. By researching what is available, evaluating your facility, and looking at your ability to integrate future technological innovations, you will be able to select and implement a system that will grow with your library and benefit your users for many years.

References

Bertot, John Carlo. "Public Access Technologies in Public Libraries: Effects and Implications." *Information Technology and Libraries*, June 2009, p. 84.

Bilal, Dania. *Automating Media Centers and Small Libraries: A Microcomputer-Based Approach*. Second Edition. Santa Barbara, CA: Libraries Unlimited, 2002.

Breeding, Marshall. "The Advance of Computing from the Ground to the Cloud." *Computers in Libraries*, November/December 2009, p. 23.

———. "Investing in the Future." *Library Journal*, April 1, 2009, Vol. 134, Issue 6, pp. 26–39.

———. "Library Automation in a Difficult Economy." *Computers in Libraries*, March 2009, Vol. 29, Issue 3, pp. 22–24.

———. "The Viability of Open Source ILS." *Bulletin of the American Society for Information Science and Technology*, December 2008/January 2009, Vol. 35, No. 2, pp. 20–25.

Cibbarelli, Pamela R., ed. *Directory of Library Automation Software, Systems, and Services: 2006–2007*. Medford, NJ: Information Today, 2006.

Dougherty, William C., "Integrated Library Systems: Where Are They Going? Where Are We Going?" *The Journal of Academic Librarianship*, September 2009, Vol. 35, No. 5, p. 482.

Gordon, Rachel Singer. *The Accidental Systems Librarian*. Medford, NJ: Information Today, 2003.

Greenwood, Bill. "ILS Roundup." *Computers in Libraries*, July/August 2009, Vol. 29, Issue 7, pp. 50–54.

Molyneux, Robert E. "Evergreen in Context." *Bulletin of the American Society for Information Science and Technology*, December 2008/January 2009, Vol. 35, No. 2, pp. 20–25.

Morgan, Eric Lease. "Open Source Software in Libraries." http://infomotions.com/musings/biblioacid. Cited December 12, 2004.

National Institute of Technology and Standards. "NITS Definition of Cloud Computing v. 15." http://csrc.nist.gov/groups/SNS/cloud-computing/index.html. Cited October 7, 2009.

O'Brien, Lynne. "Mellon Foundation Awards $2.3 Million for OLE Development." http://oleproject.org/2010/01/11/mellon-foundation-awards-2-3-million-for-ole-development. Cited January 11, 2010.

2 Evaluating Integrated Library System Software

- Chart of ILS Vendors
- Meeting with Sales Consultants
- Product Demonstration and Evaluation of Software
- Contacting Other Libraries for Information

Once you have an understanding of the types of integrated library systems (turnkey, stand-alone, hosted, SaaS/cloud computing, and open-source) that can be implemented, the next step is to evaluate the software modules, features, applications, and add-ons available. Selecting the right software and the right vendor or open-source community is one of the most important decisions you and your organization will make for the library. "The cost of acquiring an ILS represents a huge investment. Therefore, libraries take the selection process seriously" (Wang, Zhonghong, "Integrated Library System (ILS) Challenges and Opportunities: A Survey of U.S. Academic Libraries with Migration Projects." *The Journal of Academic Librarianship*, May 2009, p. 209).

It is vital that you find software that will serve your library users now and in the future. Those patrons will utilize your institution, whether they are students, faculty, parents, children, attorneys, scientists, adults, or teens. The methods your patrons use to search for and find information will be the guiding beacon to evaluating ILS software. "While designing systems and services, the primary factor to ponder over is users—their information needs and wants" (Koneru, Indira, "Integrated Library System: Selection and Design." *DESIDOC Bulletin of Information Technology*, November/December 2005, p. 8).

To view a variety of systems in an effective, economical manner, it is recommended that you attend one of the national conferences, such as of the American Library Association (http://www.ala.org), Public Library Association (http://www.pla.org), Special Libraries Association (http://www.sla.org), Association of College and Research Libraries (http://www.acrl.org), or American Association of School Librarians (http://www.aasl.org). This will give you the best opportunity to visit a wide variety of companies in a short span of time.

The benefit of attending a national conference is having access to a broad spectrum of choices. It is well worth the investment in travel and hotel costs to view demonstrations in person and speak with many vendors or open-source communities in one location. The

American Library Association, for example, has two major conferences per year, one in January and the other in June.

At a national conference, you can spend two full days visiting the vendors who sell integrated library systems, viewing demonstrations, and speaking with sales representatives. Repeat visits over the course of the conference will be common as you learn more information and develop new questions. Sales representatives serving your geographic region will want to speak with you—and that is a good thing. Sales representatives can be an important resource.

Attending professional conferences to see integrated library systems in person and to speak to vendors or OSS communities needs to become a regular activity. Conferences give you the ability to research products and keep current with new developments. If it is just not possible to attend a national conference, other options are to invite sales representatives to your library or request a Web-based demonstration. Some ILS companies have links for webinars on their Web sites.

Following is a chart of integrated library system companies and open-source software communities.

Chart of ILS Vendors

Product Name	Company	Types of Systems	Contact Information
AGent VERSO	Auto-Graphics, Inc.	Stand-alone; hosted	3201 Temple Avenue, Suite 100 Pomona, California 91768-3279 www.auto-graphics.com 800-776-6939 toll free 909-595-3506 fax
Apollo	Biblionix	Software-as-a-Service	401 Congress Avenue Suite 1540 Austin, TX 78701 www.biblionix.com 877-800-5625 toll free 512-366-9311 fax info@biblionix.com
Atrium	Book Systems, Inc.	Stand-alone; Software-as-a-Service	4901 University Square, Suite 3 Huntsville, AL 35816 www.booksys.com 800-219-6571 toll free 800-230-4183 fax sales@booksys.com
Concourse CyberTools for Libraries	Book Systems, Inc. CyberTools, Inc.	Stand-alone Standalone or Software-as-a-Service	(see above) Blanchard House 249 Ayer Rd, Suite 302 Harvard, MA 01451 http://cybertoolsfor libraries.com 800-894-9206 toll free info@CyberToolsFor Libraries.com

(Continued)

Product Name	Company	Types of Systems	Contact Information
EOS.Web Express EOS.Web Enterprise EOS.Web Academic EOS.Web Legal EOS.Web Medical	EOS International	Stand-alone or Software-as-a-Service	2292 Faraday Avenue Carlsbad, CA 92008 www.eosintl.com 800-876-5484 toll free 760-431-8448 fax sales@eosintl.com
Evergreen	Equinox Software	Stand-alone or hosted. Provides services for Evergreen open-source software.	3050 Business Park Dr., Suite A1 Norcross, GA 30071 http://esilibrary.com 877-673-6457 866-497-6390 sales@eslibrary.com
Evergreen		Open-source software	www.evergreen-ils.org feedback@evergreen-ils.org
Aleph	Ex Libris Group	Stand-alone	1350 E. Touhy Ave, Suite 200 E Chicago, IL 60018 www.exlibrisgroup.com 800-762-6300 toll free info@exlibris-usa.com
Voyager Destiny Library Manager	Ex Libris Group Follett Software Company	Stand-alone Centrally installed or hosted	(see above) 1391 Corporate Drive McHenry, IL 60050 www.follettsoftware.com 800-323-3397 toll free 800-807-3623 fax
Millennium	Innovative Interfaces, Inc.	Turnkey; Stand-alone; Software-as-a-Service; hosted	5850 Shellmound Way Emeryville, CA 94608 www.iii.com 510-655-6200 510-450-6350 fax info@iii.com
Millennium Via for K-12 Libraries	Innovative Interfaces, Inc.	same as above	(see above)
KLAS	Keystone Systems, Inc.	Stand-alone	8016 Glenwood Avenue, Suite 200 Raleigh, NC 27612 www.klas.com 800-222-9711 toll free sales@klas.com
Koha		Open-source; stand-alone	http://koha.org

(Continued)

(Continued)

Product Name	Company	Types of Systems	Contact Information
Koha and Evergreen	ByWater Solutions, Inc.	Turnkey; stand-alone; hosted. Provides services for Koha and Evergreen open-source software	ByWater Solutions 5383 Hollister Ave Goleta, CA 93117 www.bywatersolutions.com 888-900-8944 info@bywatersolutions.com
Koha & Evergreen	PTFS (Progressive Technology Federal Systems, Inc. Acquired LibLime)	Software-as-a-Service. Provides services for Koha and Evergreen open-source software.	6400 Goldboro Road, Suite 200 Bethesda, MD 20817 301-654-8088 301-654-5789 fax info@ptfs.com www.ptfs.com
Mandarin M3	Mandarin Library Automation	Stand-alone	P.O. Box 272308 Boca Raton, FL 33427 www.mlasolutions.com 800-426-7477 toll free 561-995-4065 fax automation@mlasolutions.com
Mandarin Oasis	Mandarin Library Automation	Software-as-a-Service; hosted	(see above)
OPALS	Open-source Automated Library System	Software-as-a-Service	Media Flex P.O. Box 1107 Champlain, NY 12919 www.opals-na.org 877-331-1022 toll free 514-336-8217 fax info@mediaflex.net
Polaris	Polaris Library Systems	Turnkey; hosted	P.O. Box 4903 Syracuse, NY 13221-4903 www.polarislibrary.com 800-272-3414 toll free 315-457-5883 (fax)
Symphony	SirsiDynix	Stand-alone; hosted	400 W. Dynix Drive Provo, UT 84604 www.sirsidynix.com 800-288-8020 toll free 801-223-5202 fax sales@sirsidynix.com
Carl	TLC (The Library Corporation)	Turnkey; stand-alone; Software-as-a-Service; hosted	The Library Corporation Research Park Inwood, WV 25428-9733 800-325-7759 toll free 304-229-0295 fax info@tlcdelivers.com

(Continued)

Product Name	Company	Types of Systems	Contact Information
Library Solution	TLC (The Library Corporation)	Turnkey, stand-alone, Software-as-a-Service; hosted	(see above)
Library Solution for Schools	TLC (The Library Corporation)	Turnkey; stand-alone; Software-as-a-Service; hosted	(see above)
Virtua	VTLS	Stand-alone; Software-as-a-Service	1701 Kraft Drive Blacksburg, VA 24060 www.vtls.com 800-468-8857 540-557-1210 fax info@vtls.com

Meeting with Sales Consultants

The sales representatives for each company will ask some basic questions about your library in order to determine how to best match their products with your facility. These questions will include what type of library do you represent (academic, public, school, or special), what are your annual circulation statistics, how many titles and items are in your collection, are you currently automated, and, if so, with what company, and so forth. It is best to come prepared with information about the library along with data about the library's network, Internet access, and hardware. Following is an example of the information you should provide to the sales consultant. You can use this sample chart to document information about your own facility.

Product Demonstration and Evaluation of Software

Ask for demonstrations over the following main features and take detailed notes of functionality and costs. A sample form entitled "Integrated Library System Vendors and Features" may be found in Appendix A. Use this form to keep notes on each vendor along with the modules, add-ons, features, and services that are offered. It is a visual method to compare apples to apples. For example, Company A has support-desk hours Monday through Friday, 8:00 A.M. to 5:00 P.M. Central Standard Time, and Company B has support-desk hours Monday through Saturday, 7:00 A.M. to 9:00 P.M. Eastern Standard Time, plus emergency support after hours seven days a week, including holidays.

Record any features that will help the library operate in a more efficient and cost-effective manner. Look for modules and add-ons that can save money and staff time, such as automated e-mails or telephone notification systems that notify library users of reserved materials or overdue items. These latter features save paper, envelopes, postage, staff time, and printer cartridges. Saving money on supplies and postage, along with the reallocation of staff responsibilities to other important duties, are points to drive home when justifying the expense of purchasing an integrated library system.

The following is a list of suggested information to seek when viewing a demonstration of ILS modules and add-ons:

Information for Sales Consultant Chart

Facility Evaluation	Sample Answers	Notes
Number of borrowers.	24,000	
Annual circulation.	175,000	
Number of titles in the collection,	41,500	
Number of items in collection.	44,000	
Current automation system or Integrated Library System.	Company XYZ	
Type of Internet connection and speed.	Dedicated T-1 line. Internet service provider is funded by the state's higher education consortium.	
Any branches? If so, how many branches?	No branches	
How are branches connected to the main library and to other branches?	not applicable	
Description of community, school, and/or library users that the library serves.	City population is 17,000 but service area is around 35,000. City is a suburb of a metropolitan area. Service area is rural.	
Projected growth in customers and collection over the next five years.	Expected growth is expected to be 5% annually in borrowers and collection.	
Type of operating system platform: Windows, Macintosh, Linnux, etc. Number of employees. Number of staff workstations. Number of Public Access Catalogs (PACs)	Windows platform. Current server is four years old and operating software is Windows 2003. Workstations are Windows XP Professional with service pack 3. Nine employees Seven workstations. Four PACs	

- System Administration:
  - ✓ What type of architecture(s) does the company offer: turnkey, stand-alone, hosted, SaaS/cloud, open-source, or a hybrid of more than one type?
  - ✓ If on-site servers are needed, how many and what types of servers (data server and/or Web server) are needed to operate the system?
  - ✓ If the library has a domain-controller server to manage its network, can the ILS software be loaded on the domain-controller server, or does the ILS software need its own server(s)?
  - ✓ How is the system managed?
    - Does the library need a systems administrator to manage the ILS?
    - Does the vendor provide hosting services in which they manage the ILS software on their servers?
    - If the library wants to own its own servers, does the vendor provide remote access for troubleshooting and installing software upgrades?

- Does the library have to purchase the servers from the vendor or can it use its own equipment?
✓ What operating system and hardware requirements are needed for the servers?
✓ What operating system and hardware requirements are needed for the client workstations?

- Online Public-Access Catalog (OPAC) and Web site:
✓ It is vitally important to select an online public-access catalog (OPAC) that will appeal to your users in appearance and functionality. To your end users—whether they are students on a college campus or people living in your town—the OPAC is the "face" of your library. The OPAC may also be part of the overall Web site that the vendor will design and maintain for your library. Some vendors will be able to show you Web sites that they have designed for other library customers. If not, they should be able to give you Web site addresses to visit. Sample Web sites will give you an idea of how your library's home page may look and how your Web site will operate.
✓ Ask the vendor about the features available on the OPAC.
  - What is the appearance of the search box? Is it a Google-like search box that is easy for customers to locate?
  - How is the borrower able to manage his account? For example, can the user place holds on materials for pickup later and/or renew books online?
  - Is there federated searching, which retrieves "hits" from both the catalog and the library's online databases? If so, is a subscription fee required to a third-party company in order to retrieve information from the online databases?
✓ It is also possible to purchase an OPAC or "next-generation catalog" (NGC) separate and apart from the integrated library system you select. If the ILS you decide to purchase has a Z39.50-compatible catalog, you will have options for selecting from a wide range of software and services. You may be able to purchase one of the next-generation catalogs from companies that develop NGCs exclusively, such as Aquabrowser (http://www.aquabrowser.com), Endeca (http://www.endeca.com), and WorldCat (http://www.oclc.org/us/en/worldcatlocal/default.htm). There are also open-source NGCs in various stages of development. Overall costs along with total functionality have to be considered when making this decision. Research whether or not the NGC of your choice can work in tandem with the circulation module and provide a live status of items. Whether an item is checked out or checked in must display immediately in the NGC. Again, the total cost of buying from multiple vendors as well as the staff expertise to implement multiple systems must be considered.

- Circulation Modules:
✓ It is important to choose a circulation interface that will appeal to staff. Put yourself in the shoes of circulation employees and determine the ease of use, functionality, and appearance.
  - Can you move effortlessly between check-in and check-out screens?
  - At first glance, is there sufficient information about borrowers and their items?
  - Is the information on the screen organized in a logical fashion? As one checks in materials, are the titles listed at the top of the list so that one can verify if the bar codes scanned correctly? Again, as one checks out material, are the titles listed at the top of the list so that the circulation clerk can see if the bar code or RFID tag scanned correctly? (RFID is covered in greater detail on page 25 and in Chapter 4.) The circulation module needs to make the circulation clerk's job easier, not harder. You do not want a circulation module in which scanned items appear in random order on the screen. You want the scanned items to appear at the top of the list.

- Are the fonts and graphics easy to read?
- Does the module allow both keyboard commands and mouse clicks? Having the ability for both functions allows flexibility for staff members who prefer one method of working to the other.
- ✓ How does the system manage the placement of holds?
- ✓ If the server fails, is the circulation module able to work off-line?
- ✓ Some circulation modules issue automatic e-mail notifications regarding holds and overdue materials. If a patron has an e-mail address in her record, she will be notified by e-mail that a book is waiting for her. The same is true of overdue notifications. Borrowers are notified by e-mail that their materials are late. If an integrated library system possesses this feature, ask if it is part of the basic package or if there is an additional charge.
- ✓ Note any special features that each company offers.

- Cataloging Modules:
  - ✓ If you are not a cataloger, this section of the demonstration may be challenging to understand. Read the Library of Congress's online document entitled "Understanding MARC Bibliographic: Machine-Readable Cataloging" at http://www.loc.gov/marc/umb. Katie Wilson, in her book *Computers in Libraries*, has a helpful chapter on cataloging that covers the MARC (machine-readable cataloging) record structure, bibliographic utilities, bibliographic record, authority record, and the item or holdings record.
  - ✓ Ask for a demonstration to illustrate and discuss the methods for entering bibliographic records into the database. (Be sure to follow up with other libraries that use the system you are considering on the ease of entering and downloading MARC records.)
    - How are MARC records that are purchased from other vendors imported into the system?
    - Are there templates to provide shortcuts in cataloging materials?
    - How does one connect through the Z39.50 to download MARC records from other servers, such as the Library of Congress?
    - How does authority control work? Is there an additional charge for authority control?
    - What information is available when viewing the item records?
    - Are there a variety of avenues to search for a title, such as, ISBN, UPC code, title, author, and publisher?

- Reports:
  - ✓ If there are standards reports that you need an integrated library system to generate on a regular basis, such as monthly circulation figures in call-number order, ask the sales consultant if the reports you need are currently available. Sometimes a sales consultant will state that the company is in the process of writing a certain type of report. You want to take careful notes of these types of comments. A promised feature can in reality be one, two, or three or more years in development before becoming a standard report, and there are charges for custom reports.
  - ✓ Reports are powerful tools in evaluating budget expenditures, improving services, and developing a quality collection. Reports also help communicate information about library operations to your library board or supervisor. Spend time exploring this module and noting what standard reports each vendor provides.
  - ✓ Ask if one is able to export the reports into a variety of formats, such as Excel, PDF, HTML, XML, CSV, and so forth.

- Data Conversion:
  - ✓ If you are planning to migrate from one system to another, you will need to ask the sales consultant if his or her company has experience converting records from the automation system you are currently using.
    - Ask for a list of libraries that converted from the automation system you are using to the vendor's system so that you can speak with the staff. Vendors will most likely give you the list of libraries that migrated successfully without any hiccups. It may be prudent to ask around to see if there were any problematic migrations and how the situations were resolved.
    - It is helpful when the company assigns a specific person to work with your library on data conversion. More often than not, there is some type of problem that needs to be resolved during the migration. It makes for a smoother transition to work with one person throughout the process.
    - What is the cost for the data conversion?
  - ✓ If you are purchasing an integrated library system for the first time, speak to the sales consultant on how the vendor would work with you on converting to MARC records.
- Training:
  - ✓ When purchasing an integrated library system for the first time or migrating to a new one, there is a steep learning curve. Choosing the right training module for the staff is one of the most important decisions to be made.
    - Will your staff benefit by having trainers on-site at your library or can staff be adequately trained online using a webinar format?
      - One benefit of on-site training is that trainers can troubleshoot equipment and software problems. In addition, trainers can gauge any areas in which staff are having trouble. Trainers and staff establish a rapport when trainers are at the library.
    - If a library has a system administrator, then Web-based training may be the choice. The company selling the ILS can train the system administrator who, in turn, provides in-house training for library staff.
  - ✓ You will need to establish a budget for training. Ask how much training is provided for each module: circulation, cataloging, public-access catalog, Web site modifications, reports, acquisitions, serials, interlibrary loans, and system administration. Make note of the answers because later you will ask other library directors, who purchased the system you are considering, whether or not they received enough initial training on each module. Some vendors provide one day of training with installation, and other vendors offer three days. If you must increase the amount of introductory training from what is being offered, you need to include that cost in your budget.
- Technical Support:
  - ✓ Make sure that the hours of operation for technical support match the hours of operation for your library. If your library is open on Saturdays and Sundays and the circulation module goes down, you want technical support to be available during weekend hours to help you repair the situation.
  - ✓ Where is your vendor located geographically? Time zones can affect the level of telephone support and upgrades, unless the vendor has support available 24 hours a day.
  - ✓ If the vendor has to do major upgrades in which the server will be down, are technical-support staff able to perform these upgrades while the library is closed so that it does not affect your daily operations?
  - ✓ How are requests for assistance handled? Does technical support accept phone calls and e-mails? Is there an online support center in which customers can chat online with technical support?

> ✓ What is the average response time to requests for technical assistance?
> ✓ What is the maximum allowable time that technical support must respond to a request?
> ✓ How are emergencies handled? If your circulation system fails to start up, how quickly will technical services respond to your problem?
> ✓ Do support employees specialize in the repair and operation of different products? If so, is there more than one employee for each product? For example, if there is only one support employee who works with the telephone notification system module, what happens if he or she is on vacation when your telephone notification system fails?

- List of Current Customers:
  > ✓ Ask each vendor what libraries in your state (or surrounding states) use their system. If the sales consultant cannot provide that information at the conference, he or she should be able to follow up with this afterward.
- Cost of Maintenance:
  > ✓ How much are the annual maintenance fees?
  > ✓ What type of support is provided? Are there tiered levels of support? What are the costs of the various tiers?
- Third-Party Add-ons:

  While you are shopping for an ILS, you may want to consider other products that work with each integrated library system. Ask the sales consultant for a review of equipment and software that works in tandem with the ILS. (More information about add-ons is covered in chapter 4, "Added Features.") Some of these adds-on may include:

  - Telephone notification system: This piece of equipment and software calls a borrower and leaves a prerecorded message notifying that: (1) reserved material is at the library waiting for the borrower to retrieve and/or (2) overdue materials need to be returned to the library. Notification systems also allow borrowers to renew their materials by phone. Telephone notification systems allow staff time to be re-allocated to other responsibilities and saves paper, envelopes, and postage. This is an add-on that should be considered in your budget.
    - Ask the sales consultant what equipment is needed to operate the telephone notification system, such as a dedicated computer workstation and dedicated phone line(s).
    - Does the ILS vendor install the equipment and software?
    - Does the ILS vendor provide technical support for the equipment and software? If so, what is the additional charge for this support?
  - Computer reservation system: Library customers log onto public computer workstations directly or reserve time on a public workstation. This eliminates the need for staff to monitor time limits and whether or not someone is an authorized user in good standing. The computer reservation system may interface with the ILS to authenticate library users. Customers log onto the reservation system using the bar code numbers on their library cards and/or a PIN number.
    - Ask if additional equipment, such as a stand-alone workstation, is needed to operate the system.
    - Ask if there is an additional charge for the patron-authentication software.
    - Is the software installed remotely or on-site?
    - Is staff training provided? If so, what is the fee?
    - What are the annual maintenance fees?
  - Print-management system: This system manages print jobs originating at the public computer workstations. Customers pay for printing with credit cards, account deposits, or cash payments before their requests are printed. This eliminates

customers printing sheets that they do not want. Libraries may see a decrease in wasted paper and an increase in revenues.

- Ask the sales consultant what equipment is needed to operate this program, such as a dedicated computer workstation or server.
- Does the ILS vendor install the equipment and software remotely or on-site? The former requires someone at the library to assist in the installation.
- Does the ILS vendor provide technical support for the equipment and software? What is the annual maintenance fee for this service?

■ Acquisition module:
- Check for functionality and ease of use.
- What transmission protocol does the ILS vendor use to communicate with suppliers such as Baker & Taylor, Brodart, Ingram, BOT (formerly called Books on Tape), Midwest Tapes, and others? Does the ILS vendor name particular distributors that interface with their acquisitions module? Are these the same companies that you currently use or would consider doing business with in the future? (Be sure to speak to your suppliers to obtain their opinion of a particular acquisition module. Ask if they have any problems in receiving orders or working with the ILS company.)
- When viewing the demonstration, look at the records being displayed. Are you able to determine from the descriptions which are trade editions, library editions, large print, paperback, audiobook, DVD, and so forth?
- Most acquisition modules set up purchase-order accounts for different suppliers, encumber funds, and track packing slips and invoices. If you have more than one person who orders materials, ask how order lists are kept separate. Is there a method to create an order and then have it move through a supervised approval process before transmitting it to the distributor?
- Look for acquisition modules that connect to your local catalog and multiple suppliers simultaneously. That is, when you search for a title, such as *Treasure Island* by Robert Louis Stevenson, you are able to connect with Baker & Taylor, Brodart, Ingram, and your local catalog with one typed request. This will ensure that you do not order a book that the library already owns, and you can compare prices and formats among distributors.
- Another nice feature on an acquisition module is the ability to download "on-order" records into the PAC. Customers can see that a particular title has been ordered and, if allowed, place holds to be notified after the item has been processed.

■ Inventory: Tracking materials in the library can be simplified by utilizing an inventory module. This module allows staff to input items straight from the shelf and then run reports from the resulting list to generate reports as to what items are misshelved, what items have not filled a waiting request as they should, and what items are missing (not on the shelf or checked out). Ask the vendor if the library can be inventoried collection by collection and, if necessary, across multiple locations. RFID technology makes the inventory process even easier. Refer to Chapter 4 for more information regarding RFID.

■ Serials: This add-on allows the library to acquire and manage the most troublesome of printed formats: periodicals, serials, and standing orders. The serials product should have all the typical acquisition functionalities of budget tracking, order placement, and invoice processing, but with the ability to submit claims when issues do not arrive on schedule. An "automated claims" feature tracks the arrival of each issue, and when a particular issue does not arrive, the system automatically transmits a notice to the vendor. Entry of the individual titles and issues is also an important feature. Customers and staff must have the ability to see what individual issues are in the library at any time.

- Interlibrary loan management: At this writing, many interlibrary loan programs are proprietary and can communicate only with other libraries that own the same or a compatible ILS. This is an important consideration when deciding whether or not to purchase an interlibrary loan (ILL) add-on. Library staff will also need to decide whether or not customers will have the ability to place their own ILL requests, or if all requests must go through staff. If customers place their own requests, the interface needs to be intuitive and easy to use. Customers viewing union catalogs or other libraries' catalogs need to be able to determine what titles are available locally versus what is available to borrow from another location. Ask the sales consultant how ILL materials are managed within the integrated library system so that items can circulate and overdue notices can be issued if necessary.

- RFID (radio-frequency identification): Instead of using bar codes and bar code readers, some libraries employ RFID technology to circulate books and other materials. RFID tags are attached to library materials, and when items are placed at an RFID station, the antenna reads the RFID tags and transmits the information to the circulation module. Circulation clerks do not need to take the time to scan each time. The RFID station is able to read a stack of books or DVDs at one time.
  - This functionality is often provided by one or more third-party vendors. Inquire as to which third-party companies the integrated library system will support.
  - Ask the sales consultant what equipment is needed to operate this product.
  - Is the equipment and software nonproprietary, using the latest ISO standards (15693, 18000-3, etc.)? If not, keep in mind that you will be tied to the proprietary system and any changes could involve costly equipment replacement and retagging.
  - Does the ILS vendor install the equipment and software remotely or on-site?
  - Is the hardware built into the cabinetry, or is it a detached model? The former requires carpentry and other planning assistance with furniture installation.
  - Is the library required to purchase the computer workstation from the vendor?
  - Does the ILS vendor provide technical support for the equipment and software? If so, what is the annual maintenance fee?

- Self-checkout stations: A library does not need to have RFID to have self-check stations but it is the common route to take in providing this service. If the library has space for self-check stations, this option has the potential to relieve staff for other duties. Patrons also enjoy the privacy of checking out their own materials. Ask the vendor what equipment, software, and furniture are needed to provide a self-check station.
  - How does the self-check work? Does it utilize touch screens, receipt printers, bar code scanners, or RFID technology?
  - Does the product require the library to purchase the computer hardware or cabinetry from the vendor?
  - Can library staff easily install, or does the vendor install?

- E-commerce: This add-on allows borrowers to pay fines, lost book charges, and print charges with a credit card or debit card. The software is Web based so patrons can pay charges from the public-access catalog or from their home computers.
  - E-commerce requires some type of patron-authentication software. Ask how the vendor allows for third-party authentication.
  - Library staffers make arrangements with a bank that can provide e-commerce services. The library's e-commerce software communicates directly with the bank, which approves and handles each transaction, making a direct deposit to the library's account.

- Ask the vendor what equipment, operating systems, and browser versions are required.
- Collection agency: This third-party add-on automatically sends delinquent borrower accounts to a collection agency that manages delinquent borrowers owing a certain amount of charges. Delinquent borrowers are notified by the collection agency to settle the account or to bring materials back to the library. Borrowers are notified several times and have a timed deadline to clear their account before a credit report is filed. The potential credit report is a strong incentive to return materials.
  - You will need to make sure that the ILS has a module that interfaces with the chosen collection agency. The ILS should generate a regular report of borrowers that is automatically transmitted to the collection agency. The collection agency, in turn, transmits return files that are uploaded into the ILS to clear records, amend amounts owed, and so forth. The collection agency will invoice the library for the number of records processed, but it is advisable to add that dollar amount as a processing charge to the delinquent borrower's record. It is assumed that the collection agency's charges are offset by the materials and fines that are recovered that would not have otherwise been.
- Material-vending machines: If your library is considering adding vending machines to circulate books, DVDs, and CD-ROMs at a remote location, then the library will need to employ RFID technology, a communication protocol such as SIP2 (Standard Interchange Protocol, version 2), and compatibility with the integrated library system. The Contra Costa County Library in California implemented "Library-a-Go-Go" in which commuters on the rapid-transit system or those living in underserved areas of the county were able to utilize material-vending machines to borrow items. Susan Kantor-Horning wrote about the project in the August 1, 2009, issue of *Library Journal* (pp. 16–19). Check with ILS vendors to see if they are able to support this emerging opportunity to reach patrons at shopping malls, public-transportation centers, or other locations away from the main library. Vending machines are also a secure solution for the troublesome DVD format, whether in a remote location or in the library itself.

Contacting Other Libraries for Information

As mentioned earlier in the chapter, you will want to ask sales consultants for a list of customers. It is helpful for this list to include libraries that are of the same type and serve a similar-size population. So if your facility is a school media center, you will want a list of customers who are also located in media centers that serve a similar-size student population.

If you are migrating from one type of automation system, you will want to speak to other libraries that also migrated from the same system. These individuals can give you an account as to how smooth the migration process was and if they experienced any problems. A vendor that is unable to produce a list of current customers of similar size and type is a sign that the company does not have experience working with a library such as yours.

When you call one of the contacts, ask to speak to the library director if the vendor has not given you a specific contact name. Identify yourself and the reason you are calling. The director may be able to answer some of your questions but he or she may forward you to the staffer directly involved with the network and the ILS. In any case, thank the director for his or her time and assistance.

If you discover that most or all of the people you are speaking with migrated five or more years ago, you should contact the sales consultant and ask for a list of recent customers who migrated from the system you are currently using. The people you want to speak with should have purchased their ILS in the past one to three years. Customers who purchased their system several years ago may not be running the same software version that you viewed in the demonstrations.

Important questions to ask other libraries include:

1. When did you migrate to the (name of integrated library system)?
2. What version of the software are you operating?
3. From which ILS did you migrate?
4. Do you have servers on-site, or did you purchase a hosted system?
5. Is the system stable, or do you have server or connection problems? (If it is a hosted system, ask about the reliability and speed of the connection. Do they experience downtimes or slow connection speeds at certain times during the day?
6. If the library migrated from the same ILS you are using, ask about the migration and data-conversion process. What problems, if any, did they encounter? How were issues resolved? How long did the process take? How much downtime was experienced in the transition?
7. Did the vendor create your Web site? If so, may I have your Web site address? Are you pleased with the Web site the company designed for you?
8. In what ways was the ILS company knowledgeable, helpful, and professional?
9. Were there any instances or issues that you wished the company would have handled differently?
10. Do the modules operate as you thought they would? Are staff satisfied with the system?
11. Can you provide any overall advice or comments?

If you are searching for copies of RFPs, then you should ask the person to whom you are speaking if he would be willing to share a copy of his or her RFP. Most librarians and MIS administrators are open to sharing their RFPs. After all, these individuals are in the information-sharing business and they were once in the same position of shopping for an ILS.

Time invested in researching the types of integrated library systems available, and the vendors who provide ILS products and services, will help you make the right decision in choosing the best system for your library. Communities grow and technology changes, so it is vital to choose an ILS that is flexible and can support add-ons when the library is ready to make additional purchases.

References

Kantor-Horning, Susan. "Self-Service People." *Library Journal*, August 1, 2009, Vol. 134, Issue 13, pp. 16–19.

Koneru, Indira. "Integrated Library System: Selection and Design." *DESIDOC Bulletin of Information Technology*, November/December 2005, Vol. 25, p. 8.

Library of Congress. "Understanding MARC Bibliographic: Machine-Readable Cataloging," http://www.loc.gov/marc/umb. Accessed November 9, 2009.

Robkin, Shai. "Managing Multivendor RFID Rollouts." *American Libraries*, November 2009, Vol. 40, Issue 11, pp. 44–47.

Wang, Zhonghong. "Integrated Library System (ILS) Challenges and Opportunities: A Survey of U.S. Academic Libraries with Migration Projects." *The Journal of Academic Librarianship*, May 2009, Vol. 35, No. 3, p. 209.

Wilson, Kate. *Computers in Libraries: An Introduction for Library Technicians.* Binghampton, NY: Haworth Information Press, 2006.

3 Selecting the Hardware

- ILS Determines Hardware Purchases
- Hardware Purchasing Principles: Servers
- Hardware Purchasing Principles: Workstations
- Peripheral Devices
- Backup Plans and Devices
- Networks and Network Security

The first step in selecting hardware is deciding what type of integrated library system will be purchased. This crucial decision determines not only what equipment needs to be acquired but also who will be responsible for administering day-to-day operations, software upgrades, troubleshooting, and hardware maintenance.

ILS Determines Hardware Purchases

If a turnkey or stand-alone integrated library system is chosen, then the library will need to purchase servers, workstations, and network equipment either from the ILS vendor or from a third party. Purchasing the equipment from the vendor affords the advantage that the vendor is then responsible for resolving all problems surrounding the efficacy of the ILS. Purchasing the equipment from a third-party vendor may have cost savings, but you must be sure to follow the specifications required by the ILS vendor. In addition, the servers and network equipment will be housed on-site. This means that the library director will assign or hire staff who will be responsible for operating the system and maintaining backups and server hardware, along with troubleshooting problems with the ILS vendor.

In a stand-alone purchase, the library hires a system administrator who manages both the integrated library system software and all the hardware. "The local management of an integrated library system is known as system administration. Tasks include managing the hardware, internal and external access to the system, security, backing up the databases and daily transactions on a regular basis, troubleshooting, performing system upgrades, and communicating with the vendor support staff" (Wilson, Kate. *Computers in Libraries: An Introduction for Library Technicians*, 2006, p. 32).

In small libraries, the library director or other staff person will also serve as system administrator, depending upon the complexity of the ILS software.

In a turnkey arrangement, the library purchases the hardware and software from the vendor, who installs it. In addition, the vendor assumes the major role in troubleshooting software and hardware issues and provides or remotely installs software upgrades.

A turnkey system is the choice to make when a library wants its equipment and software on-site but does not have the in-house expertise to develop and enhance the software and hardware. The library is still responsible for staffers, who operate and maintain the ILS system hardware and software; however, those staff can rely on the ILS vendor for assistance and technical support, both for operational and upgrade activities. For example, staff will monitor backup media each day to ensure that the servers are backing up the data correctly. (Refer to the section at end of this chapter, "Backup Plans and Devices.")

Servers should be rebooted at least each month for general maintenance. In addition, at least two staff members should be trained to report software issues to the vendor's technical support. Many small libraries operate turnkey systems without a dramatic impact on staff time because the vendor has the major responsibility for resolving problems. However, the person who interacts with the vendor must be comfortable working with computers and should have some expertise. Beyond the normal expectations of e-mail and office operations, staff will learn the special operations and processes that come with an ILS.

If the library chooses a "hosted" system or a software-as-a-service (SaaS) system, then the library will not need to purchase servers but will be responsible for the workstations or thin clients and the network needed to communicate with the vendor. "Thin clients are very low-cost computer stations that have very few resources of their own and rely on a server to provide the majority of their storage, memory and processing capabilities. They are basically a new form of the old-fashioned 'dumb terminals'" (Bolan, Kimberly, and Robert Cullin. *Technology Made Simple: An Improvement Guide for Small and Medium Libraries*, 2007, p. 40). In a hosted or SaaS system, the library needs to stipulate in the contract with the vendor who is responsible for managing the daily operations, performance expectations for the system, data security (backup) guarantees, expectations for scheduling software upgrades or running reports, disaster procedures, and network management issues, including network bandwidth specifications and network outage procedures. By choosing a hosted or SaaS system, the need to manage server hardware or to hire skilled staff is alleviated.

It should be noted that a network administrator is required in all instances: turnkey, stand-alone, hosted, and SaaS. The network administrator is responsible for the library's local area network (LAN). "Typically, a LAN is a network that is used by a single library or perhaps by a single college campus. The speed limitations of the cabling used for the LAN make it difficult to extend the network beyond a single organization or a small geographic area" (Burke, John J. *Neal-Schuman Library Technology Companion: A Basic Guide for Library Staff, 3rd edition*, 2009, p. 77). If a library has branches, then the network administrator is responsible for the wide area network (WAN), which uses existing communication networks.

Libraries that cannot or do not wish to have a network administrator on staff can contract for these services. Someone has to install and maintain the Internet connection, which includes the router, switch(es), firewall (for network security), and cabling, and install workstations onto the network. The workstations communicate with the library's servers via the LAN or WAN or with the vendor's servers via the Internet.

If the library has a system administrator to operate and manage the ILS, it is common for that person to also manage the network. If the library does not have a system administrator, then it is not unusual for the library to contract with an outside provider for this service. If the library opts to contract with an outside provider, a separate service agreement is advisable. The service agreement will stipulate the library's needs for installations, response time, and problem resolution, particularly for times when the library is open beyond normal business hours. If the network goes down on Saturday morning, the service agreement must state how problems will be resolved without exorbitant after-hour charges.

Hardware Purchasing Principles: Servers

If the library decides to purchase a turnkey or stand-alone system, the library director will need to purchase at least one server to house the ILS software, the bibliographic records, and the patron records. If the library plans to manage its own Web site or to make the public-access catalog available online, then a Web server is required. For security reasons, the Web site and the online public-access catalog (OPAC) should be housed on a separate Web server and not on the same server as the ILS software, unless one utilizes hardware virtualization, which is discussed later in this chapter. The Web site and the OPAC are open to the public and therefore are at risk to hackers. It is vital that the library's ILS software and records be protected from unauthorized entry. To protect the network, one needs to purchase a firewall and "demilitarized zone" (DMZ). The DMZ is a section of the network that is exposed to the Internet so that the public has fewer restrictions when accessing certain library services (such as searching the catalog), while managing more secure access to other library services.

The ILS vendor may offer to sell servers and other hardware. To select the right server and workstations, the prospective ILS vendors will ask how many borrowers are being served, how many titles and items the library owns, and what is the annual circulation. Through the request for purchase (RFP) process, vendors will provide their recommendations for minimum server specifications, such as the speed of the processor, memory requirements, workstation requirements, and other elements specified by the library.

When selecting hardware, there are two basic principles. First, buy as far into the future as you can afford to and, second, consider purchasing hardware from the vendor, especially if this is your first experience working with this company.

Whether you are purchasing servers or workstations, focus on the following three items: (1) select the highest processing power/speed, (2) purchase the most random access memory (RAM) you can afford, and (3) purchase the largest amount of hard disk memory that fits your budget. By getting as much as possible, not only will the server last longer, but your system will also function faster. The server should be a "server-class" machine for better durability and processing capabilities. Servers with dual-core or quad-core capabilities are preferred. Keep in mind that the number of processors multiplies the processing speed, so that a 2.2 MHz dual-core machine is far faster than a 3.0 MHz single processor. Quad-core will last longer than dual-core.

The recommendation to get the most you can afford relates to all three of the factors noted before (processing speed, RAM, and hard disk memory), but if your funds are limited, then some prioritization is necessary. In other words, rather than spend hundreds more to go from a 2.13 MHz dual-core processor to a 2.4 MHz dual-core processor, it may be better to get additional gigabytes of RAM. Hard disk space is relatively inexpensive and easy to upgrade, but it is still wise to purchase as much hard disk space as possible when placing the initial order. A large hard drive will not only extend the life of the system, but the server will also operate faster and create a more responsive system. At the same time, it is advantageous to have multiple hard drives for better data security and increased space. It is advisable to have a fast bootup drive (10,000 or 15,000 rpm) even if it is no more than 40 to 80 GB of space for the operating system, and then have a much larger second drive to provide the space for data. This configuration is different if you choose to have a RAID array as the method for backup (see "Backup Plans and Devices"). As of early 2010, increase the CPU to be at least a dual-core processor that is over 2.0 MHz in speed, if that is more than what your vendor has suggested. Then add as much RAM and hard drive space as you can afford, focusing on RAM first.

In addition to buying as far into the future as you can afford, the second basic principle is to buy hardware from the vendor. The advantage of making a single phone call to resolve all integrated library system problems can be a compelling reason to purchase hardware from the system vendor. If the discrepancy in costs is not too great, it is usually best to at least begin with a new ILS by purchasing hardware from the vendor. With this type of scenario, troubleshooting all hardware problems is the responsibility of the vendor's technical support staff, who contacts the hardware manufacturer.

It can also be advantageous to purchase hardware from the vendor due to the possibility of special pricing, warranty, and advantageous maintenance agreements. This is especially true of peripherals, such as bar code scanners and receipt printers, but it also holds true for workstations and servers. For example, you may be offered a deal in which all the hardware comes bundled for a better price than if you were to buy equipment separately from other companies. In addition, when purchasing hardware and peripherals from the vendor, there should be no question that the equipment will work in tandem with the software. Later, when you need to replace or add receipt printers or bar code scanners, it may be more cost-effective to purchase from another company who specializes in those peripherals. The library should track the current pricing for hardware in order to be able to compare market prices with vendor costs.

The server purchased for the library's integrated system might also provide additional functionality depending on the size of server purchased and the functions desired. For example, large libraries might require one large server for processing circulation and cataloging work, another server to provide public-access catalog services, another server to provide the library's Web site, another server for business office accounting, and yet another for e-mail hosting. A small library may be able to consolidate several major functions on a single large multiprocessor server by creating "virtual machines" within that single hardware unit.

A virtual machine is a software structure, including an operating system, which operates within a larger software environment. The larger environment may even consist of a different operating system, and can "host" several virtual machines, each running a different application at the same time on one hardware platform. Through virtualization (with software like VMware, for example), a library can have one physical server that runs an e-mail server and business applications (accounting and personnel software) at the same time. In this scenario, the hard drives of the server are partitioned, and each partition operates as if it were a separate server. Consolidating applications through virtualization can save hardware costs and reduce space requirements.

Differences in the functional needs, budgetary constraints, and staffing expertise of every library make for the need to individualize configurations to achieve the greatest effectiveness and efficiency. If the library selects a virtual server, it is recommended that you verify in writing with the vendor that the selected server will be able to manage other functions without interfering with the ILS functions. You do not want a situation in which the ILS vendor blames you for ILS software problems because of the other functionality you are performing on the server. Availability of low-cost and immediately accessible outsourcing providers for any of the functionality should also be considered. For example, there may be local businesses that could provide Web services or e-mail for the library.

Hardware Purchasing Principles: Workstations

Decisions made when purchasing servers are similar to decisions made when purchasing staff and public workstations. You may consider buying hardware from the vendor but only if it yields advantages of reduced costs for quantities and ease in troubleshooting hardware issues. Purchasing hardware from the vendor is not as important for workstations as it is for servers, since workstations throughout the industry have a lot of basic similarities. In fact, so long as you buy workstations that exceed minimum specifications provided by the ILS vendor, it is likely you will be able to spend less on workstations purchased from other computer manufacturers. It is advisable to purchase workstations that are exactly alike insofar as that is possible. Workstations that are alike are also easier to maintain, because the parts are alike and less time is required for learning the maintenance associated with a variety of platforms. Purchasing computer hardware through government consortia contracts can save a lot of money. Quantity discounts provide even deeper savings.

In library technology departments, one of the "best practices" is to replace from one-fourth to one-third of the institution's desktops every year. This means that every workstation will have a three- or four-year life cycle. This may seem to be wasteful at first, given that computers may last longer than three or four years, but the amount of money saved in maintenance and staff time in working with old computers is well worth the continual investment in newer technology, not to mention the improved performance that will be realized.

Besides having a hardware replacement schedule, it is also important to consider the reliability of manufacturers. A local provider or even an individual might be able to build computers for the library inexpensively. The reliability of the parts being used by the local provider should be examined just as carefully as the reputations of machines purchased from major manufacturers. Buying inexpensively today may cost more in maintenance and in more frequent replacements over four to eight years. Another consideration when purchasing from a local business is that it may provide a quicker response time to problems.

As of early 2010, dual processing workstations are the standard. RAM memory is also relatively inexpensive, meaning that a minimum of 2 to 4 gigabytes would be the norm with which to start. Hard drive space is also relatively inexpensive. Purchasing 250 gigabytes would be more than enough space for normal use, but getting more for a relatively small price increase will also mean the computer might last longer and operate faster. A typical workstation configuration might look like this:

Workstation Configuration

PC specifications

- Processor: Dual processor 2.5 to 3 GHz[1]
- 3 GB RAM[2]
- 20″ Monitor
- A video card that supports having two monitors
- Hard drive: 320GB SATA[3]
- Sound: internal speaker
- CD/DVD: 16x DVD+/−RW[4]
- Keyboard – USB, Mouse 2-button USB[5]
- Gigabit Ethernet network card

MAC equivalent

If you are using Apple products and installing a Mac-based network, there are some Web sites that can assist you. Apple's support site is http://www.apple.com/support. It has the latest information regarding servers, operating systems, RAID, and storage systems. Another site is http://www.macfixit.com, which is part of CNET reviews. MacFixIt has links to topics on all things Apple, such as forums, utilities, and the ability to e-mail questions and to have other Mac users respond.

Keyboards and mice are mostly a matter of personal preference, especially for staff workstations. Ergonomic "split" keyboards might be preferred by some staffers; however, others will definitely not want the split effect. One might think the least expensive alternatives would suffice for public-access workstations; however, in times of flu epidemics, there are good reasons to purchase waterproof antimicrobial keyboards for easy cleaning. Specialized mice (more than two buttons) are not usually necessary, but it may be a good suggestion to have a few USB rollerball mice available for those who have difficulty manipulating regular mice.

Twenty-inch monitors are now at a price point that makes them a good alternative. The larger the screen, the more effective the monitor is for the user. For staff members who work with multiple applications or documents simultaneously, multiple screens provide a much more effective workspace, hence the "dual DVI" graphics card in the example configuration above. For a circulation desk performing a single function most of the day, two monitors would be superfluous. Circulation desk personnel want as few obstacles as possible between them and their patrons.

If you are using a Windows-based system, ask the vendor what service pack version needs to be installed on workstations and what browser type and version needs to be installed. Web-based modules and Web-based ILS software will operate at optimum performance only with particular browsers and particular browser versions.

Peripheral Devices

There is a wide variety of additional peripheral devices possible, including cameras, headphones, fingerprint readers for authentication, receipt printers, wide-format printers, bar code scanners, document scanners, RFID antennae, external hard drives, and so forth. It may a good decision to purchase peripherals, such as bar code scanners, receipt printers, and RFID antennae/scanners from the vendor to ensure compatibility. This is especially true for libraries migrating from one system to another.

Take, for example, Anywhere Public Library and its decision to migrate from System A to System B. The bar code scanners purchased with System A are still operable;

so, Anywhere Library is considering keeping the original scanners instead of purchasing new ones from Vendor B. In its research, Anywhere Library discovers that the bar code scanners for System A are made specifically to read System A's proprietary bar code symbology. If Anywhere Library chooses to keep its original scanners, it will be locked into that technology during the retrospective conversion process to System B. If the library is not able to purchase bar code scanners from Vendor A in the future, it will have to spend additional funds and staff time to correct the problem by bar coding the entire collection. To avoid this type of scenario, library staff should consider purchasing the peripherals, especially bar code scanners and RFID scanners, from the ILS vendor.

Backup Plans and Devices

It is vital to include data backup in the planning process right from the start. If something should happen to the data server(s) due to a hardware failure, fire, or natural disaster, the library will lose all of its patron and bibliographic data without backup files available. It is best to include as much in the startup package as possible to get the most for the money spent. Consider one or more of these options: a built-in tape drive, RAID arrays, CD/DVD-writeable media, and flash or external hard drives. It is possible to subscribe to Internet sites willing to provide space for backup data. Such sites are an option, but the total cost of tapes versus subscription costs should be compared carefully. Also, the security of such sites is an important consideration. Though CD/DVD media are reliable storage for small amounts of data, they transfer data slowly and are not practical for larger amounts of data. RAID (redundant arrays of inexpensive disks) configurations are a desirable option because they provide moment-by-moment backup of work as it is performed and can facilitate faster recovery in problem situations. You will need to explore the possibilities with your vendor, as their system may work better with some backup processes than with others, or even be incompatible with some types of backup systems.

No matter which type of backup media is chosen, it is important to have well-defined procedures that are executed without fail. The data should be backed up daily. It is recommended that incremental backups be done during the day as well. A different tape is used every day so that the backup media is not overwritten immediately. You will also then have several backup copies in the event that one or more of the media devices have data errors. It is also wise to keep one backup off-site in a secure location. The off-site media should be updated weekly. Fireproof safes certified for computer data are a good idea. If tapes are used, do not use them for more than the recommended number of times, usually no more than 50 uses. It is also recommended that tapes be verified once or twice a year to assure viability. Similarly, other backup media, for example, external hard drives, should be verified. Even with multiple backups being made, you do not want to encounter the need to recover data only to find the media you have been using is bad.

Here is an example of one backup strategy using tapes: a library that is open Monday through Saturday would buy seven backup tapes. Label each tape for the day of the week plus label two tapes for Saturday. On Monday, a staff person will insert the "Monday" backup tape in the data server and take the "Saturday" backup tape to an off-site, fireproof, and waterproof safe. The "Saturday" tape that is already in the safe will be removed and utilized that coming Saturday. The process repeats itself each week. If something happens to the data server, the library will have its patron and bibliographic records saved on its collection of backup tapes. If a disaster, such as a fire or flood, hits the library building, then the library has its data protected off-site on a backup tape. To ensure that the backup tapes are functioning properly, check the backup utility each day to make sure that data is being saved to the tapes. Use the cleaning cartridge every other week to keep the backup tape drive in serviceable condition.

Networks and Network Security

The network for most libraries consists of Cat-5 (Category 5) or 5e Ethernet cabling that connects the staff and public workstations to a switch that in turn is connected to the router for access to the Internet. Category 5 (now superseded by 5e) is the designation of twisted copper wiring that is specified to handle data transmission speeds of up to 100 Mhz. Category 5 is able to transmit data of up to 100 Mbits/sec (megabits per second). Cat-5e, while still specified for 100 Mhz transmissions, is capable of gigabit (1,000 Mbits/sec) networks. Category 6 cabling is rated to guarantee 250 Mhz transmissions. Category 6 cabling is backwards compatible with lower categories. The choice of cabling is a matter of cost and plans for the future. Either Cat-5e or 6 will serve the library well into the future. Cat-6 or even Cat-7 may have the capacity for additional services desired by the library but that are outside the scope of this book. The switch may also connect the workstations to one or more servers depending upon the setup for the library. For example, a public-access catalog would be connected to the Web server via the switch.

When selecting an integrated library system, you will research what type of network is needed to operate the ILS. For example, with a software-as-a-service system, the network will consist of workstations communicating with the vendor via the Internet; so the network will consist of Cat-5 (or higher) cabling, switch, router, and a high-bandwidth Internet connection. The vendor will give specifications for the staff and public workstations along with browser specifications to access the software.

If you are purchasing network equipment for the first time or upgrading your network connection, your technology plan should cover goals for the library that could affect network equipment purchases. For example, the library will need a router to manage the network communications between servers, workstations, and the Internet. You should consider whether or not to offer wireless Internet access. If so, then you will need to consider purchasing a partitioned router. One side of the router will handle the library's network traffic and the other side of the partition will handle the public wireless Internet traffic. A partitioned router protects the library's network and prevents access from individuals using wireless laptops and other wireless devices.

To protect the security of the library's LAN, you must have a hardware firewall in place. It will prevent hackers from entering your network and ultimately your servers. It is worth the effort to have someone on staff who is trained to understand the configuration of the firewall. At the minimum, your Internet service provider should be able to either manage your firewall functionality for you or advise you of a knowledgeable network administrator in your area.

If the library is purchasing a Web server for the first time, you will need to configure a DMZ to protect it from unauthorized access. As mentioned earlier, a "demilitarized zone" (DMZ) is a section of the network that is exposed to the Internet. Adding a DMZ will make use of a third interface port on the firewall. This configuration allows the firewall to exchange data with both the corporate network and the DMZ network using network address translation (NAT). NAT allows data received on a specific port or interface to be routed to a specified network. For example, when someone visits an organization's Web site at http://www.somecompany.com, the browser is sent to the server where the site lives. If this organization keeps its Web server in a DMZ, the firewall will know that all traffic sent to the IP address associated with the Web site should be passed to the server sitting in the DMZ network rather than directly into the organization's internal network.

If maintaining a LAN is a new undertaking for you, it is advisable that you read a general overview of the infrastructure and maintenance of a network. Even if you contract with a network administrator, being able to understand and communicate with the administrator is advisable. *Networking for Dummies* by Doug Lowe (Hoboken, NJ: Wiley Publishing, 2010) is a well-written, easy-to-understand guide on the basics of a network, servers, backup storage devices, and security.

Due to continual innovations in all aspects of technology, from data storage and processor architectures to new developments in Internet services, it is essential for library staff, especially the director or system administrator, to maintain constant awareness of technological improvements. It is not too early to forecast the escalation of

Network Speed

Type of access	Transmission speed Kbps = kilobits per second Mbps = megabits per second Gbps = gigabits per second	Time to transfer files Word doc = 4 kb to 200+ kb Picture = 250 kb to 4+ mb Mp3 music = 10 mb to 40 mb Movie = 1+ gb
Typical dial-up modem	56.6 kbps (kilobits per second)	Large document = 2 to 5 secs Picture = 30 sec to 10 min Music = 25 min to 1+ hrs. Movie = 2+ hours
ISDN	128 kbps	Large document = 1 to 2 secs Picture = 15 sec to 5 min Music = 10 min to 45 min Movie = 1.5+ hours
Cable Modem	460 kbps	Picture = 5 sec to 2 min Music = 2 min to 15 min Movie = 30+ min
High-Speed Internet	Range from 756 kbps to 6 mbps	(depending on speed) Picture = less than a minute Music = 1 min to 10 min Movie = 15+ min
"T-1" line	1.54 mbps	Picture = 2 sec to 1+ min Music = 1 to 8 min Movie = 20+ min
Ethernet	10 mbps	Picture = Less than 20 sec Music = 30 sec to 5 min Movie = 10+ min
Fast Ethernet	100 mbps	Picture = less than 3 sec Music = 3 sec to 30 sec Movie = 1 to 2 min
Gigabit Ethernet	1000 mbps (1 gbps)	Music = less than 3 sec Movie = less than 15 sec

network access to gigabit network cards. While a network card that communicates at 10 MB/sec or even 100 MB/sec would be acceptable at this time, networks are increasingly moving to faster and faster speeds. Below is a table explaining various network speeds and the capabilities in downloading data:

Through research, investigation, and a close examination of your library's needs within the framework of staff expertise and financial capabilities, you will begin to see which ILS architecture will best suit your situation. Hardware and networking decisions will also begin to be clearer as you define what it is you need and what will help you and your staff function most effectively. In considering these needs and wants, there are other elements that are beyond the basics of an ILS that you may also want to consider. The next chapter describes additional elements that can also enhance your ILS implementation and help you serve your patrons in new ways.

References

Bolan, Kimberly, and Robert Cullin. *Technology Made Simple: An Improvement Guide for Small and Medium Libraries.* Chicago: American Library Association, 2007.

Burke, John J. *Neal-Schuman Library Technology Companion: A Basic Guide for Library Staff,* 3rd edition. New York: Neal-Schuman Publishers, Inc., 2009.

Lowe, Doug. *Networking for Dummies.* Hoboken, NJ: Wiley Publishing, 2010.

Wilson, Kate. *Computers in Libraries: An Introduction for Library Technicians.* Binghampton, NY: Haworth Information Press, 2006.

4 Added Features

- Online Acquisitions Module
- Serials Management Module
- Interlibrary Loan Management
- Automated Notification Systems
- Federated Searching Tools
- RFID and Self-Checkout
- Public Computer Reservation and Print Management
- E-Commerce

When considering which integrated library system to purchase, it is vitally important to look at what added features each ILS will support. The term "added features" is used for equipment and software that is outside of the standard modules of circulation, catalog, reports, and the online public-access catalog (OPAC). "Added features" are modules or functions that are requested and purchased in the contract as additions to the basic system offered by the ILS vendor. For example, an online acquisitions module would be an add-on if it were priced separately from the basic package. A vendor may charge $15,000 for the basic system and another $1,400 for the online acquisition module.

The functionality of added features may be a primary consideration in deciding which ILS is the best for your facility. Added features will not only allow you to implement significant tasks that expand the operations of the ILS, but add-ons also indicate the viability of the ILS vendor. If an ILS vendor does not offer e-mail and/or telephone notification regarding borrowers' holds or overdue materials, and does not support third-party add-ons that offer these services, this leaves the library with only a print-notification option. Printing and mailing notices is the most expensive method for libraries to contact customers. Phone calls from staff are labor-intensive and a costly alternative. However, if an ILS vendor has negotiated with a third-party company to offer e-mail and/or telephone notification, this is a good indication that the ILS vendor is aware of library customer needs and is willing to find solutions. For many ILS vendors, it is more cost-effective for a third-party company to create or manufacture the software/ hardware than for their organization to develop these functionalities.

The customer picks and chooses which added features, if any, he or she wants to include in the initial RFP or to purchase at a later date. If you are planning to purchase the add-ons in the same fiscal year as the integrated library system, you will want to check the legalities of that decision. Your organization may not be able to split the purchases. Ask your business office, administrator, or attorney for guidance.

ILS vendors will sell many of the add-ons but you do not have to purchase the added features from the same company from which you bought the ILS. You may obtain a better price for an added module from another company, but be certain to research compliance with your integrated library system. Acquiring an add-on from the ILS vendor may or may not cost more, and you have the assurance that the product will work seamlessly with your system. Again, you can research compliance by asking how long the vendor has contracted with the third-party company to provide equipment and software, who handles technical support, and whether the vendor is able to provide a list of customers who are currently using the third-party product.

If you incorporate added features into your RFP, be sure to include in the request for proposal that the vendor is responsible for handling the acquisition, installation, and maintenance of the add-ons. Write a simple statement in the opening section of the RFP that reads, "A single proposal will be received for all work to be performed. A single vendor must serve as the prime contractor for all items contained in their proposal." This will alert vendors that if they state they are able to provide a service or feature, that they will be responsible for seeing that it is implemented.

Following is a list of the add-on modules most libraries find especially useful. The list will include the description of the product, how it works with the ILS, plus information on any preparatory work before installing the product.

Online Acquisitions Module

The acquisitions module is a product that manages the fund management, selection, purchase, receipt, and invoicing of library books and materials. Some libraries are also able to use the budget-tracking feature in the acquisitions module to oversee all of the library's accounts, including personnel and supplies. The module should allow library staff to create budget categories, manage lists of desired titles, submit those lists electronically to book suppliers, track the costs of the materials ordered and received, and send claims for items that have not been received. There should also be an option to allow or not allow the public to view orders in the public-access catalog and to place holds on those items.

Most vendors today offer a Web-based acquisitions module. "Web-based" means that the product is accessed via the Internet and does not reside on the data server in your building. Staffers who perform collection development will log into the module and search for materials, place orders electronically, download MARC records into the catalog, track expenditures, input receivables from packing slips, and pay invoices.

In deciding whether or not to purchase an acquisitions module, evaluate staffing levels and job responsibilities along with the current workflow for placing, handling, and tracking orders. Most distributors, such as Brodart, Baker & Taylor, Ingram, and the like, have online ordering products for their customers to use. Some of these online components are free and some charge an annual subscription fee for features such as full-text journal reviews or the ability to download MARC records. These online ordering products allow librarians to transmit orders electronically, but the products may not track expenditures or keep account balances as an acquisition module does.

The online acquisitions module should eliminate the need for staff to maintain paper records. You want a product that will streamline your workflow at an affordable price. An effective acquisitions module will contain all information regarding orders. You should have the capability to keep several order lists. For example, you may have two juvenile nonfiction order lists that you are building. One juvenile nonfiction order list is with Distributor A and the other list is with Distributor B. You should have the ability to add and delete titles from these lists until you transmit the orders to the distributors.

You should also be able to search for a title among several distributors in one search entry and be able to compare prices, formats, and availability. So, for example, if you have accounts with Ingram, Baker & Taylor, and Brodart, you should be able to search for a title with all three distributors simultaneously. One distributor may have the title available in large print, DVD, CD-ROM, and MP3, while another distributor may just have the trade and large print editions. It saves staff time to view price and format availability in one search entry and it saves money to be able to compare prices.

Another benefit of an online acquisitions module is the ability to enter information from packing slips, cancellation notices, and invoices. Staff should be able to know at any time the status of their orders: what has arrived, what is pending, and what has been paid. In addition, staff should know what funds have been encumbered, what funds have been expended, and what funds are still available.

Some online ordering modules are complex. You will want to research the type of training and technical support that is available from the company. Staff should be able to perform all the basic functions of ordering, receiving, invoicing, setting up vendor accounts, and opening purchase orders after their initial training. The training program should also cover how to utilize the module's online help function.

Be sure to speak to your distributors and other librarians about the online acquisitions module for each ILS vendor you are considering. Ask if they are experiencing any problems with the product. You will want to have specific examples of concerns and not just generalities. This will help you compare features and speak to the sales consultants about any concerns.

Serials Management Module

A serials module is a software component that handles the library's serials, periodicals, and standing orders. Serials are volumes that are issued by a publisher on a regular basis and contribute to the overall body of work. An example of a serial would be *Something about the Author*. Every few months, a new volume is published that adds to the entire product. *Something about the Author* is a collection of biographical profiles of children's writers and illustrators. It is a reference tool for people who want to know about the lives, motivations, and interests of authors and artists. Libraries who collect *Something about the Author* do not want to miss a volume. A serials module would monitor *Something about the Author* and ensure that all volumes are received. This eliminates the need for library staff to monitor whether or not the latest volume has been delivered and to manually contact the publisher if the latest volume has not arrived at the library.

"Periodical" is another word for "magazine." Periodicals are published on a regular basis, but each issue stands alone and does not contribute to a body of work. Periodicals are received weekly, monthly, bimonthly, or on another periodic basis. *Time, Business-Week*, and *People* are examples of periodicals that are issued on a weekly basis. The serials module tracks that each periodical is received and transmits a notification of a missing issue to the publisher.

Standing orders are titles that the library wants to purchase each time a new edition is published, such as *The World Almanac* and *Guinness Book of World Records*. Both of these titles are issued on an annual basis. Unlike serials, such as *Something about the Author*, standing-order titles do not add to a body of work. Once the new edition of *The World Almanac* is received, the previous edition is weeded from the collection. A serials module tracks standing order titles to ensure that the library receives the latest edition of each title as it is issued.

Before adding the serials module to the library's integrated library system, staff need to determine the philosophy for the periodical collection plus the number of serial and standing-order titles. Not every library needs a serials module.

Staff should determine whether or not the periodicals collection is for research or for browsing and entertainment. Questions to ask are: (1) Is it important to account for the location and status of each title? (2) Will customers need to know if the latest issue of the magazine is on the shelf or if it is checked out to another customer? Many libraries today offer periodicals in full text from online databases. If a magazine is available in full text from an online database, then customers can retrieve a specific article from the online resource and the paper version can be available for browsing and circulation. If the latter is the case, then staff may decide that it is not necessary to track each individual issue. Determining a collection philosophy will help you decide whether or not to purchase a serials module.

For facilities having more than 200 periodical, serial, and standing-order titles combined, the serials module may be a vital component in organizing and maintaining these facets of the collection. If a library contains fewer than 200 periodical, serials, and standing-order titles, it may not be an effective use of staff time or money to purchase this module. Serial modules are most commonly found in large public and academic libraries.

The management of periodical titles in a small collection can be handled other ways within the integrated library system. One option is to enter individual magazine titles in the catalog and bar code each issue separately. Another option is to have one copy record that represents all issues. The public access catalog will read, "check shelf for holdings," instead of giving a detailed status for each issue. Staff will manually record the receipt of periodical titles and contact publishers or the subscription service if issues are missing. If a customer asks about a particular issue, staff can answer whether or not the issue has been received but will not be able to answer whether or not the issue is in-house or checked out to a customer. Again, library staffers need to identify the goal of the periodicals collection—research or browsing, loosely managed or tightly controlled.

If it is determined that a serials module is required, then it is helpful to understand how the serials module works. This module functions with the acquisitions module to track serials, periodicals, and standing orders. Each issue or standing-order title is tracked and the appropriate monies deducted from the account. If there is a missing issue or standing-order title, a "claim" is issued automatically to the periodical agent, distributor, or publisher. A serials module can be an important management tool for collection development and technical services. Installation involves entering the titles, expected time frames and deadlines for each title and issue, budget information, and sources for the suppliers.

A growing component of the serials module is the management of full-text electronic content. Marshall Breeding writes, "In the automation systems of today, serials content suffers from an especially disjointed state of affairs. . . . Due to the inflexibility of the original design of the ILS and the way that separate modules have been developed to handle the management of e-journals, the current picture of the management and access of serials content looks like a tangled mess" (Breeding, Marshall. "Next Generation Library Automation: Its Impact on the Serials Community." January–June 2009, p. 63). Breeding points out that the traditional management of print serials using the serials module poses difficulties for the management of e-journals (electronic journals). As mentioned before, the serials module checks in the title of the journal, tracks the arrival of each issue, and sends claim notices to vendors when an issue is missing. Discuss the management and control of e-journals with ILS vendors and third-party companies. The latter may have a solution that will work in conjunction with the integrated library system you ultimately select.

In addition, check with the periodical agents, distributors and publishers that the library uses, to see which communication protocols are necessary to interface with their systems. Ask if there are problems with any particular serials modules. You will want to select a module that interacts effectively with the companies you utilize.

Interlibrary Loan Management

The interlibrary loan (ILL) module allows staff to place ILL requests electronically. They are able to place requests, send materials, and check out the ILL materials to patrons. The work of placing requests and checking out materials to patrons works seamlessly with the integrated library system. With some interlibrary loan modules, patrons are able to place their own requests without staff intervention. Staff will want to consider the financial impact of such a decision. Sometimes it is more cost-effective to purchase the requested item for the collection. If it is an older edition, then Amazon or a used-book dealer is an option for filling the request. What is spent on postage could instead be spent on acquiring the item if the title would be useful to the collection.

The interlibrary loan management module is an area within the field of integrated library systems that is in transition. The main hindrance to purchasing an interlibrary loan module is that it is difficult to communicate with integrated library systems outside of the library's own type of ILS. For example, if the library owns "System A," then it is easy to submit and to respond to interlibrary loan requests from other "System A" libraries. It is not easy, however, to communicate interlibrary loan requests with libraries that do not own or are not compatible with "System A."

Staffers need to determine how they are going to handle their interlibrary loan business. Most libraries are involved with some type of interlibrary loan consortium within their state, region, or with OCLC (Online Computer Library Center). OCLC is a membership-based, nonprofit organization that provides many services, including interlibrary loans. Its Web site states that it is the world's largest consortium. When choosing an ILL module or deciding whether or not to purchase this module, you will need to look at the consortium to which you belong. Ask whether or not the ILL module will communicate with the consortium the library is using.

Improvements in Z39.50 protocols may improve the ability to communicate with a variety of ILL modules in the future. Until ILS vendors have nonproprietary interlibrary loan modules, you will have to be careful to select the module that is compatible with the libraries with which you work. In any case, the entire ILL procedure needs to be planned with the other libraries' structures in mind.

There are methods for tracking ILL materials in-house without having to purchase an ILL module. You can manually track a book that you receive from another library using your circulation and catalog modules. Create a temporary bibliographic record and attach a "dummy" bar code number to the item. When the patron checks out the ILL item, the bar code attaches the title to the customer's record. When the item is returned, delete the bibliographic record.

If your integrated library system allows patrons to place holds, you will need to set parameters for ILL materials so that patrons are not able to place holds on these temporary records.

Automated Notification Systems

Automated notification systems are services and processes that contact borrowers when they have books that are ready to be picked up and or when they have overdue materials that need to be renewed or returned. Notification systems may include a range of contact options: e-mail, mail, and telephone. Some libraries are beginning to offer a text to cell phone option. Borrowers or staffers select one or multiple avenues of contact.

Staff members need to consider how the methods of contact will impact the budget. Some libraries have completely eliminated the use of mailed notifications to save paper, staff time, and postage. Listed below is information about telephone notification systems, which are normally manufactured by third-party companies. ILS vendors will advertise which product works best with their system.

The telephone notification system is programmed to work with your integrated library system. The reports module generates both a contact list of borrowers who have materials on hold and a contact list of borrowers who have overdue materials. If the ILS software package includes an automatic e-mail notification feature, the phone notification system may or may not duplicate the same e-mail contact list for overdue materials and holds. If it is desired that patrons be contacted by both phone and e-mail, then you will want to list this option in your request for proposal.

The ideal arrangement for a telephone notification system is to have a dedicated computer workstation with its own high-bandwidth Internet connection and dedicated telephone jack. If your library utilizes an internal phone system, you will need to contact that company and notify them that you are adding a telephone notification system. The company will advise you if a line is available or if you will need to pay for the installation of a new line. You do not want to share a line with the fax machine or another extension, as this will interrupt outgoing calls. You will also need to know if the internal phone system programs a prefix number in order to access an outside line.

With the prevalence and portability of cell phones, some customers keep their cell phone numbers even if the numbers are long-distance numbers for the area in which they are currently living. Library staff will have to decide whether or not they are willing to pay for long-distance charges and if the phone notification system can handle an array of area codes. Encouraging library patrons to give an e-mail address for e-mail notification will solve this issue; however, not everyone will be willing or able to give an e-mail address.

If it is cost-prohibitive or space-prohibitive to have a dedicated computer workstation for the telephone notification system, you can share a workstation. However, the phone notification system cannot operate if the computer is being used for something else, such as cataloging or word processing. Most phone notification systems can be paused while the workstation is used and then restarted once the machine is free. Being able to share the phone notification workstation depends upon the size of the library and the number of patrons who need to be called on a daily basis.

It is important to purchase a good, uninterrupted power supply (UPS) for the phone notification system hardware. A lightning strike or a power surge can damage this piece of equipment. The computer workstation, to which the phone notification system is connected, should also be plugged into the UPS.

Research the parameters of the notification systems available for purchase. Determine if the phone notification system will fit your current circulation procedures regarding the handling of holds and overdue notices or if you will need to modify your procedures. An example of this would be how long a library waits after the due date to notify customers about their overdue materials. If your library waits 14 days after a due date before sending a notice to the patron, ask the vendor if one is able to program a 14-day grace period in the software. If the phone notification system that you want to purchase comes with preset parameters that cannot be manipulated, you may need to plan ahead with staff on revising circulation procedures.

Libraries may also purchase telephone notification systems that have an automated renewal feature. These systems require an additional dedicated incoming phone line for patrons to call to renew their items. The automated renewal system will tell patrons if their items have been renewed or have not been renewed and need to be returned to the library. If the items are renewed, the system gives the new due dates.

Depending upon the size of your customer base, you may need to install more than one incoming and outgoing line for the automated phone notification system. A dedicated computer workstation is definitely required for libraries with a system that allows automatic renewals because patrons will call at their convenience, so the system needs to be available 24 hours a day, seven days a week.

Federated Searching Tools

Federated searching is software that allows customers to search across multiple resources simultaneously using one search tool, usually the online catalog. Libraries, especially academic and large public libraries, are experiencing an increased demand for e-resources (electronic resources), and federated searching helps patrons acquire search results across the library's collection of print and non-print resources. "A paradigm shift in library collections has occurred in which e-resources are now the major component of new library materials, requiring new ways to manage and display them" (Wolverton, Robert E., and Jane Burke. "The OPAC is Dead: Managing the Virtual Library," October 2009, pp. 247–252).

In addition to searching a library's e-resources, patrons also have the ability to search other libraries' online catalogs. Take as an illustration the Anywhere Public Library, which subscribes to BigTime Premier database and has an agreement with the nearby Distant Public Library to include access to its online catalog in federated searching. A patron searching for information on ocean mammals types the search term "whales" into the Anywhere's public access catalog search box. The search results display book titles available at both the Anywhere Public Library and the Distant Public Library, along with DVD titles and links to electronic magazine articles in the BigTime Premier database. The patron can print some of the magazine articles plus check out materials from the Anywhere Public Library. In addition, the patron may also drive to Distant Public Library and borrow materials on whales or request the titles through an interlibrary loan.

Not every library uses federated searching to allow patrons to view other libraries' catalogs. A library may use federated searching solely for integrating its online database subscriptions with its online public catalog.

Federated searching modules may be expensive, so consider asking a company about its pricing options. A vendor may offer a discounted price for libraries subscribing to fewer than 10 online database titles. This is an affordable option for small libraries and school media centers that want to offer their patrons this powerful method of accessing information.

The library should carefully consider what other library catalogs, if any, are included in federated searching. This may increase interlibrary loan requests, which will impact staffing and postage costs. You need to make sure you have agreements with the libraries whose catalogs you want to add to the federated searching module.

RFID and Self-Checkout

RFID stands for radio-frequency identification. This technology uses radio waves to read the numbers assigned to items and then transfers that information to the circulation module for checkout and check-in. These numbers are the same numbers that are encoded into the bar codes of the items in the system, so that the process of RFID-tagging items involves scanning the bar code into software that then transfers the same number via radio waves into the RFID tag. The RFID tag contains the item number as well as a digit that manages the security status. The latter is used with security gates and other theft-prevention devices. RFID simplifies the circulation of materials because staff no longer have to scan each individual bar code, but can place a stack of materials on the RFID reader (antenna). It also simplifies self-check circulation with interfaces that can easily identify the items for checkout. Companies that provide RFID tags also provide self-check stations and all related equipment.

Opening a new library utilizing RFID technology is relatively easy to implement. If staff members have to convert an existing collection to RFID technology, it can be a lot of work and expense. At this writing, RFID technology is utilized by medium to large libraries. As RFID tags become less expensive, this technology may become a reasonable alternative for more libraries. Self-check equipment that includes specialized software and touch screens may also be cost-prohibitive for some libraries. Touch screens simplify the interface for patrons and can help make access to the network more difficult. Patrons also prefer the convenience of going through the process and answering questions by just pressing buttons on the screen.

If you plan to convert to RFID technology, here are some suggested tips:

● Closing your library may facilitate faster tagging, although many libraries have implemented RFID tagging without closing.
● Develop some method to designate which items have already been tagged (a dot on the spine) so staff can glance at a shelf and know what items have not been tagged.
● Hire additional temporary staff to tag everything on the shelves with RFID tags. Temporary staff may also be used to tag items as they are returned to the library until the majority of the collection is converted and regular staff can deal with the remaining stray items.

- It is not unreasonable to expect individual staff to tag at a rate of three to five items per minute, or 200 to 300 items per hour. A team of three or four people, two or three consistently tagging, with one managing supplies and the transfer of items back and forth to the shelves, can achieve higher rates. Such a team could be expected to tag a collection of 25,000 items in a week.
- As with the development of most technologies, the cost of RFID technology is becoming more reasonable every year. Five years ago, RFID tags cost about a dollar each. Today, they are less than 35 cents each. Tags can be as large as a credit card or small enough to fit on CDs or DVDs.
- RFID technology has inspired a variety of new appliances and pieces of equipment. There are sorting machines that will automatically check in items as they go through a book drop and sort them into ready-for-shelf and a number of other categories depending on how many bins are chosen. Wands that read RFID tags can help with shelf inventory. The "antennae" that read RFID tags can be purchased separately like bar code scanners or any other input device. The panels that staff will use at their desktops cost a few thousand dollars. There are even little RFID devices that attach to PDAs or other hand-held devices.
- Self-checkout and self-check-in machines can be relatively expensive if specialized cabinetry is desired. Touch-screen monitors that make the user interface easier are also expensive, but worth the cost. The landscape of what is possible is ever changing and always improving, so you should allow some time for evaluating options.

Once the majority of the collection is tagged, install antennas at the circulation desk and self-check stations for circulating materials. Bar code scanners are still a necessity at the circulation desk and self-check stations for library cards utilizing bar codes instead of RFID technology.

Some type of cabinetry or desk is needed for the self-check stations. Libraries can purchase furniture from the companies selling RFID equipment, build their own, or use existing desks. Self-check units purchased from the vendors may be expensive. Libraries can save money by using existing tables, desks, or cabinets. Purchasing the touch-screen monitors and related software is highly recommended.

Automated RFID check-in utilizes sorting bins, but this may be a cost-prohibitive option due to the price of conveyor systems. The workflow process may require that staff manually check in items using RFID readers. This will still be a time-saving method over the bar code-scanning process as staff will be able to read stacks of materials instead of scanning individual bar codes. Some libraries allow check-in at the self-check stations because borrowers like the assurance of receiving a receipt for returned items. The self-check-in process needs to include a slot with the RFID antenna attached. As items are dropped through the slot, they are checked in and the security is reset.

Placement is important when installing self-check hardware. A self-check station may be located anywhere in the library, as long as there is access to a network jack and an electrical outlet. Wireless is an option, but wireless connections can be unstable and unreliable. Planning the placement of self-check stations is an opportunity to examine the public-service strategy of the library. Library staff may want to consider converting a labor-intensive circulation desk into a smaller, centralized patron service station. Employees at the customer-service desk can make library cards and handle other account-related questions while borrowers use the self-check stations for the majority of their circulation transactions.

In addition to circulation duties, RFID technology is also used to inventory the collection. Vendors offer portable RFID inventory stations. A laptop with an RFID antenna on a wheeled cart with battery power can move among the library stacks. Staff runs the antenna wand across the shelves to read the RFID tags in the books. The scanned results are downloaded into the inventory module that interfaces with the integrated library system. Staff can then generate a report of missing and misshelved items.

Public Computer Reservation and Print Management

Libraries that offer public-access computers usually need some way of managing patron registration and usage statistics. Computer reservation software allows borrowers to reserve the next available computer or to reserve a future time slot. This software allows patrons to make reservations without staff interaction. Users enter the bar code number on their library cards at either a central computer workstation or at one of the public Internet workstations available for use. In some libraries, patrons will go to a reservation computer, reserve a time slot, and receive a receipt telling them which computer to use and what time they can use it.

Computer reservation software is a time-saver for public-service staff. They do not have to monitor whether or not an individual is a legitimate cardholder in good standing with the library. In addition, they do not have to monitor time limits as the software takes care of this process.

Print-management software regulates printing requests generated by patrons at the public workstations. Customers have to pay for their print jobs before the printing takes place. Staff release the print job once the fees are paid. With a coin-operated machine, the print job can be automatically released after the money has been put in. This software program saves ink, paper, and headaches, as staffers do not have to deal with customers who want to dispute charges.

Usually third-party companies, not the ILS vendors, sell the computer reservation and print management software. Some companies have products and pricing for small libraries. The program settings may not be as flexible as the other versions they carry, but it is an affordable option for small libraries.

It goes without saying that you need to choose add-on products that will work with your integrated library system. The computer reservation system needs to access the customer database for patron authentication. This means that the software identifies that the person reserving the computer is a patron of the library. Some software can also determine whether or not the user is in good standing with the library and can block individuals with overdue materials, lost materials, or excessive fines from using the public workstations. These types of blocking or notification parameters are set by a library's computer-use policy.

Computer reservation systems can also limit the maximum number of hours a person can use the computer each day. This allows more customers to utilize the library's resources. Again, the type of parameters one can set on computer reservation system varies from one company to another.

E-Commerce

E-commerce encompasses the many ways libraries allow patrons to electronically manage payment for services. Customers can pay for their fines, printing, and other charges either by using a credit card at a service desk or by accessing a secured Web-based procedure. E-commerce can also include deposit accounts and smart cards that allow patrons to deposit money in advance of future charges.

Implementation of e-commerce involves the installation of a software interface that accesses both the customer's credit card/debit card account and library account through SIP (Standard Interchange Protocol) or other authentication. Once authenticated, the software processes payment through an agreement with a bank. The bank that processes the payment has a contract/agreement with the library to provide such services. Banks normally levy a basic charge per transaction for providing this type of online service. It is imperative to install a security certificate on the server utilizing the e-commerce software. Library staff should compare costs and services provided by banks that are able to process electronic payments.

In Conclusion

Added features can greatly boost the effectiveness of an integrated library system. Careful consideration and research should be conducted into which added features, modules, and software an ILS vendor can utilize. Part of the ILS selection process should include a comparison of how flexible each integrated library system is and how easily it can accommodate improvements that might be arranged through third-party providers. The research, comparison, and analysis of all the functions and other data can be very complicated depending on the needs of your library. It is important to have a good, though always objective, relationship with the sales consultant for the prospective ILS.

References

Breeding, Marshall. "Next Generation Library Automation: Its Impact on the Serials Community." *The Serials Librarian*, January–June 2009, Vol. 56, Issue 1, pp. 55–64.

PLA Tech Notes, http://www.ala.org/ala/mgrps/divs/pla/plapublications/platechnotes/index.cfm. Published by the Public Library Association. Contains tech notes on the following add-ons: E-Commerce, PC Reservation and Print Management, and RFID Technology.

Wolverton, Robert E., and Jane Burke. "The OPAC is Dead: Managing the Virtual Library." *The Serials Librarian*, October 2009, Issue 3, pp. 247–252.

5 Working with the Sales Consultant

- Seven Stages of the Working Relationship
- Introduction
- Questions and Answers
- Demonstration
- Product Demonstration Review Form
- Request for Proposal
- The Contract
- The Invoice
- After the Sale

It is important to develop and maintain a good working relationship with the sales consultant assigned to your geographical area. Unless you encounter some kind of problem, you will work with this individual from the moment of introduction through the request for proposal (RFP) stage. After the RFP process, you will work with the sales consultant of the winning bid through the final steps of the sale.

It is important to remember that sales consultants are paid by how much they sell and for what price. Each individual is eager to create a good working relationship with you. He or she is either building a reputation or keeping his reputation polished and glowing. It is vital that you speak favorably of him or her to your colleagues so that he or she has the opportunity to make future sales. "If a business is managed poorly, no customer relationship wizardry will help. If managed well, customers will notice and the business will thrive" (Coe, George, "Managing Customer Relationships: A Book Vendor Point-of-View," 2006, p. 44). Due to the prospect of additional business with you and your colleagues, the sales consultant can be your advocate and may provide assistance down the road if needed.

Often an organization utilizes a fraction of a vendor's capabilities. If you develop a relationship with the vendor, you can discover all the products and services available through the company. Vendor relationship management is a way of achieving this (Brevig, Armand, "Getting Value from Vendor Relationships," October 2008, p. 34).

It is essential to be mindful, however, that this is a professional relationship, not a personal one.

Seven Stages of the Working Relationship

1. Introduction
2. Questions and Answers
3. Demonstration
4. Request for Proposal (RFP)
5. The Invoice
6. The Contract
7. After the Sale

Introduction

When you contact an ILS company for the first time or approach an ILS exhibit booth at a conference, introduce yourself and give your library name, city, and state. This will immediately connect you with the sales consultant for your geographic area and/or type of library (public, academic, school, or special). If your sales consultant is not immediately available, someone else will begin the demonstration and answer your questions until your sales consultant becomes available. Remember, he or she has other clients, so you may want to schedule a particular time to come back and meet with him or her.

If you are attending a conference and there are ILS companies that you are interested in visiting, then it would be beneficial for you to contact them ahead of time. You can visit the vendors' Web sites or call them to find the representative for your area. E-mail or call the person to see if you can make an appointment at the conference to meet. That way you receive 30 minutes or more for a thorough demonstration of the product. It will also establish you as a potential customer—someone the sales person is willing to invest time and effort in providing the information you need.

During the initial visit with the sales consultant, he or she will ask questions about your facility, such as the number of titles and items in the collection, annual circulation, number of borrowers, and number of staff members. This helps the consultant decide whether or not the company is a good fit for your library and if so, what type of system (turnkey, hosted, etc.) would work well for your facility. A good sales consultant can be helpful in providing useful information and guidance.

Questions and Answers

After your initial contact with a vendor, you will have follow-up questions as time progresses. Some of these questions can be answered by visiting the company's Web site. Other questions will require feedback from the sales consultant. He or she may recommend that you participate in a webinar.

The webinar is a demonstration over the Internet. You will need a workstation or laptop with Internet access plus a telephone with speakerphone capabilities. At a scheduled time, you will log on to a designated Web site to view the demonstration. You will also call a phone number to communicate with the webinar presenter.

Webinars are an excellent opportunity to include other staff members in evaluating potential systems. For example, you may want to include a staff member from the circulation desk to view the circulation modules for Vendor X and Vendor Z. You and your staff can view the webinar demonstrations for each vendor and discuss which features you like or do not like. (Refer to the Product Demonstrations Review Form on page 54.) Feedback from staff will help you write the RFP and select circulation features that are workable for your facility.

Remember that the webinar presenters will not be able to present all aspects of their modules. If one vendor demonstrates a feature that another does not, it does not mean that a particular feature is not available in both systems. So if Vendor X says its system automatically transmits e-mail notification regarding holds and overdues but Vendor Z never mentions this feature, it does not mean that Vendor Z does not offer this capability. So if you write "automatic e-mail notification of holds" into your RFP, Vendor Z may respond "yes" to this feature. Of course, you can also ask Vendor Z if the company has automatic e-mail notification, but this can become a time-consuming process. The RFP places the burden on the vendors to tell what features they do or do not have.

Also, when purchasing or migrating to a new system, it is important to involve staff in webinars and demonstrations. A new system will change how processes are done. Employees will experience changes in their routines. For example, a system that issues automatic e-mail notices regarding holds or overdues will drastically reduce the number of phone calls that employees will have to make to patrons. Some staff will worry that if they are not spending time calling customers, then what will they do with their time? Will some of them lose their jobs? Other employees will be glad that they will not have to make phone calls and that they will have more time to provide quality customer service, process materials, register people for programs, and the myriad of other duties performed by circulation staff.

Choose a lead employee who is experienced, knowledgeable, and will ask good questions to join in the webinars and demonstrations. A lead employee will help prepare other staff for change and generate excitement about a new system and a new way of doing business. Also, a sharp, intelligent employee will ask good questions and will think of aspects you have not considered. This will prevent pitfalls later on in the process. Do not select a negative employee to participate in the selection process. He or she will only highlight the "difficulties" of installing or migrating to a new system.

Lastly, most sales consultants are happy to answer your questions, but it is advisable that you try to compile a list of questions instead of contacting the consultant each time you have an inquiry.

Demonstration

There are two opinions on when the vendor demonstrations should take place:

1. When acquiring information BEFORE writing the request for proposal, and
2. AFTER writing the RFP. Only the finalists meeting the RFP parameters will have the opportunity to give a demonstration.

There are several benefits in inviting the vendors to your site before writing the RFP. After visiting the exhibit booths and asking questions, you probably have a good idea of two to four systems that will work at your facility. It is useful to have the vendor visit your site so that other employees can view the product and the sales consultant can tour the facility. The latter is useful because he or she can see the equipment you are currently using and make recommendations.

In addition to purchasing the integrated library system software, it may be necessary to buy hardware and peripherals. You will need to determine if your workstations, servers, bar code scanners, receipt printers, switches, and firewalls will work with a new system. If the existing equipment will not work with the new system, then you need to budget for these items. A sales consultant may not always be an expert in network and hardware issues, but he or she can track down the needed information and provide hardware specifications.

Due to the costs involved with traveling, many sales consultants will schedule their site visits so that they are able to meet with others in the area at the same time. As a courtesy to vendors, do not arrange for a site visit unless you are close to writing your RFP. If you are just at the stage of gathering information for a budget proposal, then use the webinars as a method of extracting more data and introducing the product to staff.

Vendors who offer to make a site visit or agree to a site visit are those who are interested in your business. "Vendors aren't the only ones who run substantial operations. So do libraries. The complexity of behind-the-scenes library operations is always a surprise to outsiders, who might guess that maintaining an OPAC or mounting a database requires considerable expertise, but who in general would have no idea what it takes in people, processes, systems, and equipment to put a book on the shelf, let alone tens of thousands of books" (Coe, George, "Managing Customer Relationships: A Book Vendor Point-of-View," 2006, p. 46). Sales representatives understand that no matter the size of the institution, library employees are managing a multitude of processes and services. Companies that display a willingness to invest time and resources in contacting libraries will be more successful in presenting modules, features, and services that fit the library.

During the site visit, the representative will go more in-depth in demonstrating modules than time allows at exhibits or webinars. Most consultants will schedule several hours with you and your staff to cover the circulation, cataloging, reports, and public-access catalog modules, plus add-ons such as federated searching, serials, and acquisitions. The vendor may not be able to demonstrate third-party software such as an automated phone system, but he or she can describe how it will work with the ILS software.

It is imperative to take good notes so that you can remember which vendor offers what features and how those features are visually presented. Following is a suggested review form that can help you document each demonstration.

Product Demonstration Review Form

Product Demonstration Form

Reviewer's Name _____ System _____ Sales Rep. _____

1. What types of systems does this vendor provide (turnkey, hosting, etc.)

2. How are MARC records entered into the catalog? How are MARC records imported from another server via Z39.50? How are MARC records imported from book distributors?

3. Is the Circulation Module easy to operate? What are the best features? What are the drawbacks to this module? Will the staff like this module?

4. Why would the public like or not like this the PAC?

5. Is the Reports Module easy to operate? Does the system currently create reports useful to this library?

6. Does the vendor create and maintain a Web site for the library at no charge?

7. Were there any awkward operations within or between functions or modules?

8. What are some of the system functions that would be beneficial for the library?

9. What aspects of the system that would be a hindrance to staff or customers?

10. What do you like best about this system?

11. What do you like least about this system?

12. What are the best overall features of this system?

13. What did you find cumbersome or awkward within or between functions?

14. Were there any problems with the demonstration?

15. List functions or operations that could not be demonstrated.

16. General comments.

Company specifics:

17. How long has the sales consultant been employed with this company?

18. How long has this company sold integrated library system software?

19. What types of libraries does this company mainly serve?

20. How many integrated library systems has the company installed for similar-size public libraries?

21. What comments does the sales representative make about the overall financial health of the company?

22. What is your overall impression of the sales consultant?

From *Integrated Library Systems: Planning, Selecting, and Implementing* by Desiree Webber and Andrew Peters. Santa Barbara, CA: Libraries Unlimited. Copyright 2010.

It is important to see how your staff react to different products. You want to choose a product that helps staff perform their duties more efficiently and with ease. Again, ask a lead employee to join the product demonstrations.

An on-site presentation gives you an opportunity to visit with the sales consultant. Ask questions about the history of the company and plans for the future. Is the company working on a major upgrade in software, and, if so, when is the scheduled release? This latter question is very important as you may not want to install or migrate to a system that is a recent, major upgrade for the company. This question can also be addressed in the RFP. The upside to purchasing the latest software version is having all the newest bells and whistles. The downside is working with technical support staff who are not fully versed in troubleshooting problems and trainers who are not able to train on all aspects of the software. Other problems include functions that do not work properly or that do not work at all.

Between the time of your initial contact with vendors and the site visit to your facility, you will have contacted other libraries that have purchased the integrated library systems you are reviewing. If at all possible, visit these libraries in person so that you can spend time visiting with employees who use the software. Note any problems or concerns that they experience. Discuss these concerns with the sales representative to see if the company is aware of the issues and if there are plans to address the problem in future software upgrades or patches.

During the product-demonstration period, the vendor may also negotiate with you regarding the price or a discount. Some sales consultants may ask what the dollar amount is for which you must legally issue a bid. So, for example, if your organization has a policy in which all purchases of $25,000 or higher must go out for bid, anything under $25,000 can be bought directly from a company without a bidding process. Some ILS companies will offer to come under the bid amount in order to obtain your business. An ILS vendor may also offer a discount, such as 15 percent or more, if the library eliminates the RFP process and chooses to purchase the integrated library systems from them.

Overall, the on-site demonstration is like a job interview. Library staff are interviewing the sales representative because this individual is a reflection of the company with which you may be working. Judge whether or not the consultant operates in an ethical, professional manner. An integrated library system is a major purchase and you want to choose a product and a company of the highest caliber.

Request for Proposal

Be knowledgeable about the laws and policies regarding requests for proposal or "bids" for your organization. Some cities, states, school districts, or universities have laws or internal policies forbidding the acceptance of gifts from companies seeking to do business. Do not accept offers to lunch or dinner. Even if you plan to pay your own way, it can be easy for the representative to insist upon picking up the tab, or to make arrangements with the wait staff to pay the bill. Then you have been placed in a compromising position of having broken a law or policy. It will damage your reputation and it signals to the sales rep that you can be persuaded to lower your guard.

All sales reps want to create a close working relationship with you. Keep it professional. If your employer discovers that you have broken a policy, you may suffer the consequences, and if another vendor discovers you have broken a law or policy, he or she will cry "foul" and insist that the bidding process is tainted—especially if his or her company is not chosen.

There needs to be ground rules for the RFP process. You want to ensure that all vendors participating in the bidding process are treated fairly and equitably. When issuing the RFP to vendors, there needs to be a statement in the cover sheet about how vendors can contact the library director, media specialist, management information systems director, and so forth, regarding questions and clarifications. Refer to the example given below, which is from the cover sheet for an RFP issued by the Anywhere Public Library. (A copy of the RFP in its entirety may be found in Appendix D.)

Example of Contact Information for Request for Proposal

Contact for further information:

For further information, contact Rob Payne, Library Director, Anywhere Public Library, 1201 N. Anywhere Blvd., Anywhere, USA 92020, or 617-000-4444 or jmaddox@cityofanywhere.org. Any questions regarding discrepancies, omissions, or clarifications within the request for proposal must be submitted in writing either at the above listed address or e-mail no later than [date]. The words "Integrated Library System Inquiry" should appear on the envelope or in the subject line of the e-mail. The source of the question will not be revealed, and answers to all inquiries will be made available to all vendors.

The purpose of this statement is to give vendors two to four weeks to read the RFP and respond with any questions or clarifications. Give a deadline as to when all questions or inquiries must be made and allow yourself one week after the deadline to answer all questions. After the cutoff date for questions from vendors, you will no longer accept or respond to any questions or comments.

Responding to an RFP is a time-intensive and time-consuming process for the vendor. Companies invest staff time in a proposal for which they may not be successful. It is the cost of doing business in this field and explains why the process is very competitive, with each vendor wanting to acquire your business. Respond to questions and inquiries for clarification as quickly as possible. If the answer requires research on your part, send a quick response that you received his or her question and will respond as soon as you have an answer.

The contact information example above also reads that the questions and responses will be distributed to all the vendors, but that the source of the inquiry will not be given. Again, in the spirit of fairness and openness, you will e-mail all vendors with the question asked along with your answer.

In the course of responding to questions, do not be tempted to answer questions or give information to a sales representative informally. You may like one company over another, but do not give inside information. If you do, you are showing that the bidding process is unfair and that you are not a professional in your conduct. This can work against you as the vendor may wonder what else you have done to taint the bidding process. And, if for some reason the consultant to whom you gave inside information is not chosen, you will hear from this individual and so will the administrators above you.

Detailed coverage of the RFP, the RFP process, and the contract is covered in Chapter 9.

The Contract

Once the RFP process is complete, the sales consultant for the company being awarded the bid is contacted. As a courtesy, all vendors should be notified and thanked for submitting a proposal for consideration. Some vendors may contact you and ask why their company was not successful. Be prepared to give an answer. (The evaluation process is covered in detail in Chapter 9.) The answer may be as simple as the winning bid met all the requirements and was the lowest price.

Following notification of being awarded the bid, the sales consultant will transmit an electronic copy of the contract. The contract is a negotiation phase among you, your facility's attorney, the vendor's attorney, and the vendor's management. The sales consultant is normally the contact person with whom you communicate questions and your facility's version of an approved contract. Sometimes the contract process may be lengthy and difficult, but keep in mind that the sales consultant also wants a successful resolution to the contract process. He wants to move along, issue the invoice, and receive his commission.

Once a contract is signed and approved by both parties, the next step is the invoice.

The Invoice

The sales consultant will send you an invoice giving the details and prices for the software, hardware, add-ons, peripherals, and any other items that you are purchasing. Compare the specifications for each item submitted in the RFP and contract to the specifications given in the invoice. Make sure that everything matches. For example, if you are purchasing a data server, compare every specification line by line. If you discover any discrepancies, contact your sales consultant and request a corrected invoice. If your sales consultant cannot provide the equipment or software as detailed in the RFP, then you have a major problem. Do not be talked into something less than what was awarded in the bidding process. You will need to drop this company from consideration and document your reasons why.

The invoice may request partial payment upfront. Check with the finance or business office for your library. In some states, it is illegal to pay for undelivered products or services. Payment can be made only after the system is installed and operating properly. In this situation, the library could order, receive, and then pay for peripherals, such as bar code readers and receipt printers, so that the vendor has some type of commitment from the library before proceeding with the data migration and installation.

After the Sale

Once the invoice is accepted and the library places the order for the integrated library system, this marks the end of your contact with the sales consultant. A good consultant will explain the process that lies ahead, who will contact you regarding the implementation, and will thank you for your business. Be sure to thank the sales consultant for his time and assistance.

As mentioned earlier, the sales consultant wants to maintain a good working relationship with you so that you will be satisfied with his or her efforts and the system you have purchased. This will help with future sales. Librarians who are pleased with the ILS they have bought will repeat this information to their colleagues. Therefore, if you encounter any problems after implementation and are unable to resolve the issue within the company, you will want to contact your sales representative. He or she may be able to act as your advocate and help to have the problem fixed.

The relationship with a sales consultant is a unique one. A successful and effective consultant will help you find the best system to fit your facility. He or she can provide good advice and options. By nature, sales representatives are friendly and can be a pleasure with which to work. Their personality characteristics are the attributes that make them successful in their chosen profession. That is why it is important to be mindful that sales representatives make their livelihoods on how much they sell; keep the relationship on an equally friendly, but always professional, level.

References

Anderson, Rick. *Buying and Contracting for Resources and Services: A How-to-Do-It Manual for Librarians*. New York: Neal-Schuman, 2004.

Anderson, Rick, Jane White, and David Burke. "How to Be a Good Customer: Building and Maintaining Productive Relationships with Vendors." *The Serials Librarian*, 2005, Vol. 48, Issue 3/4, pp. 321–326.

Brevig, Armand. "Getting Value from Vendor Relationships." *Searcher*, October 2008, Vol. 16, Issue 9, pp. 28–34.

Brooks, Sam. "Introduction: The Importance of Open Communication Between Libraries and Vendors." *Library/Vendor Relationships*, 2006, Vol. 44, Issue 3/4, pp. 1–4.

Coe, George. "Managing Customer Relationships: A Book Vendor Point-of-View." *Library/Vendor Relationships*, 2006, Vol. 44, Issue 3/4, pp. 43–55.

Gagnon, Ronald R. "Library/Vendor Relations from a Public Library Perspective." *Library/Vendor Relationships*, 2006, Vol. 44, Issue 3/4, pp. 95–111.

Stanison, Christine. "What They Never Told You about Vendors in Library School." *The Serials Librarian*, Vol. 56, Issue 1–4, pp. 139–145.

6 Timeline for the ILS Project

- Quick-Scan Timeline
- Timeline with Details

A timeline is like a road map for the planning, purchasing, and implementing the library's integrated library system. It will help you see what needs to be accomplished at each stage of the venture. The timeline will help you forecast into the future how you will manage your time over the course of the project. A schedule also gives you benchmarks to check off as you progress with the enterprise.

Nothing better insures success than planning and having the assurance of knowing the road. Unexpected occurrences can happen on any road trip, but knowing that you will depart from Point A and will arrive at Point B helps you navigate through tasks efficiently.

There is not a calendar or time schedule associated with this timeline. The optimum time is allowing 18 to 24 months for the planning process through the installation. Sometimes, manna falls from heaven and we are told that capital project funds are available and need to be spent by a deadline—usually a fast-approaching deadline. When that happens, be prepared for a stressful but exhilarating ride. You may not have to write or update a strategic plan, but all the other steps will need to be followed. Otherwise, the wrong decisions will be made, the network and hardware will not be in place at the right time, or, worst-case scenario, the wrong system for your library will have been purchased.

What follows is a timeline that can be quickly scanned. It can be printed and posted on your bulletin board or inserted in the front of your ILS project notebook. Following the quick-scan timeline is the same timeline but with details and short explanations. The details will give more information on what needs to be accomplished.

Quick-Scan Timeline

- Visit Integrated Library System vendors at a professional conference
- Assessment at Library location
  - Hardware
  - Software
  - Network
  - Customer needs
  - Staff needs
- Planning
  - Strategic Plan
  - Technology Plan
  - Develop budget
- Research
  - Visit other library sites
  - Develop list of questions for vendors
  - Webinars
  - Site visit by sales representatives
- Capital Request to Funders
  - Submit budget request with justifications for purchase
- Prepare Collection
  - Weed collection
  - Inventory collection
- Prepare borrower database
  - Delete borrowers who have not used their accounts recently
- RFP Process
  - Research RFP samples
  - Write RFP
  - Review of RFP
- Evaluate submitted RFPs
  - Evaluation Tool
  - Presentations by vendors
- Select vendor for Integrated Library System
  - Contract
  - Order
- Implement installation
  - Develop the schedule of activities and tasks that need to be completed
  - Network installation or upgrade
  - Electrical wiring
  - Retrospective Conversion
  - Bar code Collection
  - Hardware
    - Upgrade existing hardware
    - Purchase needed hardware
  - Add-ons:
    - Telephone Notification System

- Phone line(s) for telephone notification system
- Workstation for telephone notification system
  ○ Decisions regarding Web site
    ■ Appearance
    ■ Content
    ■ Photographs
    ■ Messages from the director and other staff
- Plan marketing of system to customers
- Plan "thank you" to acknowledge funders
- Installation of hardware and peripherals
- Installation of software
- Staff training
- Going live
- Evaluation of migration
- Final payment to vendor
- Celebrate
  ○ Thank funders
  ○ Thank staff

Timeline with Details

- Visit integrated library system vendors at a professional conference:
  ○ The American Library Association Conference holds two conferences per year (http://www.ala.org), one in January and the other in June. Both are well attended by vendors who serve a variety of libraries: academic, public, school, and special.
  ○ There are also professional conferences for specific types of libraries:
    ■ Academic libraries: Association of College and Research Libraries (ACRL). Information can be found at http://www.acrl.org.
    ■ Public libraries: Public Library Association (PLA). Information can be found at http://www.pla.org.
    ■ School media centers: American Association of School Librarians (AASL). Information can be found at http://www.aasl.org.
    ■ Special libraries: Special Libraries Association (SLA). Information can be found at http://www.sla.org.
- Assessment at library location:
  ○ Hardware: If the existing staff and public workstations are three to four years old, then you will want to consider replacing or upgrading them. Review hardware and specifications from the vendor against the specifications of your current hardware inventory.
  ○ Software: Note the operating system and check to see if the latest service packs for your operating system have been installed on the workstations and servers.
  ○ Network: Is your network in place? Do you need to install additional drops for staff workstations or public-access catalogs? If the ILS vendor will remotely access the server(s) to troubleshoot problems or install software upgrades, those server(s) need to be connected to the Internet.
  ○ Customer needs: Do you have enough public-access catalogs or will you need to purchase more?

- ○ Staff needs: Are you planning for expansion into the near future, such as installing another workstation at the circulation desk? If so, you need to purchase enough client licenses for all staff workstations.
- Planning:
  - ○ Strategic plan: a long-range plan covering what goals and objectives need to accomplished over the next 5 to 20 years.
  - ○ Technology plan: a three-to five-year plan on projected technology needs and staff training.
  - ○ Develop budget: calculate costs of the integrated library system plus any hardware, software, peripherals, add-ons, and network needs that are required to make the ILS operable.
- Research:
  - ○ Visit other library sites—ask prospective vendors to provide you a list of similar-type libraries that have the systems you are interested in researching.
  - ○ Develop a list of questions for vendors.
  - ○ Develop a list of questions for other libraries.
  - ○ Schedule webinars.
  - ○ Schedule site visits with sales consultants.
- Capital request to funders:
  - ○ Submit your budget request with justifications for purchase; justifications should include how the ILS will help provide effective library service to users. It should also include how the new system will help staff use their time more effectively and perhaps save money.
- Prepare the collection:
  - ○ Weed the collection: To prepare for retrospective conversion, it is important to deselect outdated and damaged materials. There is no reason to pay for records you will not use.
  - ○ Inventory: This step is not always a practical one, but in an ideal situation, it is good to inventory your collection to see what is missing before proceeding with the retrospective conversion process.
- Prepare borrower database:
  - ○ Check the instruction manual for your current automation system on how to delete old borrower records. You will want to submit an up-to-date customer database for conversion to the new integrated library system.
- RFP process:
  - ○ Research RFP samples: Ask colleagues for copies of their RFPs. Technology changes rapidly, so if the RFP is more than five years old, it is probably outdated.
  - ○ Write the RFP: After reviewing other RFPs, develop the RFP that will purchase the right system for your organization.
  - ○ Review of RFP: Proofread—ask someone to read through the proposal for accuracy.
- Evaluate submitted RFPs:
  - ○ Evaluation tool: The evaluation committee reads through the bids and scores the results on the evaluation form.
  - ○ Presentations by vendors: Only those who met the criteria in the evaluation stage will need to make a presentation.
- Select vendors for the integrated library system:
  - ○ Contract: Read through the contract that the vendor submits to you. Make changes that protect the interests of the library. The vendor must be contractually liable to information submitted in the RFP. Work with an attorney.
  - ○ Order: Place the order. Double check that the invoice matches the RFP.

- Plan marketing of the system to patrons: Let your library users know that the library is migrating to a new system. Emphasize the benefits to borrowers. Advertise any dates that the library will be closed.
- Plan "thank you" to funders: Think of ways to appropriately thank the people who approved the funding for the capital project, such as a banner in front of the library, a reception to unveil the new system, thank-you notes, press releases to area newspapers, posters, flyers, announcement on the Web site, and so forth.
- Implement installation:
  - Work with the vendor to develop the implementation schedule and communicate the schedule to staff and administration.
    - Decide whether or not the library will close for certain events such as bar coding, installation of software, or staff training.
    - If the library closes before "going live," stagger due dates so that items are not due the first day the library reopens.
- Retrospective conversion: You will work with a cataloguer, so brush up on your cataloging knowledge. Read the Library of Congress's online document "Understanding MARC Bibliographic: Machine-Readable Cataloging" at http://www.loc.gov/marc/umb. Katie Wilson, in her book *Computers in Libraries*, has a helpful chapter on cataloging that covers the MARC record structure, bibliographic utilities, the bibliographic record, the authority record, and the item or holdings record.
  - Bar code collection
  - Hardware and peripherals
    - Upgrade existing workstations, servers, and so forth.
    - Purchase needed hardware and peripherals (servers, workstations, bar code readers, receipt printers, routers, hubs, firewalls, UPSs, and so forth.
  - Add-ons
    - Telephone notification system example
      - Phone line for telephone notification system
      - Workstation for telephone notification system
      - Uninterrupted power supply
  - Network installation or upgrade: If you are adding more workstations, you will need to run Cat-5 cabling and install jacks. Work with your technology staff to see if the firewall and other equipment will be compatible with the new system.
  - Electrical wiring: Do you have enough outlets (and the proper type of outlets) to handle any new equipment?
  - Decisions regarding the Web site: If the vendor is designing the Web site for the library, you will need to decide on a color scheme, photographs to use, plus the content—what information do you want to impart and how do you want to say it?
    - Appearance.
    - Content.
    - Photographs.
    - Messages from the director and other staff.
    - Which staff will have their contact information posted on the Web site?
- Installation of hardware: Everything has to be ready for the installation of the server(s) and workstations. Do you have UPSs, rack mounts for the server(s), access to the Internet, and other equipment in place?
- Installation of software: The vendor will work with you on the installation of software.
- Staff training: Where is the training going to take place? Do you have workstations set up in the training area for hands-on learning along with laptops and LCD projectors? Feed

the staff. This is a stressful time that can be relieved with food. Have snacks and drinks available. Cater in lunch, even if it is ordering pizza.

● Going live: After months of planning, the day has finally arrived. You will want a vendor representative on hand to troubleshoot any problems.

● Evaluation of migration: How did the process go? Were the vendor representatives/trainers helpful? Did you encounter problems with the bibliographic records, patron records, or bar codes? If so, were issues handled to your satisfaction? If not, contact the vendor's implementation project director for resolution.

● Final payment to vendor: Make sure that everything is operating as promised in the contract. Do not make the final payment until all outstanding problems/issues have been resolved.

● Celebrate:
   ○ Thank funders: see previous page.
   ○ Thank staff: Your employees have been on the front line. Thank them for their patience, professionalism, and hard work. If possible, keep snacks and beverages on hand for the first couple of days.

References

"Understanding MARC Bibliographic: Machine-Readable Cataloging" by the Library of Congress in collaboration with The Follett Software Company. http://www.loc.gov/marc/umb.

Wilson, Kate. *Computers in Libraries: An Introduction for Library Technicians.* Binghampton, NY: Haworth Information Press, 2006.

7 Planning Creates Success

- Strategic Plan
- Strategic Plan Example
- Technology Plan
- Technology Plan Example
- Approval Process

If the library's current long-range strategic plan does not include the purchase or upgrade to a new integrated library system, then you will need to update your plan. The same holds true for the library's technology plan. These two plans are important to the success in funding and implementing the project. It is essential to convince the library board, city manager, college president, school board, or other funders to purchase an integrated library system; so the ILS must be part of both the long-range strategic plan and the technology plan.

The strategic plan is the business tool to seek approval from those who have the power to approve or reject the project. Your technology plan serves as the road map for the selection and implementation of hardware, software, wiring, and other components needed to operate the integrated library system.

Strategic Plan

"Strategic planning can be a significant opportunity to unify management, staff members, stakeholders, and customers through a common understanding of where the library is going, how everyone can work to achieve a common purpose, and how the library will measure and report its progress and levels of success. . . . one of the most important perspectives that must be maintained in the planning process is a focus on the customer" (Matthews, Joseph R. *Strategic Planning and Management for Library Managers*, p. 58).

The difference in strategic planning, as opposed to long-range planning, is that the library is projecting its services and collection far into the future. Businesses create strategic plans that steer them 20 years into the future. Libraries need to look beyond the three- to five-year time frame and visualize past the horizon. Even the smallest library has a multitude of responsibilities to manage, a patron base, an inventory of materials, services, and programs to fund, personnel to supervise, and an administration or board to which it must report. The library must envision its business of serving patrons 10 or more years into the future. And, most specifically in regard to this chapter, the strategic plan must incorporate the integrated library system (the engine of the library) into the library's future goals.

Technology is intertwined in nearly all aspects of library service, and technology costs money. The library builds support in providing excellent service and delivery of information on a daily basis. You must ask representatives of those you serve to help with strategic planning in order to learn what patrons want and to ask for their support.

A successful strategic plan is one that is developed by a planning committee. The committee should consist of those who will assist and support the library in moving forward. In a public library setting, this will include members of the library board, friends of the library, active community residents, library patrons, city council officers, and library staff. The group does not need to be large; in fact, a group of 10 or fewer is more effective. The strategic plan will cover all aspects of planning for the library's future, such as staffing levels to meet customer demand, types of services to provide or eliminate, allocation of funds, building upgrades or expansion plans, furniture purchases, and, of course, the acquisition of an integrated library system.

When the planning committee discusses the ILS, the library director or network administrator gives a presentation about an integrated library system and how it will benefit the library and those it serves. The presentation to the planning committee will include: (1) a description of the integrated library system and the projected outcomes (benefits) if purchased, (2) the proposed costs for the project, and (3) possible sources of funds for the system.

A description of the integrated library system must include highlights of the product that will interest the committee. Most planning-committee members will find features that directly benefit library borrowers, or that save money or staff time, as beneficial. An example of this would be an integrated library system that provides e-mail and telephone notifications to patrons regarding materials waiting for them at the library and/or overdue materials. (Some e-mail notification systems also send courtesy notices to patrons before their items are due.) These features will pique the interest of the planning committee as the library director presents not only the customer-service benefits of e-mail/telephone notification, but also presents how these features eliminate the need for library staff to call patrons, thereby saving staff time. In addition, the library director may point out that e-mail and telephone notification systems will allow funds budgeted for postage, postcards, paper, and envelopes to be reallocated for other purposes.

The proposed budget for the ILS should include a breakdown of software, hardware, add-ons, annual maintenance fees, and any other costs affiliated with installing and implementing the ILS. It is important to provide a complete picture of the project to the planning committee so that they are informed about all the costs involved. Refer to Chapter 8 for details on constructing a budget and a justification statement. Planning committee members are your base of support in seeking approval for a new integrated library system. It is vital that members be able to speak in an educated, informed manner to the administration members who will approve the funding request.

As the library director or network administrator, you are the expert in choosing the type of integrated library system to purchase for the library (turnkey, hosted, and/or SaaS). Do not provide choices of types of systems to the planning committee—present the specific type or specific system that you want to purchase. If members of the planning committee are familiar with different types of integrated library systems, be prepared to support your choice with comparisons in features, the ability to add components, and the overall costs involved. If you are not able to provide all the answers at a particular meeting, take note of the questions and return to the next meeting with answers.

Strategic Plan Example

The following is an example of a long-range strategic plan for a public library that aspires to purchase a new integrated library system. The wording of the plan is not elaborate. It includes the goals, objectives, outcomes, and proposed budget in simple, direct statements. The budget presented in this example is for a medium-sized public library seeking a robust ILS along with a telephone notification add-on.

The purpose of the following example is to give a template for writing the section of the strategic plan that addresses the goal of purchasing an ILS. There are a variety of integrated library systems and a number of price structures. The dollar amounts in the following example should be read as placeholders for the amounts that you will plug in for your own purposes. A complete long-range strategic plan may be found in Appendix B.

Anywhere Public Library

Strategic Plan 2011–2021

Goal #1: Library customers utilize current technology to access information.

Objectives:

1. By December 2013, select, purchase, and implement an integrated library system that includes a telephone notification system.
2. By December 2013, replace the Web server and data server with those that are compatible with the new integrated library system.
3. By June 2014, customers of Anywhere Public Library will be able to manage their personal accounts online from the library's Web site, such as reserving materials and renewing items from home, school, or work.
4. By December 2014, the Anywhere Public Library will have its Web 2.0 technologies available via its Web site.
5. By December 2014, the Anywhere Public Library Web site is the location people access daily for information.
6. By December 2015, add public computer reservation and print management software.
7. Schedule replacement of staff and public computer workstations and software on a three-year basis so that both staff and patrons have access to current technologies.

Outcomes:

1. The library will provide an economic benefit to the city of Anywhere and the Anywhere Chamber of Commerce by hosting a Web site that provides full-text magazine and newspaper articles, community information, a calendar of events, and links to recommended reading lists, news, weather, and ready-reference Web sites. The library's Web site will be visited daily by those seeking current information.
2. The library provides an economic benefit to the community by providing computers, software, and high-speed Internet access for continuing education and job-seeking purposes.

3. Borrowers reserve materials, renew materials, and otherwise manage their accounts utilizing the library's Web site.

4. Borrowers will utilize Web 2.0 technologies such as library blog(s), social network sites, e-mail references, and RSS feeds.

5. Borrowers receive timely overdue remainders by e-mail or telephone notification via the integrated library system. This feature saves paper, envelopes, and postage and uses staff time more effectively for other responsibilities.

6. Borrowers are quickly notified of materials on hold by e-mail or telephone notification via the new integrated library system. Circulation staffers no longer have to call patrons; therefore, their time is used more effectively in assisting customers and performing other duties.

7. Library usage will grow by 3 percent annually due to patrons discovering the wealth of materials available at the library via the new online public-access catalog.

8. Public computer (PC) reservation and print-management solutions will help staff better assist patrons in using the public computer workstations for recreational, business, job-seeking, and continuing-education purposes.

Budget Impact:

1. The initial cost for an integrated library system is approximately $37,935. This price includes software ($25,500), a data server ($7,400), Web server ($3,565), and a telephone notification system ($1,470). The data server manages the ILS software, bibliographic and patron records and the Web server hosts the library's Web site. The library director will seek capital funds from the City of Anywhere and/or utilize state funding for public libraries and seek financial assistance from the friends of the library.

2. The software maintenance agreement for the ILS will cost approximately $5,000 per year. City and/or state funds will be utilized for this purpose.

3. Approximately $4,000 per year will be budgeted for equipment (computer workstations, scanners, printers), replacements, and software upgrades.

4. PC reservation and print management software, projected to be added in 2014, will have an initial cost of $7,500 plus $2,200 for a reservation workstation and receipt printer. (Network cabling is already in place.)

Technology Plan

The library's technology plan also addresses the need for an integrated library system. The technology plan covers the goals and objectives in improving library services through computer equipment and software, Internet access, the library's Web site, online resources, electronic-based marketing (such as social networks), and other technology-based services. "Since technology is now so tightly interwoven with all library functions, planning for the future of technology means planning for the library itself" (Gordon, Rachel Singer. *The Accidental Systems Librarian*, 2002, p. 169).

Public libraries and school systems are required to write technology plans every three to five years if they apply for federal e-rate discounts. The technology plan should really be viewed as a vehicle to improve library services and should be a formal planning process undertaken by all libraries. It is important that the library strategize how it is going to spend its funds, allocate staffing and training to incorporate technology in operating the library, and serving its patron base.

The plan should cover three to five years into the future. Technological innovations make it difficult to write a plan that covers more than five years. Input from the community and library staff can assist in writing the technology plan. Joseph Matthews writes in his book *Technology Planning: Preparing and Updating a Library Technology Plan* that "the critical audience for a technology plan is the library stakeholders and funding decision makers who will determine the fiscal and other resources that are allocated to the library on a yearly basis. These decision-making individuals will, as a result of reading the plan, have a better understanding of how technology is used by the library to deliver services that are designed to meet the needs of its customers and will therefore be in a better position to allocate the necessary resources to fulfill the plan" (2004, p. 3).

A library can host public meetings, lead focus groups, or conduct surveys to acquire information from the community (public, student/faculty, and corporate) that the library serves. In addition, the library director must keep current with technology through books, journal articles, Listservs, blogs, conferences, and interaction with MIS administrators employed by similar-type libraries. Staying current with technology will not only help the library director to write a technology plan, but will also assist the director in seeking approval for the plan. The director is the spokesperson for the library and must be able to translate technological advances into language understandable to staff and administration.

The information that goes into the technology plan regarding the integrated library system, of course, reflects the type of ILS the library is considering. If the library is planning to purchase a software-as-a-service system, then the technology plan will address the network infrastructure, workstations, operating systems, browser versions, and so forth, needed to implement this type of system.

To ensure a successful implantation, the plan includes all the components that need to be in place for the ILS to operate. These components include the network, security of the network, the equipment room, cabling, electricity, uninterrupted power supplies, the bandwidth of the Internet connection, the computer workstations and their operation systems, the servers and their operating systems, methods for data recovery, browser versions, peripherals, and staff training. Planning for the technological aspects of the ILS helps the library director to think through all the steps that need to be taken and all the hardware, if any, that needs to be acquired.

The following is an example of what may be written in a technology plan concerning the purchase of a turnkey integrated library system. A sample technology plan may be found in Appendix C.

Technology Plan Example

Anywhere Public Library

Technology Plan 2013–2018

- The library will investigate the purchase of a new integrated library system (ILS) that will better serve the community.
    a. The library will work with the City of Anywhere and outside funding sources to purchase an ILS that meets the needs of future challenges.
    - Library staff will research ILS software and prices.
    - The library director will present this plan to the library board of trustees at its February 2013 meeting.
    - The library director will present this plan to the city manager and friends of the library to ask for financial assistance at March 2013 meetings.
    - If needed, outside funding sources will be researched and pursued beginning in July 2013.

Budget impact: The integrated library system that is purchased will be one that best serves the community and can be operated with little impact on staff time. Systems being considered are those in which the hardware and software are located on-site and in which the vendor has remote access to troubleshoot the hardware and software. Estimated software costs are $25,000, with $5,000 in annual maintenance fees.

Evaluation: The Anywhere Public Library's board of trustees approved the library's long-range strategic plan for 2011–2021. This plan calls for the purchase of a new integrated library system with features to better serve the community, along with modules that save staff time and money spent on postage and paper supplies. The Anywhere Public Library will be successful in purchasing an ILS that provides excellent customer service and is easily operated and maintained by the library staff. The library will be successful in attaining the necessary funding through the City of Anywhere and the Friends of the Anywhere Public Library.

● The library will select an integrated library system that will be robust in features but simple in operation and maintenance.
   a. The ILS software will be housed on-site.
      ● The library will replace the existing data server, which is six years old.
      ● The library will replace the existing Web server, which is four years old.
      ● The uninterrupted power supply will be replaced and upgraded to a better model.
      ● A turnkey ILS will be explored in which the library purchases the hardware and software from the vendor. The vendor loads the software on the servers before shipping to the library and handles any server issues with the hardware manufacturer.
      ● The library will work with the city's MIS administrator and the ILS vendor to ensure that the ILS can utilize the current network as the switches, router, and firewall are current and in good working order.
      ● The ILS will utilize the current staff and client workstations as the operating system, processing speed, memory, and other specifications exceed the vendors' requirements.
      ● The latest service packs and browser versions will be installed on each staff and client workstation.

   b. A telephone notification system will be purchased so that library patrons are notified of overdue materials and items on hold for them through an automated calling system.
      ● The library will purchase the telephone notification system from the ILS vendor to insure compatibility. The ILS vendor will install and maintain the telephone notification system.
      ● The telephone notification system software will be installed on an existing workstation in the staff work area. This workstation is currently on the network and no additional changes need to be made. The ILS vendor will install software to troubleshoot the notification software remotely.
      ● One dedicated telephone line will be installed at the location of this workstation. The library will work with the phone system company to ensure compatibility with the proposed telephone notification system.
      ● The existing uninterrupted power supply will be utilized for the telephone notification hardware and computer workstation.

   c. An automatic e-mail notification system will be purchased so that library patrons receive courtesy notices regarding upcoming due dates, notices regarding overdue materials, and notices for materials on hold.

- The library will select an ILS in which these features do not require staff interaction. E-mails are generated automatically by the ILS software.
- The library staff will work with the MIS administrator and the ILS vendor to ensure that the city's exchange server and its operating system version are compatible with the e-mail notification system.

    d. Library will select an ILS vendor who provides a Web site as part of the ILS package.
- Borrowers will be able to manage their accounts online: place holds, renew materials, check fine payment history, and so forth.
- Staff will implement Web 2.0 technologies:
  1. The youth services librarian will start and maintain a blog page for teens to discuss books, authors, and programs. Links to blogs will be featured on library's Web page.
  2. Library staff will create and maintain a social networking site promoting materials, services, and programs. Link to the social networking site on the Web page.
  3. Create a link on Web site for borrowers to e-mail reference questions. Reference librarians will read and respond to e-mailed inquiries.
  4. Library staff will work with the ILS vendor to implement RSS feed technology.

Budget Impact:

- The library will replace the existing data server and Web server. The library will purchase hardware that allows for future growth in patron records, bibliographic records, and Web traffic. A separate Web server is necessary for the security and integrity of the data server. The library needs to replace the existing firewall in order to protect the Web server from unauthorized access. The estimated cost for both servers is $11,000 and the estimated cost of replacing the firewall component is $2,860.
- The MIS administrator for the City of Anywhere will assist the library director in writing the technology portion of the RFP at no additional charge. In addition, the MIS administrator will update any service packs and browser versions at no additional charge to the city or the library.
- The MIS administrator will be on-site for the installation of the new data server and Web server plus the installation of the client software on the staff and public workstations. The latter requires turning off the security software on the public workstations to allow for the installation of new software. An estimated $2,400 will be budgeted for the services that fall outside of the City's contract with the MIS administrator.
- The library will budget $1,500 for the purchase of a telephone notification system along with $200 in annual maintenance fees. The ILS vendor will install the notification system at no additional charge. The ILS vendor will maintain the telephone notification system and work directly with the manufacturer in troubleshooting any software and hardware issues without additional costs to the library other than the annual maintenance fees.
- The library will notify the company that manages the City's phone system regarding the installation of a telephone notification system to ensure compatibility plus the access of another dedicated phone line for the library. Have $100 budgeted for the installation of a dedicated telephone line.
- A new uninterrupted power supply (UPS) will be purchased for the equipment closet to handle the larger data server and Web server needed for the new ILS. The existing UPS will be utilized for the telephone notification system hardware.

Evaluation: The new servers will handle growth in patron records, bibliographic records, and Web traffic over the next four to six years. The new Web site, telephone, and e-mail notification systems will move the library into a new level of service for the community. The library will realize a net growth of 3 percent each year in the number of cardholders along with a growth of 3 percent annually in the circulation of materials. Web site usage will increase by 5 percent each year.

e. Staff training:
- The ILS vendor will provide on-site training for all modules and components. Training will be provided to all circulation, reference, and administrative staff, and a training day will consist of an eight-hour day.
- The ILS vendor will train and advise staff on the daily backup routine for the servers.
- The ILS vendor will train staff on any on-site server maintenance that needs to occur.
- The ILS vendor will train staff on operation and maintenance of the telephone notification system.

Budget Impact: Approximately $4,500 will be budgeted for three full days of staff training along with training instructors on-site for "going live" with the new integrated library system. The vendor will also quote follow-up training costs for a 12-month period following the installation of the system in case additional training is needed.

Evaluation: Staff will receive training that will provide competency in the following areas:

- Operate daily circulation functions with ease: check-in, checkout, add new patron records, update patron records, place holds, and handle fines and lost-book charges.
- Ability to perform original cataloging, copy cataloging, use of cataloging templates, import MARC records from another server using Z39.50, and to import MARC records from vendors. Ability to use authority control functions.
- Working knowledge of public-access catalog, including search strategies, managing patron accounts, and placing holds.
- Working knowledge of utilizing library's Web site, including accessing electronic resources and other links. Ability to update Web site information.
- Staff are able to perform daily backup routines on servers and is able to confirm that backup functions are operating correctly. Staff are able to perform routine maintenance on servers.
- The vendor will set up the telephone notification system, including recording messages. Staff will have working knowledge of running the notification system for holds and overdue materials and will be able to run daily reports on results of phone contact and attempted contact.

Approval Process

The final step in creating the long-range strategic plan and the library's technology plan is seeking final approval or acceptance by the administrative body that oversees the library's budget. This step is vitally important, especially with the long-range strategic plan. Just by virtue of having conducted a planning process and of having written a plan will establish the library director as a leader and the organization itself as a professional entity. This impression of the library director by the administrative body will assist in approving the purchase of the integrated library system and other projects outlined in the strategic plan.

Both plans can also be utilized as garnering support among other departments, in the community, or within the organization. Present the plan in a professional format and, at a minimum, use word-processing software and graphics to create attractive covers for three-ring binders. Do what is needed and appropriate for your type of organization to promote the plan—press releases to the media, speaking to local civic organizations, or making presentations to faculty, alumni, and parents.

In Conclusion

Writing a strategic plan and a technology plan takes time and planning. One has to plan *to* plan. Investing in the time to plan at the beginning will ensure a successful purchase and implementation in the end. It is well worth the time and thought that it takes to form a planning committee, gather patron and staff input, research the current technology, work with the network administrator, and research the variety of integrated library systems available. Planning also gives you a timeline from which to work. (Refer to Chapter 6.)

The next step is to work within your fiscal-year constraints to write a capital budget request and justification statement to submit for approval. The justification statement, which is covered in the following chapter, is a short document that accompanies the budget and explains the benefits of the integrated library system to the board or administration. Submitting a budget for approval tells the administration how much the project costs but does not detail the benefits to the staff and patrons and the savings that new technology can provide.

References

Bolan, Kimberly, and Robert Cullin. *Technology Made Simple: An Improvement Guide for Small and Medium Libraries.* Chicago: American Library Association, 2007.

Gordon, Rachel Singer. *The Accidental Systems Librarian.* Medford, NJ: Information Today, Inc., 2002.

Matthews, Joseph. *Scorecards for Results: A Guide for Developing a Library Balanced Scorecard.* Westport, CT: Libraries Unlimited, 2008.

———. *Strategic Planning and Management for Library Managers.* Westport, CT: Libraries Unlimited, 2005.

———. *Technology Planning: Preparing and Updating a Library Technology Plan.* Westport, CT: Libraries Unlimited, 2004.

Nelson, Sandra. *Implementing for Results: Your Strategic Plan in Action.* American Library Association, 2008.

Nelson, Sandra, for the Public Library Association. *Strategic Planning for Results.* Chicago: American Library Association, 2008.

New Jersey State Library, Library Development Bureau, http://www.njstatelib.org/LDB/E-Rate/utechpln.php. Several links on technology planning and sample technology plans.

North Central Regional Education Laboratory, http://www.ncrel.org/sdrs/areas/issues/methods/technlgy/te300.htm. Technology plans for public schools.

Techsoup.org, http://www.techsoup.org/learningcenter/techplan/index.cfm. Web page with article links on technology planning for nonprofits.

WebJunction, http://www.webjunction.org/techplan. Web page with links on creating and writing a technology plan.

8 Creating the Budget

- Vendor Price Comparison Grid
- Preparing the Budget for Approval
- Sample Budget
- Description for Each Budget Line Item
- Justification Statement
- Sample Justification Statement
- Divulging the Proposed Budget for an ILS Project

Once you have written or updated the long-range strategic plan and the technology plan, and have had both plans approved by the library board or other administrative body, then the next step is to make the capital request in your annual budget submittal. A capital request is a request outside of the normal, routine funds to operate the library. Operating funds are for personnel, materials for the collection, database subscriptions, office supplies, utilities, Internet access, and building maintenance. Capital funds are one-time requests for special projects such as replacing a roof, purchasing a vehicle, or, as in this example, purchasing an integrated library system and its related equipment, hardware, and peripherals.

Prices for integrated library systems vary widely among vendors and also upon what type of ILS is selected. An effective method for comparing companies is to create a grid.

Vendor Price Comparison Grid

Create a grid that compares prices for the software, hardware, services, add-ons, and training among the companies you are considering. This organized compilation of information will help you write a proposed budget for the ILS capital request. Once you have a good estimate of the funds needed to purchase the ILS for your facility, you can write the budget and the justification statement.

Please note that your board or administrator may want to see a list of vendors you have been researching for the ILS project. This presentation should include only companies from which you want to receive bids. Do not include vendors whose products do not fit your

Vendor Comparison Grid

Company Name	Product	Price	Second Year Costs	Comments
Company A (Turnkey System)	ILS software	$25,500.00	$5,100.00	Basic package includes circulation, offline circulation, cataloging, reports, patron authentication, public access catalog, Web site and inventory modules. Price includes unlimited PAC licensing; 7 staff workstations.
	Z39.50 server	$0.00	$0.00	Included—no additional charge
	Acquisition Module	$3,000.00	$800.00	Software-as-as-Service product
	Telephone Notification System	$1,470.00	$294.00	Third-Party Company—ILS vendor installs and provides technical support
	E-mail Notification System	$0.00	$0.00	Included—no additional charge
	Federated Searching	$3,950.00	$3,950.00	Annual subscription fee for up to 10 databases
	OPAC Enrichment	$995.00	$995.00	Annual subscription fee
	Copy Cataloging Product	$495.00	$495.00	Annual subscription fee per user
	Authority Control	$0.00	$0.00	included—no additional charge
Note: Vendor sells a combined data/Web server for libraries with less than 50,000 titles for $5,000	Data Server	$7,403.00		3-year warranty—vendor ships server with software pre-installed; vendor handles all hardware issues directly with manufacturer
	Web Server	$3,547.00		3-year warranty - vendor handles all hardware issues directly with manufacturer
	Retrospective Conversion	$4,435.00		$0.10 per record
	On-site Installation	$3,200.00		
	On-site staff training	$4,500.00		3-days training; include going live
	Total Initial Costs	**$58,495.00**		
	Total Second-Year Costs		**$11,634.00**	

Company B	ILS Software	$20,250.00	$5,715.00	Basic package includes circulation, offline circulation, cataloging, Web site, inventory, acquisitions, patron authentication, OCLC Inter Library Loan Interface modules. Price includes unlimited PAC licensing; 7 staff workstations
	Public Access Catalog			Web-browser application
	Authority Control	$0.00		Included—no additional charge
	Reports Module	$3,000.00	$750.00	
	E-mail notification	$0.00		Included—no additional charge
	OPAC Enrichment	$0.00		Included—no additional charge
	Data Server	$12,605.00		
	Retrospective Conversion	$7,500.00	$0.00	Includes bibliographic records, patron records and circulation transaction migration
	On-site installation	$4,500.00		
	Source Code Maintenance	$700.00	$1,500.00	
	On-site training	$18,000.00		2-days training; include going live
	Total Initial Costs	**$66,555.00**		
	Total Second-Year Costs		**$7,965.00**	
Vendor states that the library must arrange purchase and installation of third-party products				

(Continued)

(Continued)

Company Name	Product	Price	Second Year Costs	Comments
Company C (no servers on-site)	ILS Software	$18,400.00	$3,700.00	Price based on number of bibliographic records
	Hosting Fees	$1,200.00	$1,200.00	Annual fee
	Installation	$2,900.00		
	Retrospective Conversion	$4,435.00		$0.10 per record
	Federated Searching	$3,950.00	$3,950.00	Annual subscription fee for up to 10 databases
	OPAC Enrichment	$1,050.00	$1,050.00	Annual subscription fee
	Authority Control	$1,500.00		Annual subscription fee
	On-site training	$2,500.00		2-days, include going live
Vendor states that the library must arrange purchase and installation of third-party products	**Total Initial Costs** **Total Second-Year Costs**	**$35,935.00**	**$9,900.00**	

operations. If administrators look solely at the bottom line, the vendor with the lowest price may suddenly become the only choice available to you. Administrators may also think that if you have a vendor on the list, then you must be considering the company as an option.

Prices for integrated library systems vary by 50 percent or more. If you are proposing a budget that is at the higher end, a detailed budget and justification statement must show how the higher price tag will purchase a better system and benefit the library.

Preparing the Budget for Approval

After you have gathered information about the integrated library systems available and asked vendors for estimated costs, it is time to create a budget to present to the administration or the board for approval. A budget lists all the expenditures necessary to implement the project. This would include the ILS software, the hardware needed to operate the software, preparation of space to house the hardware, the retrospective conversion, peripherals, subscription fees for copy-cataloging services, installation, maintenance, training, and add-ons such as a serials module, federated searching software, or a computer reservation system.

Present a detailed budget listing the price for each item. This will help to justify the amount of funds you are requesting. It is important to show that you have given thought and consideration to your budget proposal. Any kind of fluff will cause administrators or board members to question the entire document.

Another benefit of presenting a detailed budget is assisting in the difficult choice of making cuts if the total amount requested cannot be approved. If the administration is not able to fund the entire amount, a line-item budget will assist you in discussing what features can be set aside for implementation at a later date. Libraries can start with a basic system and purchase additional features later. A detailed budget will also prevent cuts so deep that it keeps you from purchasing the ILS system that is needed.

Following is a sample of a detailed budget request for a turnkey integrated library system. The sample budget coincides with the strategic plan and technology plan examples given in Chapter 7. In this illustration, the library director is proposing that the library purchase the ILS software, hardware, add-ons, and peripherals from one vendor. The add-ons include (1) the acquisitions module, (2) a telephone notification system, (3) federated searching software, and (4) enriched content (book jackets, reviews, and summaries) for the public access catalog. The library currently has a local area network with access to the Internet, so equipment costs include only expenses to install the data server and Web server in the server room.

Sample Budget

Sample Budget Request for the Integrated Library System

	INTEGRATED LIBRARY SYSTEM COMPONENTS	COSTS	SECOND-YEAR COSTS
1	ILS Software—second-year costs include annual support renewal	$25,000.00	$5,000.00
2	Z39.50	$0.00	$0.00
3	Data Server (3-year warranty)	$7,500.00	$0.00
4	Web server (3-year warranty)	$3,500.00	$0.00
5	Installation of servers on-site	$3,200.00	$0.00
6	Data Preparation of MARC records@ $0.10 per record	$4,435.00	$0.00
7	Online Acquisitions Module	$2,300.00	$500.00
8	Cataloging Authority Control	$1,500.00	$0.00
9	Bar code Scanners (3)	$1,280.00	$165.00
10	Telephone Notification System	$1,350.00	$200.00
11	Federated Searching Software	$2,000.00	$2,000.00
12	Enriched content on public access catalog	$1,050.00	$1,050.00
13	On-site training for staff (3 days)	$4,500.00	$0.00
14	**Total first-year costs**	**$57,615.00**	
15	**Total second-year costs**		**$8,915.00**
16	**Equipment Costs for Server Room**		
17	Firewall to protect Web server	$2,860.00	
18	Uninterrupted power supply*	$800.00	
19	KVM (Key Video Mouse) Switch **	$120.00	
20	KVM Rack Mount	$125.00	
21	Cable Kit for KVM	$96.00	
22	DMZ Switch***	$800.00	
23	Contract network administrator (3days)	$2,400.00	
24	Contingency for unforeseen problems	$1,000.00	
25	**TOTAL**	**$8,201.00**	
26	*Need to upgrade current UPS to a better model.		
27	**KVM switch minimizes space, hardware, electricity, and cabling by leveraging just one keyboard, monitor, and mouse for multiple servers		
28	***DMZ—place additional security between library's network and the public Internet.		

Description for each budget line item:

Line 1: $25,500 is the proposed cost of the basic integrated library system software, which includes circulation, catalog, public catalog, inventory, Web site, and reports modules. (In this particular example, the library director is looking solely at ILS vendors who include the Web site as part of the basic package.) Second-year costs include the annual software maintenance and license renewal fee.

Line 2: Z39.50 is the communication protocol that allows your data server to communicate with other servers to exchange information such as MARC records. Most ILS vendors do not charge extra for this software program.

Line 3: The data server will house the ILS circulation and catalog software along with the library's patron data, transaction data, and bibliographic records. Most vendors are offering hardware with a three-year warranty; hence, there are no second-year costs.

Line 4: The Web server will house the library's Web site and online public-access catalog.

Line 5: Installation charges by the ILS vendor for installing the data server and Web server at the library.

Line 6: Data preparation of library bibliographic records has been quoted at 10 cents per record. The library currently has 44,350 titles for a cost of $4,435.

Line 7: The acquisitions module has an initial cost of $2,300 with an annual maintenance license renewal fee of $500 per year.

Line 8: Cataloging authority control is offered by most vendors at no additional charge. As MARC records are added to the catalog, they can be checked against national authority files such as Library of Congress authority files.

Line 9: Bar code scanners. In migrating from one integrated system to another, the library needs to purchase three new bar code scanners for the circulation desk. The current bar code scanners are proprietary and will not work with new software. An annual maintenance agreement of $165 covers all three scanners.

Line 10: The telephone notification system costs $1,350, which includes the hardware and software costs. The library director will choose an ILS vendor who supports this add-on and who will also install and configure the equipment and software. The annual maintenance fee is $200 per year.

Line 11: Federated searching software will be from a third-party company that can function with the chosen ILS. The estimated cost is $2,000. This is special pricing for utilizing 10 or fewer online databases.

Line 12: Enriched content for the public catalog features book jackets, reviews, summaries, and table of contents. This product has an annual subscription fee of $1,050 per year.

Line 13: On-site training is the best option for library staff. It is estimated that it will take two full days of training plus a third day having the trainers on-site for going live with the new system.

Line 14: Total first-year costs. This is the total amount the library director is requesting in her or his capital request to purchase an integrated library system that is best for the library. Reasons for this system will be outlined in the justification statement. Lines 16–20 include the additional equipment that will be needed to operate the new integrated library system.

Line 15: Total second-year costs. These costs include the renewal fees for maintenance (technical support), software licensing renewals, and subscription renewals. It should be estimated that these costs may increase in year three or four.

Line 16: Equipment costs for the server room. This category will include all the additional equipment, hardware, and cabling that needs to be acquired to operate the proposed integrated library system.

Line 17: Firewall to protect the network and Web server. The library in this example has Internet access, so it owns a firewall. However, the ILS vendor and the library's network administrator state that a different firewall model needs to be purchased to handle the proposed Web server. (If the library does not have a DMZ switch, it should consider installing one for additional network security.)

Line 18: Uninterrupted power supply (UPS). A higher-power UPS needs to be purchased to handle the additional data server and Web server.

Line 19: KVM (keyboard video mouse) switch. With the purchase of the data and Web servers, the library will have a total of three servers. (The third server manages the local area network.) To save space, the library plans to purchase a KVM switch in order to use one monitor, mouse, and keyboard to manage the three servers.

Line 20: Rack mount for the KVM switch.

Line 21: Cable kit for the KVM switch.

Line 22: DMZ Switch—additional security of library's network. Refer to Line 28.

Line 23: Estimated fees for the contract network administrator to work with the ILS vendor in installing the servers on-site and connecting to the library's LAN.

Line 24: It is important to include contingency funds to cover unexpected costs.

Line 25: Total equipment costs for preparing the server room for the proposed ILS software and hardware.

After presenting the budget in the example, the library director is told that that the total budget request is more than the administration can approve at this time. The administration is able to fund the request, with the exception of the Web server, the three bar code scanners, and the online acquisition component. Since a friends-of-the-library representative was a member of the planning committee, the representative asks the group to help with funding part of the project. The library director foregoes the purchase of the online acquisition component until the next budget cycle, and the friends of the library are asked to purchase the Web server and the three bar code scanners. The purchase price for the Web server includes technical support, on-site repairs, and replacement parts for three years. The administration agrees to pay the annual maintenance fees for the bar code scanners.

Due to a budget presentation that included a line item for each component of the ILS, the library director was able to negotiate the needed funds for the project through both the administration and the friends of the library. It is important not to become discouraged if approval for the project does not happen on the first request. Library directors have had to write grants, seek gift money from private individuals, or host fund-raisers to raise the money needed for such projects. Individual schools or school districts can enlist help from their parent-teacher organizations. Academic libraries can solicit help from the development office or form a friends of the library group using alumni as members. Capital funds may be raised to purchase the ILS, but the library director must have a commitment from administration for the annual maintenance fees for the software and hardware.

Justification Statement

A vital piece of every budget submittal is the justification statement. Those with the power to approve your budget requests are most likely not experts on integrated library systems and how an ILS affects the daily operations of a library. It is your job to educate them. The justification statement is a one to two page document that states succinctly why an integrated library system needs to be purchased. This is the opportunity to present the research you have invested into the process and to illustrate how this ILS is going to improve the delivery of library services to your patrons.

A thoughtful, detailed justification statement attached to the capital budget request will help improve your opportunity for approval. A justification statement allows administrators to read the story behind the numbers. It answers the questions of how this capital project will improve library operations and the people it serves. Even if you are given a chance to speak before the budget committee, the finance director, the library board, the college president, or another administrator, not everyone is an effective listener. Having the information in written form gives the board an opportunity to peruse the justifications for the project on their time frame.

Answer the following questions in the body of the justification statement:

- Why is a new integrated library system necessary and why is it necessary at this time?
- Who will benefit from a new ILS—staff, borrowers, or both?
- State if a new system will save money and, if so, be ready to provide figures to support these claims.
- How will the ILS software and hardware be paid for? Are there options for funding sources?

Following is a sample justification statement for a medium-size public library that is seeking approval to purchase a new ILS in order to migrate from a simple automation system to a complex ILS offering more features. The statement begins with the declaration that the library must purchase a new system in order to meet the demands of serving patrons. This assertion is followed by specific examples of how a new ILS will improve operations. End the justification statement with possible avenues for funding the project such as capital funds, lease options, friends of the library, parent-teacher organization, grants, or donations.

Sample Justification Statement

The Anywhere Public Library must upgrade to a more robust automation system to handle its circulation, catalog, and online catalog functions. A new integrated library system is necessary because the library has outgrown the product it uses. The current software lacks features that a busy public library needs. For example, only one staff person at a time can make or a revise a library card. The software does not allow for multiple users to enter customer information, so staff members must wait on others to finish before they can enter the customer database. Staffers make approximately 250 new cards each month and manage a database of 25,000+ cardholders. A new ILS would greatly improve the staff's ability to serve borrowers more effectively and efficiently.

Library users are also not able to renew their materials online and this is a feature they request. Approximately 50 percent of phone calls made to the library are to renew materials. Online renewals will free up our telephone lines for other calls and allow the circulation staff to better serve customers at the desk. A new automation system will notify customers by e-mail or telephone that their materials are overdue or that reserved materials are available for them to pick up. This feature will save hundreds of dollars annually in paper, envelopes, and postage because library staffers will no longer mail overdue notices or bills each week. Customers will receive an e-mailed courtesy notice that items are almost due followed by three subsequent overdue notices every two weeks by e-mail or automated telephone notification if materials are not returned.

Another important feature of a quality automation system is federated searching. Federated searching will combine all of our electronic resources with our print resources. For example, if someone searches for information on how to build a barn, not only will they find books about building a barn, but also magazine articles and electronic books. Currently, the library has several databases on its Web site that must be searched individually. Federated searching allows patrons to search the online catalog, the library's databases, and e-books simultaneously—the customer does not know this is happening, he just sees the results.

Another attribute of a quality integrated library system is patron authentication. This feature allows patrons to access electronic resources on the library's Web site remotely from home, work, or the local coffee shop. For example, the library provides two genealogical databases on its Web site but the databases cannot be used outside of the library because the current ILS software does not authenticate patrons visiting the library's Web site. With an upgraded, robust integrated library system, patrons will enter their library card number and password and be able to use all of the electronic resources the library offers on its Web site. This makes information available to library users 24 hours a day, 7 days a week, 365 days a year.

An attractive, easy-to-use Web site is a requirement in today's society. Many ILS vendors create an attractive Web site for the library that is made to specification at no additional cost. It will utilize the city's graphics to make the library's Web site visually compatible with the city's Web site.

The Anywhere Public Library is a busy library with limited staff. The type of ILS that staff recommends is a turnkey system. Hardware and software purchased from the vendor. The company loads the software at its site and, once installed at the library, is able to remotely troubleshoot both hardware and software issues. Technical support is available 24/7/365 via a toll-free number. The data server comes with four hard drives and therefore patrons and staff should not experience any downtime. For the benefit of all staff, the vendor selected should provide on-site training.

In regards to paying for a quality automation system, the City of Anywhere may be able to enter a lease purchase option if capital funds are not available. Funds for the capital or lease purchase options may include money from the library fund, state aid, donations, or grants. Annual maintenance fees also would need to be considered if the capital project is approved. Details are provided in the attached capital budget request.

In addition to submitting your budget to your administration or board, you may have to make a formal presentation or defend your request. Write a list of questions you may be asked and practice your answers aloud until you are comfortable and know your material. Exhibiting confidence is crucial. Your request is in competition with other departments on campus, other departments within the city, or other facility needs. The administration is dependent upon you to convince them that the project is vital to delivering needed services to library users.

Divulging the Proposed Budget for an ILS Project

Remember that the budget you present for approval may change during the RFP process. For one thing, it depends upon how much time passes between the time you create the budget and when the RFP solicitations are issued. Competitive bidding may cause prices to come in lower, or economic factors may cause prices to rise. In the bidding process, however, vendors who want your business will make every effort to offer their best price.

During your interaction with sales consultants, do not divulge the ballpark budget figure. It will take away your ability to receive or negotiate the best quote. Sales representatives may ask what type of price range their competitors are giving. Play your cards close to the vest. Do not give sales reps information regarding other companies—it hurts your bottom line in the long run.

Some tax-supported organizations, such as a school district, have a dollar amount for which items must go through the bidding process. For instance, Generation X School District must put out to bid any equipment, service, materials, or software that exceeds $25,000. Some ILS vendors have been known to ask what this dollar amount is and then offer to come in under that ceiling in order to make the sale. If the ILS system is on your list of finalists, you may want to give this company's offer serious consideration.

Writing the Request for Proposal and Reviewing the Contract

9

- Overview of the RFP Process
- RFPs from Other Libraries and Vendors
- Be Specific about What You Want and How You Want It to Work
- Writing the RFP
- System Specifications
- Basic System Requirements
- Modules
- Project Management and Organization
- Project Deliverables and Requirements
- Instructions to Vendors
- Evaluation Process
- The Contract

Overview of the RFP Process

The request for proposal (RFP) for an integrated library system is a formal announcement to vendors asking them to respond to your stated needs. The complexity and length of the RFP depends on the specifics that are included within the proposal. Vendors answer whether or not their product can perform all the circulation, cataloging, acquisition, online public access, Web site, automated telephone notification, and other functions that you require and request. The vendors also provide the costs for the software, hardware, installation, data conversion, hosting services, add-ons, training, and other services.

It should be noted that not all libraries elect to go through the RFP process. Depending on the purchase policy defined by the board, administration, or state laws, you may have to go through the RFP process. Without those restrictions, some directors negotiate pricing with vendors and then choose the product that they want. Some companies will offer discounts if you purchase from them without going through the RFP process. One of the benefits of an RFP is that you have in writing from the vendor what the integrated library system will or will not do. The RFP can be the foundation of the contract. It should be written into the contract that the vendor will provide the features and services as submitted in its RFP.

For both you and the vendor, the RFP is the culmination of research, demonstrations, and discussions. It is a serious enterprise for vendors because they are competing among themselves for your business.

Once the RFP is issued, there are no "do-overs." For many organizations, it is a legal process that follows strict guidelines. It is vital that the RFP ask the essential questions and provide the necessary instructions for vendors to follow.

This chapter will discuss the details of what information needs to be in the RFP, how the process works, how to handle questions from vendors, and how to evaluate RFPs to select the best bid. A sample RFP is listed in Appendix D.

RFPs from Other Libraries and Vendors

If you have never written an RFP before, it is helpful to look at other RFPs before writing your own. Ask for sample RFPs from similar-type libraries. If you are a medium-sized, single-site public library, then you will want to seek RFPs from medium-to-large, single-site public libraries. If you are a school district purchasing an integrated library system for the media centers in your district, ask other school districts for copies of their RFPs. The same example extends to academic libraries and public libraries.

In addition to asking for RFPs from facilities that are the same size as yours, you should also ask organizations that are somewhat larger than yours for copies of their RFPs. This is especially true if you are in a high-growth area in which you expect to see sustained increases in materials and patrons. Larger organizations tend to have more robust budgets so they are on the cutting edge of technology that you can plan to implement at your facility in the future. It is important to know what larger organizations have requested from vendors in services, software, and equipment. It never hurts to ask for cutting-edge technology in your RFP, as some companies may provide it at no additional charge.

Sample RFPs may be obtained by calling the library director and asking directly or by posting a request on a Listserv. Chapters 1 and 5 discuss researching different ILS companies by contacting other libraries that use their software. Utilize these contacts to request a copy of their RFPs. Most library directors are more than happy to extend this courtesy as they were once in the same position or have been helped by other directors in the past.

Vendors will also provide a sample RFP, but remember that these sample RFPs are geared toward the benefit of each particular vendor. They do not ask all the questions that need to be asked. Some vendors will later ask not be held accountable for the information placed in the RFP. This exclusion will appear in the contract that is presented by the vendor. This clause makes the RFP worthless and a waste of careful consideration and research. The RFP is an important tool to be used in selecting the best system for your library.

Review other RFPs to gain an understanding of what can be included and the best format to provide it to the vendor. Afterward, you are ready to use your information to write the RFP for your purchase needs.

Libraries also hire consultants to write their RFPs to work through the process. Consultants advertise at the professional conferences, such as the American Library

Association. You can also contact library directors for referrals. Consultants are an additional cost but can provide a useful service if library staff do not feel they have the time or expertise. Take note if a sales representative asks if you are hiring a consultant. If a vendor knows a consultant is producing the RFP, he or she will be on his or her best behavior. For example, experienced consultants know what cost price should be for an ILS and can warn directors if pricing is way out of line. However, the purpose of this book is that you will be knowledgeable and experienced in dealing with both ILS vendors and consultants.

Be Specific about What You Want and How You Want It to Work

The beginning of the RFP should state what type of RFP is being issued. The following example is the opening statement for the RFP issued by the Anywhere Public Library:

> **Notice is hereby given that sealed proposals for the purchase, installation, and maintenance of a client-server integrated library system for the Anywhere Public Library will be received at the office of the City Clerk, City of Anywhere, 1501 N. Anywhere Road, Anywhere, CA 92590, until 5:00 P.M. Pacific Time, September 25, 20XX.**

The opening paragraph tells the vendors that the bids are sealed and must be addressed to the city clerk, City of Anywhere. It also states what type of ILS for the Anywhere Public Library is looking. In this particular example, the library is requesting bids for a client-server integrated library system. In the client-server arrangement, the server is on-site and holds the catalog records, patron records, ILS software, Web site, and so forth, and communicates with the client workstations within the library at the circulation desk, reference desk, online public access catalog, and technical services. If the library is interested in software-as-a-service (SaaS), in which the library's bibliographic records, patron records, and so forth, are on an external server, it would be stated here.

Sales representatives view the beginning of the RFP to determine whether or not their companies are able to bid. If a company offers only SaaS, then the sales representative will not bid on an RFP seeking a client-server system.

The library should clarify in the opening statement whom should be contacted regarding questions that arise during the reading of the RFP. There should be only one designated person representing the library, such as the MIS administrator or the library director. The latter may seek clarification from different sources within the library (circulation, cataloging, etc.) but the vendors should deal only with one person when they have questions. You do not want the vendor contacting staff members in various departments, such as circulation, and asking questions. It could create a situation in which the vendor receives the wrong information from a circulation desk member and the person overseeing the RFP process is unaware that the conversation even took place.

This kind of miscommunication can also have legal ramifications. The vendor can claim that his or her company was treated unfairly because its response to the RFP was based on the "incorrect" answer from a circulation clerk. Stating the designated contact person for the library in the RFP protects you legally because that individual is responsible for insuring that the vendors receive answers to their inquiries and that all vendors have access to the same information. Refer to the example below:

Contact for further information:

For further information, contact Rob Payne, Library Director, at 951-XXX-XXXX or rpayne@cityofanywhere.org. Inquiries arising from any discrepancies, omissions, or other needs for clarification in this document should be submitted in writing either by mail at the above listed address or by e-mail to rpayne@cityofanywhere.org no later than 3:00 P.M. September 25, 20XX, Pacific Time. The words "Integrated Library System Inquiry" should appear on the envelope or in the subject line of the e-mail. The source of an inquiry resulting in a clarification will not be given.

This RFP and all subsequent modifications thereto are hereby designated as the sole reference and authority for the preparation of proposals. Clarification and/or addenda will be distributed to participating vendors who have indicated their intent in writing to submit a proposal.

The RFP should state how inquiries will be handled and give a deadline for receiving questions. The library's contact person provides both the questions and the answers to all vendors participating in the bidding process. This insures that all companies are treated equally in receiving the same information. This can be accomplished by e-mailing all the vendors simultaneously. Keep file copies of the e-mails to document that all vendors received the same information. It is important to note that ALL questions from vendors must be submitted in writing—questions by phone or in person will not be accepted. It is also crucial that you adhere to the deadline stated in the RFP. If you bend or break the rules at any time during the RFP process, vendors can later cry foul.

It is important to keep the source of the questions confidential. In the response, enter the question followed by the answer. The sample below is a question from a vendor followed by the response from the library's contact person:

TO: Vendor A, Vendor B, Vendor C, and Vendor D
FROM: Rob Payne, Library Director

Question: In regards to section 1.7, "Time for RFP and Project," is it necessary for you to meet a particular deadline?

Answer: It is necessary to implement the project within the 2012–2013 fiscal year. The fiscal year ends June 30, 2013.

Writing the RFP

When writing the RFP, be specific about what you want and how you want it to work. To help both you and the vendor, organize the RFP by main topics and modules.

General Description and Background

- **Statement of Overall Purpose and Objective of the ILS Project**

  This is a short, comprehensive statement about what type of system the library is planning to purchase. If you are looking to buy a software-as-a-service system, then you will write that information in this section. If you want an ILS in which the library owns and houses the servers and software, then you will state that request clearly in the "Statement of Purpose and Objective" section. Vendors will read this section and know whether or not they can compete in the RFP process. It takes a lot of time to research and write a response to an RFP, so you want to be clear in your expectations and desires.

- **Overview of the Library, Branches, and Populations Served**

  Give a description of the community and surrounding area(s) that the library serves. If your library is located in a rural area that is a growing suburb for a nearby city, you will want to include this information. Include the population of the service area plus the estimated population five years into the future. This will signal that you are in an area serving a rapidly growing population. This type of information will affect the size of the server you choose to purchase or lease. You will want to select a vendor who can provide the amount of memory and RAM that will be needed to handle the circulation transactions and the patron and catalog databases into the future.

  If the library has branches, give the number of branches and a description of the area and populations they serve.

- **System Capacity Requirements for the Library**

  Provide details on the annual materials budget plus the number of bibliographic records, item records, patron records, staff workstations, public Internet workstations, and online public access catalog. You will want to include your annual circulation figures and any other statistics that will affect or utilize the integrated library system. In addition to providing the most current numbers, you will need to estimate your growth over the next five years.

  To determine the projected growth in the number of bibliographic and patron records, review the library's statistics for the previous five years. What type of growth are you seeing in your collection and the number of borrowers? For the most accurate results, it is important that the library deselect on a regular basis and annually delete borrowers from the database who have not used their cards over the past four or five years or whatever is the standard determined by your library.

  Example for determining projected growth for bibliographic records:

Average Bibliographic Records

Year	Number of Bibliographic Records	Percentage of Growth
2006	31,689	
2007	32,957	4%
2008	34,934	6%
2009	37,379	7%
2010	39,662	6%

In the example given above, the average annual growth in the collection is 5.75 percent. So, unless the library is projecting a dramatic increase in the budget through increased allocations or fund-raising, staff can estimate that in 2015, the collection size should be around 49,602 bibliographic records.

Projected Growth in Collection

Year	Number of Bibliographic Records	Percentage of Growth
2011	39,662	
2012	41,943	5.75%
2013	44,355	5.75%
2014	46,905	5.75%
2015	49,602	5.75%

- **Goals of the New Integrated Library System**
  List the functions, attributes, and features that staff are looking for in a new integrated library system, such as catalog enrichment features with book jackets, reviews, main character biographies, and listings of series titles in order.
- **Description of Library's Computer Network, Hardware, and Software**
  Work with your technology person on this part of the RFP. Give information on the library's hardware and software, including the equipment that runs the library's network and current automation system or ILS. You will need to include the operating systems for the servers, staff workstations, and public access catalogs. If you have servers at the library, describe their location. For example, "Servers, routers, firewall, and switches are located in a secure equipment room that is air-conditioned and has access to a T-1 connection. All equipment is connected to an uninterrupted power supply." If you have any special computer security in place, you will want to mention it. The vendor may follow up with more detailed questions, such as service pack and browser versions being utilized. Responding vendors will need to provide information about how their equipment and software will fit within your network.
- **Current ILS or Automation System**
  Provide details about the current ILS or automation system being used. This will include the version you are running and the basic capabilities on the system. If the collection has never been bar coded and you are not using an automation system, then you will need to provide this information as well. It will require additional time and expense to prepare the collection and patron records. If they will be migrating from an ILS you have been using, they will need to describe how the transition will be made. You should also ask for references for any migrations they have already accomplished from the system you have been using.
- **Timeline for RFP and Project**
  A timeline for the project gives the vendor an idea of the time frame under which the library is operating. You need to pick deadlines that are workable for the library. Select the month that is best for the library to migrate to a new system and work back from that date. It is not advisable to convert to a new software platform during the library's busiest times of the year. If you are a public library, for example, migrating to a new system during the summer months would be the least advisable time period, but if you are a school media center or an academic library, the summer months would be the ideal time to migrate to a new platform. If you will be implementing an acquisition system, you may want to also consider timing that installation around the change of fiscal years.

There are always "bugs" to correct when converting from one type of integrated library system to another. Automation companies have proprietary software that can sometimes cause difficulties in the conversion process until everything is fine-tuned. In addition, the conversion process can be more pleasant and less stressful for staff if they do not have to deal with large numbers of patrons while at the same time learning new ways of doing their jobs. Ask yourself if the chief executive officer of a large department store would migrate to a new software platform during the holiday shopping season.

Below is an example of the format in presenting a timeline to vendors:

Deadline for submission of questions regarding the RFP	August 15, 20XX
Deadline for response to vendors' questions	September 10, 20XX
Due date for proposals	September 25, 20XX
Evaluation of proposals and selection of finalist(s)	September 27–October 4, 20XX
Vendor demonstration by finalist(s) (the Library considers this step optional in making a decision)	October 13–October 17, 20XX
Award bid	October 24, 20XX
Project commences	December 8, 20XX
Training	May 1, 20XX

Include a statement with the Timeline for Project that dates may be revised if any steps take longer than anticipated. Actual project commencement and completion dates will be determined through contract negotiations. Also, state in the RFP that the library reserves the right to postpone the award.

System Specifications

- **General Description of Desired System**

  State your overall expectations for an integrated library system. If you are only going to consider Web-based modules in circulation, cataloging, and so forth, then this is the time to make that information known. If you are migrating from one system to another, you want to select vendors who have the experience in migrating from the system you currently own.

  Other statements may include that you want the ILS to be compatible with your existing hardware, unless your workstations, server, and so forth, are three-plus years old and you know that they need to be upgraded or replaced. Any hardware and software must be installed by experienced staff. Vendors who have experience working with and have software development priorities for your type of library (public library, school media center, or academic) will be given preference.

  All equipment and materials must be new, free of defects, and of the most current design and manufacture. Vendors must also discuss how software upgrades will be handled and any costs involved.

- **Vendor Implementation Plan**

  Request that the vendor supply detailed information about the project timeline and how components of the process will be handled.

  - What type of staffing will the system require? Does the ILS require an MIS administrator to manage the system, or can the company's technical support personnel remotely log into the library's servers and workstations to help troubleshoot problems?
  - How will the library's policies regarding circulation, patron types, and remote patron authentication (or remote database access) configure with the proposed ILS? For example, if you allow materials to circulate for two weeks with a maximum of two renewals,

and only if no other patron is waiting to borrow an item, will that policy transfer to the new system without any type of staff intervention? In addition, if the library later changes its policy to allow only one renewal, will library staff be able to easily to modify the policy within the software?

- Does the vendor assign a single staff member to work with the library during the retrospective conversion process? What are the qualifications of this person? Is he or she well versed in cataloging standards and MARC records?
- What are the requirements for the library in preparing the site for the hardware, network, wiring, electricity, equipment closet, cooling capabilities in the equipment closet, and so forth? Will the vendor inspect the site in preparation for the installation of equipment?
- What type of training will the vendor provide for the library staff? Will the training take place on-site or will it be Internet-based? Will training DVDs or other learning tools be provided? If additional training is needed later, how will that be accomplished and at what costs? How many of the staff will be trained by the company? Will the trainers work with all staff or will they train a few library staff members and then expect the others to train the rest of the staff?

- **Vendor Responses to Specific Questions about the ILS**

  Some libraries want vendors to give specific answers as to whether or not the integrated library system can perform particular functions at the time of purchase. Again, the RFP is the basis for the contract. If a vendor states that a feature is functioning within the system, then he or she will be held contractually to that response. Below is an example of response codes:

Request for Proposal Response Codes

Code	Meaning
1	Function or service is available as specified and is fully operational in the product being offered.
2	Function or service is available but with modifications. Vendor describes what is and is not available.
3	Function or service is scheduled for a future release. Vendor will give approximate date of scheduled release.
4	Function or service is planned for a future release but a release date is not known.
0	Function or service is not available.

Basic System Requirements

It is important that you communicate the basic requirements that vendors must meet. You will want to document that the vendor must quote prices for all the equipment, functions, and services that are required to install and operate the integrated library system. Assurances need to be given that the system being proposed by vendors is fully operational and is not in the experimental or testing stage of development. If a vendor wants to use your library as a test case, you should expect compensation or deep discounts.

You do not want any surprises after a vendor is awarded the bid. In the RFP, ask vendors to respond to the question that no additional purchases will be required to make the system operational. What the vendors quote in the RFP as to equipment, software, and so forth, is what is needed to run the ILS at your library.

The library needs to retain ownership of its own data and to be able to easily export bibliographic and customer records with no additional charges. If, after several years, library staffers decide to migrate to another system, you do not want to pay the vendor to export information that belongs to the library. This clause should also be repeated in the contract.

If you are purchasing hardware from the vendor, you will want the company to respond to specific questions. If you need the vendor to install the servers and to load the software, you need assurances from the RFP that the company has qualified technicians to perform that service. Vendors need to describe the minimum hardware and software requirements to support the library's ability to serve patrons and manage bibliographic records into the future.

You will also want assurances that the hardware and software is "scalable." The library wants to be in the position of easily adding additional modules, add-ons, workstations, and even other servers if necessary.

Power failures or other unforeseen events can cause servers to fail. A backup plan is needed to keep the circulation module functioning until the server is restored. Ask vendors to describe in the RFP whether or not the proposed server(s) utilizes RAID (redundant array of independent disks), dual power supplies, and so forth, and whether or not offline circulation functions can be utilized by client workstations in the library.

Be sure to give the communication speed of your network (for example, 100 Mbps Ethernet) and have the vendor state that the proposed system can communicate at that speed.

It is very important that your library's server have the ability to communicate with other libraries' servers. This is necessary for cataloging and interlibrary loan functions. Request that the system be Z39.50-compliant (the latest version).

Nearly all libraries will want borrowers to be able to access the online catalog and online databases from home, school, office, or other off-site locations. It is important the system allow remote log-in using a variety of browsers. Vendors can tell you which browsers do not work with their system. This information will become important later on in troubleshooting patron login problems. Even older versions of standard browsers can cause problems for borrowers, so that information is important as well. Many subscription database publishers will not allow remote access to their products unless the library's integrated library system performs patron authentication. This means that every remote patron who uses the databases can verify that he or she is a library customer by entering his or her borrower identification number. If these functions are important to your library, then you will want to ask in the RFP whether or not the vendor supports remote access and patron authentication.

System security is a very important aspect of the integrated library system. First and foremost, the network needs to have firewall protection so that hackers cannot access any of the servers. Depending on the size of your ILS, you may have three servers: the data server, the Web server, and the domain-controller server. The data server houses the ILS software along with your patron and bibliographic records. The Web server hosts the library's Web page, and the domain-controller server handles the network and e-mail functions. Depending upon the size of the library and the type of ILS, one server may be able to handle all three. In any case, it is vitally important that the network be protected from external and internal intrusion.

Can the vendor provide all security at the ILS network level, database level, and application level? Ask the company to provide a description as to how security is accomplished. Does the system allow the administrator to restrict access to specific functions, such as cataloging or system administration, by log-in and password?

Library patrons must be able to access and utilize online resources from remote locations. If you want the access to be restricted by a user identification number, that requirement should be in the RFP.

Statistics

Statistics are useful management tools that can help administrators provide better services and plan for the future. What statistics are critical to operations and for reporting purposes? Of course, keeping count of how many items circulate per day, week, or month is essential because that is the basic number by which most libraries justify their usefulness to funders. It is also important to know what search terms are by used by patrons in the PAC and which searches retrieve zero results. This information is critical to collection development. Limited resources in the materials budget need to be directed toward the subjects, titles, and formats that your library users need and want.

While speaking with vendors at conferences or on-site demonstrations, ask them what type of statistical information is provided by their systems. Speak with colleagues and read the literature on types of statistical information that are being gathered and used. Some integrated library system companies have the ability to write custom reports for a library or to create a report based on demand from patrons. So, if there if there is a report that will generate statistical information that you can use, request it in the RFP and vendors may be able to make it available at no additional charge.

Training and Documentation

Training staff on how to use the new integrated library system is one of the most important implementation facets of your new system. Employees are the most essential asset of every library. If you have great people, then you have great programs, professional customer service, and effective resources that meet the needs of the users. Consider what is the best method of training for your staff and for your organization has a whole. If it is important that all staff receive on-site training, then state that requirement in the RFP. Consider what modules need to be covered and how many days of training will be needed. You will also want to request that the vendor provide trained personnel to be at the library for a full day when you "go live" with the new system.

The vendor should provide a list of all expenses related to training, including any travel, hotel rooms, and meals they plan to add to the cost of the training sessions. You will also want a quote up front for any additional training that you may need over the following 12 months. Have the vendor commit to a price. If you do not ask for this information in the RFP, you may end up paying more if additional training is needed.

If the vendor provides training DVDs or other training documentation, ask that a description be provided in the RFP. Some companies also offer online training courses, workshops, and conferences at additional costs. These can be beneficial in keeping up with new technologies and upgrades, so it is worthwhile asking about these courses or checking company Web sites for this information. Sometimes Web sites are restricted only to customers, so ask the sales representative if a guest log-in can be extended for a limited time.

Whoever is responsible for managing the library's network and servers will need training on how to operate the system on a day-to-day basis. For example, how are backups of files achieved? How does one shut down or start up the system? How are software updates received and installed? Where do staffers find documentation online, and how are they notified of technical bulletins?

System Support

If the library has existing electronic customer and bibliographic records, you will want these records to be loaded into the new ILS. Ask in the RFP if the vendor is able to load the current records and if bibliographic records will be loaded and indexed according to standard USMARC format. You also want the vendor to provide at no additional cost a gap file, which consists of the records that had been created after the initial extraction file for the vendor's conversion.

The vendor will typically extract your data at a particular point in time so that the bulk of the migration can be accomplished without interrupting your day-to-day services. You will send your borrower records and bibliographic records to the new company to convert them into their format so they are readable by the new system. While the new vendor is working on the records it has received, the library is still using its current system, adding, modifying, or deleting records until the company requests that no additional bibliographic records be added to the system. The latter records are called a "gap" file. Right before the library goes live with the new system, the vendor converts the gap file to the new system. The library opens for business with its new system and with all its bibliographic records and patron records converted and readable by the new system. You will want the vendor to describe the amount of time required for the conversion, especially the amount of time library functions need to cease, so staff and patrons can understand the process.

Other important requests to include in the RFP that the software provided is of the latest released version and that the software maintenance agreement will be provided for 12 months at no additional charge. Future maintenance fees should include all future releases of the initial software at no additional charge.

If you have servers on site at the library, you may want the ILS company to have the ability to connect remotely to the servers in order to troubleshoot problems, install upgrades, or perform routine maintenance.

Hours of operation for the company's technical support may be of critical importance. If technical support needs to be available 24/7 during emergencies, make that request in the RFP. If the business hours of technical support need to be from 8:00 A.M. to 8:00 P.M. Monday through Saturday, state that information in the RFP. Vendors will find some way to accommodate the request via Web site access, telephone, or pager.

The vendor should be responsible for all hardware that it provides and give assurances that the equipment is new, not used or reconditioned. In addition, the vendor should be responsible for contacting the third party when repairs are required. If you have specific requirements regarding the warranty of hardware, this should be stated in the RFP with specific information on start and end dates and what is covered and not covered under the warranty.

Modules

The RFP should list requirements for each of the modules and add-ons that the library plans to purchase from an ILS vendor. Basic modules may include cataloging, circulation, public access catalog, and reports. Add-ons may include serials, acquisitions, automatic phone and e-mail notification, and other specialized functions. The RFP should address each module and add-on separately. The following example is for the circulation module:

- **General Functions of the Circulation Module**
  If the library's collection is already bar coded, you want the new ILS to be able to read the library's current bar codes. Otherwise, it will require the expense and staff time of bar coding the entire collection. The library will need to provide samples of all of the differing types of bar codes in its collection. If you purchase materials that are cataloged by

different publishers or distributors, then you will need to provide a sample for each of those bar codes in the RFP. These samples will give vendors the opportunity to see if it will be easy to convert the existing bar codes to the new system or whether there will be an additional charge involved.

It is also important to ask in the RFP if the library's current bar code readers will work with the proposed system or if new bar code readers are required. This is one example of a very crucial point to be made about equipment compatibility. Some vendors adapt the reading of the bar code not only to their software but also to the bar code reader being used by the library. When converting to a new system, you may need to purchase the bar code reader from the new vendor to ensure there are no problems with new software reading the existing bar codes that the library purchases from publishers or suppliers. You do not want the problem of having the new company tweaking the software to fit your existing bar codes and bar code readers and then being in a position of replacing the bar code reader in the future with a model that does not work with your ILS. It may not be possible to switch to the vendor's bar code reader at the time of replacement because the software has been programmed for the old equipment. It will take time and money to fix the problem. It is better to decide which bar code readers to use at the beginning of the project. You may want to verify the information given to you by the sales representative with the staff who actually perform the conversion process.

Other general functions to include in the RFP for the circulation module would be:
- The ability to easily toggle from the check-in screen to the checkout screen.
- Printing of date-due receipts on the current receipt printers or to notify the library that the receipt printers must be replaced.
- Circulation transactions are immediately updated on the online public access catalog,
- The circulation module will continue to perform at the circulation desk and self-serve workstations in the event of a loss of connection to the network or server, and that the transactions can be loaded onto the server at a later time.

● **Policies and Loan Rules**

This section of the RFP deals with the circulation policies and procedures that the library is using or wants to utilize at its facility. You want to be able to easily set and change parameters regarding types of patrons, lending periods, fine rates, and adjusting the calendar for times when the library is not open. Staff may also want the ability to restrict or suspend borrowing privileges along with a comment area for messages on the borrower's record.

● **Checkout**

It is helpful to have a system that can search for borrower records by various fields besides last name, such as phone number, e-mail address, or driver's license number. You may want the ability to create and save brief patron records so that you can create borrower records for in-house uses such as reference desk, display case, story time, and repair. Brief patron records are accounts without an address, telephone, or birth date—just minimal information such as a name and bar code number.

If library staff are planning to add self-checkout stations in the future, then you will want to be assured that the system you are purchasing has that capability.

● **Check-In**

To conserve paper and the expense of purchasing receipt paper, it is important that the circulation staff have the ability to print or not print a receipt. Most customers will not want a receipt for a 10-cent fine payment, so a system that does not automatically print receipts for every transaction is earth friendly and considerate of a library's budget.

A busy library requires the ability to change the due date in order to check in materials from the book drop. Some software does not have this feature but it certainly streamlines the check-in process if the software has this capability.

The check-in process also needs the ability to check in an item by title, ISBN, author, and so forth, in case the bar code is missing.

Borrower Records

If it is in your circulation policy to block customers from checking out materials if they have overdue materials, lost-book charges, or fine charges, then you want the circulation module to notify employees of a block when viewing a borrower's record. Staff should have to respond to the block before proceeding with the transaction. The system should allow staff to view information about the block without having to leave a borrower's record.

Other helpful alerts in the circulation module are:

● Messages
● Overdue items
● Renewal limits
● Arrival of reserved materials

Each of these alerts can be addressed in the RFP. For example, you may want an automatic e-mail issued to patrons when items have been returned for them. You may also want a notice printed automatically for items that need to be placed on the hold shelf.

Fines and Overdues

Flexibility in fine payments is important. Fines may vary by material type. Books may be fined at 10 cents per day but DVDs are fined at $1 per day. Fines may also vary by borrower type. Faculty are not charged fines for overdue materials but students are. Sometimes fines need to be removed, so you may request the ability to delete fines and lost-book charges with password access.

If a detailed receipt for payment needs to be provided to patrons, make that request in the RFP. To save paper, you may want the ability to only print receipts on demand.

Patron Information

Vendors must tell you whether they can accept your current patron records in the format you can provide or if there will be problems in importing the existing records. Request a detailed description regarding the ability to import existing patron records and what charges, if any, will be imposed.

It is critical to have the ability to export patron records into database or spreadsheet software. For reporting purposes, you may want to sort patron records alphabetically or count records by borrower type, city, or zip code.

Consider what fields are needed in a borrower's record, that is, last name, first name, street address, e-mail address, phone, gender, bar code number, birthday, and parent's name. It may be necessary to have more than one line for an address, one for the physical address, and one for a post office box, or one for a temporary address and one for a permanent address.

Request the ability to search for a borrower's record by a variety of methods, such as e-mail address or phone number.

If a patron claims to have returned an item or claims to have never checked out an item, it may be important to your operations to be able to note this information on the borrower's record.

Notices and Other Functions

Overdue notices, billing notices, and hold notices are the most common type of notices generated by the integrated library system. Each library has a workflow regarding the issuances of notices. Some issue an overdue notice at some point after the materials become overdue. The time period may be one week, two weeks, or more. Whatever the workflow is for issuing overdue notices, you want the ILS to be able to replicate this pattern.

List requirements in the RFP regarding the workflow for overdue notices, bill notices, and hold notices. Such requirements might be that overdue notices are issued by phone or e-mail every two weeks and that a patron will receive a maximum of three overdue notices. The system will then allow library staff to print a final billing notice listing replacement costs. If the library refers accounts to a collection agency, you will want to list that request in the RFP as well.

You may also want the system to issue friendly notices reminding customers of upcoming due dates. The ability to create and edit messages on such notices is also a plus.

If the library issues print notices, you may want the notice to fit in a #10 window envelope or have flexibility in choosing a notice format that will similarly save staff time preparing notices for mailing.

Points to Consider on the RFP for the Public Access Catalog (PAC) Module

After reviewing demonstrations of vendors' public access catalog, note the requirements you are looking for in a system. It is essential that changes made in the circulation and public access catalog modules happen in real time. The library should have the ability to control the look of the PAC, such as colors, font size, graphics, photographs, and layout. If you wish to make use of book jackets, reviews, content summaries, series information, and other third-party PAC-enrichment features, list that request in the RFP. You will want to make sure that the system you choose can utilize these features if you wish to have them now or at a future time.

The vendor may have demonstrated that they create a Web site for the library. Ask for a detailed description of the work that the vendor provides in updating and making changes to the Web site. What costs are involved if changes are made?

Patron authentication is a requirement in most libraries today but it is a feature that may increase the price of the ILS you consider. Patron authentication is a software feature that takes a borrower's library card number and compares it to the library's database of customer records. If there is a match between the customer database and the bar code number, then the customer is allowed to use the electronic resources, enter the Web site, and access his/her account. Vendors who sell electronic resources such as genealogy databases, electronic magazine articles, or e-books require patron authentication if a library wants to allow their users to access these items remotely from the home or office. Patron authentication may also be required if you plan to add a computer reservation system or print management system to the integrated library system.

Points to Consider on the RFP for the Cataloging Module

A cataloguer should assist with writing the RFP requirements for the cataloging module. He or she will know what is needed to import or create bibliographic and authority records, cataloging templates, and other considerations. If you are a library or media center without a cataloguer, you have to consider how staff will enter bibliographic records.

You may buy bibliographic records, join a consortium and download records, or have library staff create bibliographic records using a MARC template. The latter is necessary because there will always be local histories, self-published books from local authors, and other donations that require original cataloging. The cataloging templates need to contain the required and recommended bibliographic fields. Staff should have the ability to create or modify cataloging templates, such as adding and deleting fields.

Ask the sales representatives to demonstrate how records are entered by hand and how records are imported into the bibliographic database. You will want to see the template and review whether or not your staff can utilize it or if additional training on this component will be necessary. If the latter is true, determine who will conduct this training (a local cataloguer) and how soon the training will take place after the installation of the ILS.

The cataloging module must have the ability to search and import records from outside sources using the Z39.50 communication protocol. There are libraries throughout the United States that allow other libraries to download their bibliographic records to their databases at no charge. Discuss this option with vendors and ask what information is needed in order to download records from other servers and if the vendor makes this information available to its customers along with instructions for importing the needed communication profiles.

Reports Module

The reports module needs to create reports that are required by your facility. List the required reports in the RFP so that each vendor can respond whether or not that report function is currently available. Some vendors may state that certain reports are in the process of being created or that customers can request custom reports. You will have to decide whether or not that status is helpful and if any charges are involved with custom reports.

Vendors should be required to describe and provide a list of reports that can be generated by the system. In addition, vendors must submit sample reports for review. Staff should be able to generate and print reports on demand at any time of the day or night. Reports need to be displayed on the screen before choosing to print, and staff must have the ability to export reports in an electronic format to a storage device. The system also needs to provide the ability to display the reports in a variety of formats, such as PDF, HTML, CSV, or XLS, to open in a spreadsheet program.

The RFP can also list requirements needed for each of the modules, such as reports related to circulation, cataloging, patrons, and collections.

Project Management and Organization

The RFP states that the selected vendor will designate a single project manager to work with the library throughout the installation process. In addition, the library will state in the RFP who will serve as the project manager for the implementation. The project manager can be someone such as the library director or the MIS administrator who in turn directs the work of other staff members as needed during the migration to the new system. The project manager also reports to the management team on the progress of the implementation and the status on meeting stated deadlines. Both the vendor's project manager and the library's project manager should communicate with one another on a weekly basis to ensure that the implementation is on schedule and that each party is taking care of its respective duties and responsibilities.

Once the contract has been awarded to a vendor, the project managers for both parties will hammer out an implementation plan. The plan will include when equipment is delivered to the library, when the library delivers bibliographic and patron records to the vendor, when software is installed, when training takes place, and when the library "goes live" with its new integrated library system. (Refer to page 93 in the section entitled "Vendor Implementation Plan.")

The library's project manager will be responsible for seeing that key responses to the RFP by the vendor are performed. This statement should be included in the RFP so that vendors are fully aware that the library's project manager will monitor what was promised in the RFP.

It is vital that the implementation plan be in writing with specific dates for delivery of equipment, delivery of records, training, and so forth. The implementation plan will identify what work must be completed and by when. Project managers will also want to issue weekly status reports stating what work has been accomplished and what problems and issues need to be resolved before moving to the next step in the implementation process.

Project Deliverables and Requirements

The library will want to state in the RFP that all hardware and software installed will be tested and certified to be operational by the library's project manager before the project is deemed complete and any payment is issued. The installation must meet manufacturers' recommendations along with any applicable safety standards.

This section should also state that the vendor will complete all training outlined in the RFP and contract. The training must also meet the expectations of the library before the project is deemed complete and payment is issued. Any promised documentation for the hardware, software, and training will be delivered to the library by the stated deadline in the implementation plan.

Instructions to Vendors

Every RFP needs to contain a section with instructions to the vendor regarding the submission of the RFP, how the proposal will be evaluated, and who to contact if the vendor wishes to submit questions, lodge a protest, or conduct a site inspection. Other general requests to the vendor may also be covered in this section. Library staff will want information about each company, its financial stability, and accessibility to source codes should the vendor go out of business.

State the submission deadline for the RFP, including the date and time, along with the mailing address and information for the opening of the sealed proposals. Envelopes must be clearly marked "Integrated Library System Proposal." See the example below:

Submission Deadline and Proposal Opening Date

The proposal must be submitted no later than 3:00 P.M. on January 25, 20XX, at which time all proposals will be publicly opened and read. Proposals received after 3:00 P.M. on January 25, 20XX, will be returned unopened.

Return your proposal in a sealed envelope to:
    City of Anywhere
    Anywhere Public Library
    Attention: City Clerk
    1501 N. Anywhere Rd.
    Anywhere, CA 92590
    Proposal opening will be held at the City of Anywhere City Hall, which is located at 1501 N. Anywhere Road. Proposals must be sealed. Proposals submitted via fax or e-mail will not be accepted.

Vendors may choose to be at the opening of the sealed proposals, but most likely they will not. It is important to have more than one individual at the opening of the sealed bids to be a witness that the procedure followed the legal guidelines set by your administration, city, school district, or state.

As the RFPs arrive at the library, staff receiving the packages should note the date and time received in ink or with a date/time stamp. Some vendors wait until the last possible moment to submit their proposals. If the RFP arrives past the deadline, it must be rejected from consideration.

Instructions to the vendor should also include the library staff contact for the RFP. It is important to restate that all questions regarding the RFP be submitted in writing via e-mail to the designated employee and that no other library staff member will answer questions regarding the RFP. Also state the deadline for the submission of questions along with the final date by which the library will respond to them.

If the library chooses to purchase the ILS software, then it is important to protect your access to the source codes. Companies that create ILS software protect their software from duplication by not releasing the source codes. If the ILS company goes out of business, then the library needs to have access to the source codes. Many libraries request in both the RFP and the contract that a copy of the source codes be placed in escrow and will be released to the library only in the event that the vendor goes out of business, discontinues maintenance, or declares bankruptcy. Open-source software, as a comparison, makes its source codes available to the community of users so that it can be modified or expanded.

Evaluation of the proposal is the sole responsibility of the library. The evaluation process must be fair and the same standards applied to each proposal. The library may wish to publish its evaluation process so that each vendor knows the criteria by which it will be judged.

Purchasing an integrated library system is a substantial investment in money, staff time, and other resources. It is important to choose a system with a company that has a track record of stability and success. Ask the vendors to provide information about their companies' backgrounds, such as the date established, type of ownership, location of headquarters and major offices, and number of employees engaged in systems development and technical support. Companies should provide a copy of their most recent financial statements and auditors' reports. A contract should be awarded only to a company that can confirm its financial solvency and stability.

It is also important to ask how many systems each company has installed over the past four years that were similar in size and scope to your library, along with a list of four to five references who may be contacted. Require that references be current clients from a similar type of library to yours. References should include a contact name, mailing address, e-mail address, and phone number.

The vendor should provide a list of the key personnel who will be assigned to the project along with assurances that they will work with the library's designated staff through the duration of the implementation. It is also prudent to require assurances that the vendor's personnel will be experienced with the same type of library as yours and/or have experience migrating from the vendor you have been using. Every library should expect and require top-notch service from experienced staff and not be a training ground for new, inexperienced employees.

Cost Proposal

The cost proposal must state all costs associated with the system, including but not limited to the installation, software, hardware, data conversion, migration, training, maintenance fees, and any other miscellaneous charges, such as shipping and travel.

Vendors need to state in the RFP any requirements expected from the library, such as preparing the site, hardware specifications, operating systems, browser types and versions, wiring, cabling, telephone lines, and anything else specific to the installation and operation of the ILS.

Public Records Requirements

If the library is supported by tax dollars, then all business transactions are subject to the open-records laws of your state. Vendors may offer your library a deep discount if the price paid for the system is not disclosed. This is an impossible promise to make, as any library, competitor, or taxpayer can request this information through the open-records law.

If a vendor wants other information in the RFP kept confidential, besides the costs quoted, then the vendor should mark each page as confidential. Check with your administration and state laws regarding the guidelines on confidentiality of submitted bids.

Evaluation Process

This section explains how library staff should select and evaluate RFPs. There are usually three phases to the selection process: (1) vendors meet the deadline with completed proposals, (2) proposals undergo a detailed evaluation, and (3) finalists may or may not be invited to present a demonstration of the integrated library system depending on if the library deems it necessary. It should be stated in this section that the library is the final judge of determining whether or not a proposed system meets requirements and will perform as needed.

The first selection criterion is that the submitted proposal must have arrived by the deadline and must be complete. The vendor must have answered all of the questions and submitted any detailed descriptions as required in the RFP. This is a pass-or-fail process. The vendor has either submitted a complete RFP on time or not.

Proposals that pass the first phase of the evaluation process will then undergo a detailed evaluation process. A copy of the evaluation may be published in this section of the RFP. Following is a sample evaluation process. The published evaluation begins with four categories and the weighted value of each category. In this illustration, the cost of the ILS has a weighted value of 25 percent and the ability to meet the specifications outlined in the RFP has a weighted value of 50 percent. It is more important for this library to purchase the system that meets the needs of the facility. Price is a secondary concern. What this evaluation process signals to vendors is that the library will purchase the best system it can for the best price. Sometimes there is an assumption that library staffers are looking strictly at the bottom line and so features are eliminated in order to provide the lowest price possible in competing for the bid.

Weighted Value for Each Category

A. Financial history of company and its customer base — 10 percent
B. Project management and references from similar-type libraries — 15 percent
C. Cost of the integrated library system — 25 percent
D. Ability to meet specifications in the RFP and support — 50 percent

Below the weighted categories are the sample evaluation criteria that library staff may use when reading the RFPs. The matching category for each criterion is listed at the end of each sentence. In responding to the criteria, the library can create a point system of one to five, with one being the lowest and five being the highest. Points can be added up within each category to determine which vendors received the highest evaluation score.

Evaluation Criteria

1. The ability to meet or exceed the functions specified in the RFP (D).
2. The ILS is able to use the library's existing network and infrastructure (C and D).
3. The vendor's ability to implement the hardware and software, provide technical assistance in a timely manner, and support the add-ons detailed in the RFP (B, C, and D).
4. The ability of the ILS to meet future growth in materials and borrowers, and the capability to remain current with technological innovations (D).
5. Total costs in procuring the system along with hardware and software maintenance and support for five years (C).
6. The vendor's experience in successfully implementing integrated library systems that communicate with current suppliers, interlibrary loan consortia, and so forth (B and D).
7. The number of implemented systems similar to our type of library and the ability to provide customer references for similar-type libraries and systems (A and B).
8. The financial stability and history of the vendor (A).

Prior to awarding the contract, the library reserves the right to request a demonstration of the proposed system before the selection of a finalist or finalists has been completed. Failure to demonstrate the system would forfeit the proposal (make the proposal nonviable).

The Contract

Once the library has evaluated the RFPs, a vendor is selected and notified. The contract process is the next step. The contract process is a negotiation of what the final contract will be. The vendor issues the contract—a standard contract that benefits the company. The contract is issued in electronic format because it will be modified by both parties. The library receives the contract, reads it carefully, and then begins the process of revising it. The library, of course, will use an attorney to read the contract. The attorney will read it from the viewpoint of protecting the library but will not know the intricacies of the RFP. The latter is the responsibility of the library's project manager.

Under no circumstances should the vendor be allowed to keep the following statement in the contract: "The vendor will not be held accountable to the contents of the RFP." This statement may be written in legalese, such as, "The terms inconsistent with those stated herein, which might appear on the library's formal order or RFP, will not be binding on the [vendor's name]." This statement gives the vendor the ability to not live up to the information submitted in the RFP. The whole purpose of the RFP is to verify in writing, in an atmosphere of competition with other vendors, what kind of system the company will provide, how that system will perform, and the technical support and software upgrades it will furnish. The vendor should absolutely be held accountable to the contents of the RFP and will suffer monetary consequences if it does not live up to the proposal it submitted.

The contract should also read that all bibliographic, fine, patron, and other records entered into the library's database, or supplied to the vendor, are and shall remain the sole property of the library. In addition, the library has the right to extract its data without the vendor's permission, and if the library seeks assistance in the extraction of data, the vendor agrees to provide assistance. The caveat regarding any charges or "at no charge" should also be placed in the contract.

It is important that the software perform as shown in training manuals, demonstrations, and other documentation. The contract should state that the licensed software will not suffer from systemic error that renders it unable to perform as intended. The vendor should also cover all costs, including travel, if the system has to be repaired on-site due to the errors in the software or hardware.

Software updates should also be addressed in the contract. The library should receive the most recent software version available and should continue to receive updates to that version at no charge if the maintenance fees are paid. If mandatory software upgrade results in the mandatory upgrade or change of hardware, then the vendor must provide adequate notice of this pending upgrade to allow the library time to plan for this expenditure. Adequate notice would be a minimum of 12 months.

Note what the contract states about third-party add-ons, such as computer reservation, print management, or telephone notification software. Does the vendor cover third-party software that it installs? It should take responsibility for the installation, successful integration, and operation of third-party software it sells to the library.

There can be a section on the patent and copyright of the integrated library system software. The vendor may write that it will defend the library against any claim that its licensed software is infringing upon a patent or copyright. However, the vendor will not protect the library against such claims if the library has altered the software. A savvy attorney will include the comment that the vendor will protect the library against patent and copyright infringement if the library performed an alteration to the software under the vendor's guidance, assistance, and/or consent.

Check the contract for accuracy in the stated figures or statistics, such as the estimated number of patrons and bibliographic records that the vendor will enter into the new system. Make sure that you have the correct number of staff workstations that will be licensed to operate the ILS.

All costs involved with the purchase, maintenance agreement, installation, training, and so forth, will be detailed in the contract. Compare all software, hardware, and other specifications to the information in the RFP. If you are purchasing a turnkey system that includes the hardware and software necessary to operate the integrated library system, make sure that the hardware specifications match line for line, item for item with what was quoted in the RFP. Does the RAM memory match the quote? Are the product names for the processors, hard drives, and backup devices the same as stated in the proposal? Does the technical support and replacement support match the length of years that was quoted? Review the details of the training schedule and length of training. How many days are you purchasing and how many hours are in each day? Make sure that future training costs are listed in the contract so that if additional training is needed within the following 12 months, the library is not stuck with a monstrous training charge.

The contract should also state how the escrow account is set up should the vendor declare bankruptcy or go out of business. The library needs to protect its access to the software source codes in the event something happens to the company.

Human error can occur anywhere and at any time. To rectify human error, it is important to double check information. The library must vigilant in protecting its interests and holding vendors responsible for the products and services that they sell. Work closely with your attorney and keep copies of contract revisions as you work through the contract negotiations.

Reference

Boss, Richard W. "Negotiating Contracts with Integrated Library System Vendors." http://www.ala.org/ala/mgrps/divs/pla/plapublications/platechnotes/negotiatingils.cfm. Cited November 24, 2009.

10 Implementation, Installation, and Training

- Network Installation and Upgrades
- Electrical Wiring and Cable Installation
- Peripherals
- Add-Ons
- Retrospective Conversion
- Managing Existing Bar Codes in the Collection
- Circulation Rules
- Implementation Meetings with Staff
- Marketing a New Integrated Library System to Patrons
- Plan to Thank Funders
- Planning the Appearance of the Library's Web Site
- Installation of Hardware and ILS Software
- Staff Training Sessions
- Migration of Data
- Going Live
- Final Payment to the Vendor
- A New Level of Service

The moment has finally arrived. The contract has been signed by both the library and the vendor, and the invoice has been submitted. Now begins the process of implementing the system.

Most of the larger ILS vendors will assign a project manager to work with you through the implementation phase. The software and maintenance fees are higher for these companies but customers receive guidance during the installation and migration process. For vendors who provide a project manager and guidance through the implementation phase, they invest a lot of upfront expenses in personnel to install the hardware and software. Vendors who sell less expensive integrated library system software may not provide all the services listed in this chapter. However, the software is much easier to install for libraries that want or need to do it themselves.

You will want to develop a schedule of activities that need to be accomplished, along with due dates for those activities. Monitor your progress each day. It is easy to let a step slip by you, if you are not proactive in managing the project.

What has to be accomplished depends upon what type of system has been purchased. The following will cover a majority of the activities that take place when installing or migrating to a new integrated library system. Not every library will utilize each step. If the library opts to purchase a hosted or SaaS system, for example, then steps regarding the installation of a server are eliminated from consideration.

Network Installation and Upgrades

The vendor will have questions regarding the configuration of the network, the IP address and port for communicating with the router. You will also be asked to check hardware and software specifications on the client workstations. The MIS administrator or contract network administrator can help you answer these questions. Begin now to schedule upgrades and/or the purchase of new workstations. If you are purchasing new servers, such as a data server and a Web server, then check preparations for equipment room.

- What are the dimensions for the servers? Is there a need to purchase mounting racks, sturdy desks, carts, or other furniture to keep servers off the floor and provide a location for monitors, keyboards, and mice?
- For multiple servers it is recommended to purchase a KVM box. KVM stands for "keyboard, video, and mouse." Connect the servers to the KVM box and you have to use only one monitor, keyboard, and mouse. You are able to toggle from one server to another to access the log-in screen and desktop.
- Check to see if the uninterrupted power supply (UPS) needs to be replaced. A larger, more powerful model may be needed.
- Evaluate the bandwidth of your network. Are your Internet speeds fast enough to accommodate the additional workstations and servers you have planned? If you are planning a network of more than 25 computers, consider having at least an Ethernet connection (T-10 line).
- What is the status of the hub(s), router, DMZ, and firewall? Make sure that your current firewall can handle the incoming and outgoing traffic to and from the servers, including any Web-based applications coming from the vendor's servers.
- Do you need to obtain a URL for the library's Web site?
- The vendor will need name and contact information for your Internet service provider.
- If you are planning the equipment room from scratch, make sure that it has adequate ventilation. Servers generate a lot of heat, and a hot equipment closet can cause equipment not to function at its best and can shorten the lifespan of hardware.
- The equipment room needs to be a locked, secure location. This area houses expensive equipment, not to mention the importance of the library's data.
- Check with the vendor to see what type of backup utility the company provides: backup tapes, Web-based utilities, RAID, external drives, flash drives, and so forth. If subscribing to a Web-based storage site, research the company's own plan for backing up data. If using backup tapes, flash drives, or other physical storage devices, there should be a backup tape for each day of the week that the library is open plus one extra tape. The extra tape will be kept off-site in a fireproof safe and will be replaced on a weekly basis.

Take for example, a library that is open Monday through Saturday. In this case, one would buy seven backup tapes, flash drives, and so forth. Label each tape for the day of the week plus label two tapes for Saturday. On Monday, a staff person will insert the "Monday" backup tape in the data server and take the "Saturday" backup tape to an off-site, fire-proof, and waterproof safe. The "Saturday" tape that is already in the safe will be removed and utilized that coming Saturday. The process repeats itself each week. If something happens to the data server, the library will have its patron and bibliographic records saved on its collection of backup tapes. If a disaster, such as a fire or flood, hits the library building, then the library has its data protected off-site on a backup tape. To ensure that the backup tapes are functioning properly, check the backup utility each day to make sure that data is being saved to the tapes. In addition, backup tapes should be replaced annually to ensure that they are in good working order. Use the cleaning cartridge every other week to keep the backup tape drive in serviceable condition.

- The vendor will discuss when the servers will be delivered and when they will be installed. Prepare an area for the delivery of the servers. These will be large boxes. Coordinate with the MIS administrator or contract network administrator for installation date(s). Your network administrator will need to be on hand during the installation process to make sure that the server is connected properly to the network. Have the vendor give you an estimated time frame for when the contract network administrator needs to be on-site. Let the vendor know that this is a contract person and that time at your facility costs you more money. This should generate a more accurate time frame.

Electrical Wiring and Cable Installation

Any improvements in electrical wiring and cabling should be planned from the beginning. If you are installing new workstations for staff or public access catalogs, you will need to schedule early with electricians and network cable installers. Make sure you have sufficient electricity in the places you have planned for workstations and servers. It is safe to plan on one 20-amp circuit for every four computers. Printers, especially large printers for public use, require more electricity than computers. Plan to install one large printer and two workstations per 20-amp circuit.

All workstations (public, staff, and online catalogs), printers, and peripherals need to plug into surge-protective power strips and not directly into electrical sockets. This will protect the hardware and equipment from power spikes and lightning storms. It is also wise to invest in uninterruptible power supplies (UPSs). These battery backup units supply electricity to keep your computers operational through a power spike and sustain equipment long enough after a power outage for you to gently shut down everything. It is especially important for servers to have this power protection. If a server crashes due to a power outage, serious problems may result from the potential corruption of your data.

If you are installing a network for the first time, there must be a RJ45 jack for each piece of equipment that will connect to the network. This means that there will be a RJ45 jack for each staff workstation, each public workstation, each online catalog, plus each printer on the network. Receipt printers, bar code scanners, and RFID readers will connect to the CPU for each individual staff workstation, so, at this writing, RJ45 jacks are not needed for these peripherals. However, peripherals will connect to the CPU through USB ports. Make sure your CPU has plenty of USB ports. Plan to install more network nodes than initially required so that you allow room for growth.

A contract network administrator will need to be hired to install the network. What platform will you use—Windows-based, Linux, or Unix? (This will have been decided earlier upon the selection of the integrated library system software.) Cabling should be fiber optic using Category 5, 5e, 6, or 7. (How do you select which kind? Rachel Singer Gordon states that "Pricing, ease of installation, and institutional needs will affect the choice.") Discuss with the Internet service provider regarding which router to purchase so that it communicates with their system. If you are planning to offer wireless Internet service in the future, you will need to purchase a partitioned router to protect the library's network from unauthorized access by laptop users. If you plan to purchase a Web server for the library's Web site and online catalog, you will need to purchase a DMZ and firewall to protect the server from unauthorized access. The network administrator will guide you in what equipment is needed. If you are planning to expand the number of staff and public workstations in the near future, purchase a switch with additional ports that are open for additional connections to the network.

Install enough electrical outlets in the equipment closet to allow for future growth. All of the equipment and servers needs to plug into an uninterrupted power supply, so you may need more than one UPS to handle all the pieces of equipment. If you install only one outlet, for example, and have two UPSs, you have no outlets for future growth. You can piggyback UPSs, connecting one UPS to another, but this is not an ideal situation to protect your expensive investment in hardware.

If you are using desks or counters that were not manufactured for network cables, you may want to consider having holes drilled in the furniture. This will accommodate the cables and power cords that run from the monitors, receipt printers, scanners, keyboards, and mice to the CPU workstations.

Peripherals

Order any scanners, RFID readers, and receipt printers that are needed for the project. Take into account all workstations that will need these pieces of equipment. Secure a location for the delivery of peripherals. These items will arrive before the installation, so you need to find an area in which to store the boxes.

Add-Ons

Some add-ons will take planning in the purchase and installation of hardware, cabling, electrical outlet, telephone lines, and coordination with other companies. Obtain detailed instructions from the vendor of what infrastructure is needed to install and operate the add-on equipment.

If one is purchasing a telephone notification system, for example, one will need to have (1) a computer workstation; (2) a UPS for the telephone notification equipment and computer workstation; (3) a desk for the monitor, keyboard, and mouse; (4) an electrical outlet; (5) CAT-5 cabling and an RJ45 jack to connect the computer workstation to the network; and (6) a telephone line or lines. In addition, if the library is using a phone system, the phone system company will need to be notified that a telephone notification system is being installed. The phone system company may need to be on-site during the installation of the telephone notification system to ensure that it is communicating properly.

Be assertive with the ILS vendor in obtaining all the information needed for a good installation of your ILS hardware, equipment, and add-ons. Put questions and requests in writing and ask that their responses be in writing as well. That way, if a delay occurs because the vendor omitted necessary information, you have a paper trail that you were not notified of needed information and the vendor cannot charge you for the delay.

Check and double check that everything is in place. Communicate with the vendor and network administrator on a weekly basis. Review what steps have been taken and will be taken to have the network infrastructure and necessary equipment in place to operate the ILS. Have all tasks, checklists, and deadlines in writing.

Retrospective Conversion

Retrospective conversion means to change the bibliographic records from one data format to the format of the new integrated library system you have just purchased. Software developers create integrated library systems that are proprietary, and each ILS has a different method for reading the MARC record fields and local holdings information. The more robust the software is, the more fields within each bibliographic record are used for searching. A simple system might index only the author and title fields, but a more sophisticated system will allow searching by format, publication date, call number, series, keyword, subject heading, and more.

It is helpful if the vendor assigns one staff person from their company to work with your library through the retrospective conversion process. This will help as each party has questions through the retrospective conversion process and then with the final migration to the new system.

As an initial step in the retrospective conversion process, library staff may be asked to submit paperwork that lists all the collection areas of the library (including branches), the call number for each collection area, and the circulation time period for each type of material. Staff who catalog and process materials will be the most familiar with all the different collections. It can be staggering how many collection areas a library can possess. A public library might have areas such as fiction, young adult fiction, juvenile fiction, Spanish fiction, Spanish young adult fiction, Spanish juvenile fiction, nonfiction, Spanish nonfiction, audio books, young adult audio books, juvenile audio books, Spanish audio books, downloadable audio books, e-books, music CDs, juvenile music CDs— and this is just the tip of the iceberg. Academic libraries can have special collections, government documents, sheet music, artifacts, and other unique items. It is recommended that once a staff member has made a list of all the collection areas, this list should be double checked by two additional staff members. Collection areas can be added and deleted in the future, but the best plan is to do it right the first time. This is also a great opportunity to consider consolidating collections to simplify access for patrons.

The vendor will also request information about patron types, such as faculty, students, and staff. You will also need to send circulation rules governing patron types. The latter is only necessary if there are different checkout periods for patron types. For example, a faculty member may be able to check out material for an entire semester, while a student or staff member is given two weeks.

You may also be asked information regarding what fields are used in the patron records. These fields could include name, address, phone number, bar code number or identification number, date of birth and so forth. Depending on the software, you may have an opportunity to request fields that you would like to have, such as permanent address, parent's name, comment field, and driver's license number.

Managing Existing Bar Codes in the Collection

Library staff will be asked to submit examples of all the bar codes in use. It is vitally important to submit samples of all the bar codes in your collection. There may be a variety of bar codes in the collection if you: (1) order materials from publishers or distributors that arrive processed; (2) order bar codes from library supply companies or the ILS vendor; or (3) print bar codes in-house using your ILS software. Some libraries have used a combination of all three processes over the years and have bar codes from multiple sources.

If staff do not submit samples of all the bar code types in the collection, then the missed bar codes will not be readable after the migration to the new ILS. Missed bar codes can be fixed, but it is better to provide the ILS vendor with as much information in the beginning as possible. That way, the vendor will strive to make the existing bar codes readable by the ILS software and there is less work later on for the library staff to repair unreadable bar codes.

Ask the vendor what should be done if the software does not read bar codes that were missed in the initial migration. It may just be a matter of opening the bibliographic record in the circulation or cataloging modules and scanning the bar code to make it readable by the new software. (The ILS software converts the bar code symbology to a readable format). Or staff may have to replace an item's existing bar code with a new bar code label that is readable by the system.

It is important to keep records of the bar code number ranges that are ordered from each vendor and printed in-house. So, for example, you may have records such as the following:

- 0–10000. Bar codes from a variety of sources.
- 10000–80000 reserved for Company A.
- 100000–200000 reserved for Company B.
- 300000–400000 reserved for printing bar codes in-house.

In this particular example, the library director would provide three different bar code samples (Company A, Company B, and an in-house bar code) and inform the vendor that there are bar codes in the collection from a variety of unknown sources. In dealing with bar codes from unknown sources, the options will be to: (1) weed the collection of these older materials if they are no longer needed; (2) photocopy as many different bar code types as possible to send to the ILS vendor; or (3) replace the bar codes as needed when the items circulate. One should be able to search by title, author, ISBN, and so forth, in the circulation module so staff can circulate the item to a patron and then repair the bar code issue when the item is returned. Eventually, through weeding, scanning, or replacement, the bar codes that were not converted in the initial retrospective conversion process can be repaired.

Bar codes used on library cards will also be submitted to the vendor. There may be a variety of library card bar codes if you (1) ordered library cards from more than one company in the past; (2) printed more than one type of bar code in-house; (3) ordered bar code labels from a library supply company; or (4) have a combination of all three types.

Some libraries opt to switch patrons over to the current library card by making new cards for customers as they come into the library. This is an internal decision that needs to be made before the retrospective conversion process. If you opt to switch patrons to the current library card, you may need to order an additional supply of cards or carefully monitor the inventory of library cards.

When the library is near to migrating from the old integrated library system to the new ILS, there will be a cataloging cut-off date. The library will provide the new ILS vendor with a full MARC file extraction from the old system. The vendor will mostly notify the library not to edit its MARC records after this cut-off date as any new changes to existing bibliographic records will not appear in the new bibliographic database being created by the ILS vendor. This means that employees cannot edit the MARC record and cannot change call numbers, add or delete item-level holdings, or change bar code numbers. **It is very important that all employees who have access to the circulation module (circulation desk, technical services department, reference desk, children's services) understand these instructions as well.** Changes to the bibliographic record, especially at the item level, can often be made utilizing the circulation module. So, even if a limited number of employees have access to the cataloging module, be aware that modifications to bibliographic records can occur through the circulation module.

If the library is able to export MARC records by date range, then you should be able to catalog new titles. Check with the vendor on what they recommend. If the vendor accepts new MARC records after the cut-off date, then materials catalogued during this "gap" period will be added to the bibliographic database. The gap is the time period from the "cut-off" date to the "cease all cataloging" date. That is why it is so important that no editing be made to existing bibliographic records once the MARC file is sent to the vendor. There is no overlay of records later in the system migration. The vendor will only add the gap file to the database.

Machine-readable patron and checkout files will also be sent to the new ILS vendor for migration to the new system. Sometimes it is not possible to migrate all of the transaction data to the new ILS. This information can be obtained during the RFP process, but if not, the vendor should let you know what patron or transaction information will not transfer over to the new ILS. This will give staff ample time to run reports on holds, lost-book charges, fines, and so forth. Once the migration is complete, check a few patron records (such as staff members' records) for accuracy. Check that the address, telephone number, and other contact information is correct, along with the number and/or titles checked out to each individual.

Circulation Rules

The vendor should ask library staff about the circulation rules so they can configure and/or train the library staff on how to configure the software to match how the library does business. The ability to configure the software will depend upon the complexity of the software. With most automation systems, the status in the public-access catalog changes from "checked out" to "available" once materials are returned to the library. However, some ILS software is so sophisticated that it has the ability to create a lag time before the items displays as "available" in the PAC. This lag time gives library staff a day or two to reshelve the item before it displays in the PAC.

Several weeks and months can pass from the time the library signs the contract to the actual delivery of the software. In the meantime, upgrades to the ILS software may have occurred since the product was last demonstrated to library staff. Ask the vendor to work with you to obtain all the new bells and whistles that are available. If you are a small library with limited staff, you will want to ask the vendor to provide as much assistance upfront as possible in configuring the software for your library so that it is ready for "going live."

Following is an example of information vendors may request regarding circulation rules:

- Patron types (faculty, student, adult, child, or interlibrary loan).
- Checkout time frame by collection and/or patron type. For example, nonfiction books circulate for 14 days but DVDs circulate for seven days. Interlibrary loans have a 30-day checkout.
- Fine amount imposed, if any, by collection and/or patron type. For example, students pay overdue fines but faculty do not.
- Grace periods, if any, before fines are imposed.
- Charges for replacement library cards.
- Card expiration time frame. For academic libraries, cards may expire at the end of every semester, while public libraries may expire every year or two.
- Expiration time period for holds/reserves.
- The number of overdue and bill notices issued.
- The interval between overdue notices and bill notices.

Again, the types of information you provide to the vendor depend on the ability of the software to be configured. Library staff may find themselves having to review and modify their circulation policies due to the restrictions imposed by the ILS software.

No ILS software is perfect in that it meets the all demands and requirements libraries would like. Whatever ILS software a library can afford to implement, it certainly beats the old-fashioned card system in every aspect.

Implementation Meetings with Staff

Another initial step in the installation process is preparing staff and patrons for change. The latter is true if library users will see a new public access catalog, a new Web site, and enjoy new services.

It is important to be cognizant of the fact that not everyone likes change. Even if the changes will benefit library borrowers and staff, change still engenders stress. It is important to recognize this reaction and work with staff, patrons, and others to overcome concerns and prepare for the future.

Communication is one of the best tools in dealing with change and stress. This is important with both staff and patrons, but the first step is working with the library staff. Hold an initial staff meeting and inform all the staff about generalities concerning the overall project, including:

- The approximate time frame
- What hardware and software will be installed at their workstations
- What new and improved features will benefit staff
- What new and improved features will benefit customers
- Acknowledge any outside funders for the project, such as grants or gifts
- What major changes the staff might experience
- Proposed training schedule
- Proposed date for going live

When discussing dates for the project, be sure to state that it is an approximate time frame. It is a good idea to allow for more time than you think is needed. It is better for staff morale to under promise and over deliver. Unforeseen issues may occur, but staff should know that the library and the vendor have an agreed-upon schedule that will be adhered to as much as possible. Assure staff that you will keep them current with monthly staff meetings. Even if you have department heads, it is important to build a team approach to the implementation process so that everyone knows they are a vital part of the library and not just part of an individual department, such as circulation or reference.

The more complex the project, the more information should be imparted to employees. For example, a library converting RFID technology and self-check stations will be involved with tagging the collection, installation of new equipment, and the reassignment of duties for some individuals. Staff is always concerned that their jobs will be lost. They need to know that positions will change but that they will have still have a job. Circulation staff, for example, may move from checking out materials to becoming more involved with customer-service duties or working in collection management.

Employees are interested in what hardware and software will be installed at their workstations. Let people know if computer technicians will be at the library to install new software or new equipment such as bar code readers and receipt printers. Give employees an idea of when this will take place and how they will be assigned to other duties/work areas during the installation. If the library is purchasing new hardware for its public areas, inform staff about where, when, and why this will occur. Your frontline public-service staff will interact with the public and pass along information about when and why changes will transpire. It is very important for staff to project a positive attitude toward the changes.

People want to know that changes are being made for a reason. Review the incentives as to why the library is purchasing a new integrated library system. Highlight new features or modifications that will benefit library staff. These could be improvements such as the ILS printing hold slips instead of staff handwriting customer names and contact information, or that staff will be able to easily copy contact information from one borrower account to another when making library cards for family members.

Discuss new and improved features that will benefit customers. Library patrons will want to know why the library is installing a new system (and spending institution or tax dollars.) A patron-oriented staff will be excited and proud that their library is offering new and improved functions and features for their customers. Such features could be the opportunity to use online resources from home because the new ILS has patron-authentication software. Customers will enter their library bar code numbers to access the online databases. A new function could be the ability to check out their own materials using self-check machines. To assist staff in answering questions from patrons, create tabletop signage or a flyer listing the benefits of the new integrated library system. Acknowledge funders for the project. If the city funded through a capital project, thank the city. If the ILS was funded by grants, gifts, the parent-teacher organization, or the friends of the library, acknowledge and thank the funders on the same signage used to advertise the benefits of the new system.

Cover major changes the staff will experience with the new integrated library system. These changes could encompass the appearance of the modules, moving from one screen to another, entering information, using the Z39.50 communication protocol to download MARC records from another server, the cataloging template, or patrons being able to manage their accounts from the library's Web site. Reassure employees that they will receive training in each of the modules they will use in their job responsibilities. Acknowledge that change can be stressful, but that information about the product, communication about the implementation process, and training on the modules will help to ease concerns.

Encourage questions and comments. If someone asks something about a procedure that was not considered, thank him or her for the suggestion and say that you will look into the issue and respond. It is good to have a team to help think of all the possibilities that can prevent problems down the line. Thank all the employees for their patience and stress your excitement about the new features that will help staff and patrons alike.

Go into details regarding the training schedule. This will reassure employees that they will have an opportunity to learn about the new system and how to do their jobs. Tell them whether or not the library will be closed for training or if staff will be trained in groups during normal hours of operation a few days before migrating to the new system. If at all possible, provide lunch and refreshments during the training sessions. This will lighten the atmosphere and create a mood of camaraderie. It also signals that the administration/ library director values staff and wants the transition to be as comfortable as possible.

Give the proposed date for going live with the new integrated library system. This will establish the goal and prepare employees for the upcoming changes. If the library is an academic or public facility, switching to a new system by Wednesday or Thursday will give employees a couple of days with full staffing before the weekend arrives with abbreviated staffing. The library director or project director should assure staff that he or she will be there over the weekend to assist with any problems, provide additional training, or answer questions. Just the presence of the project director or library director will be reassuring and give employees confidence in dealing with the new ILS.

At a regularly scheduled staff meeting, the library director can give updates on the implementation process and field any questions staff may have as time progresses. For example, before transmitting patron records to the ILS vendor, it may be decided that the patron database will be updated and that inactive or expired borrower records will be deleted. Staff will need to know about this decision in order to field questions from borrowers who suddenly appear with library cards in hand after a long absence. There will also be a time when staff can no longer add new bibliographic records to the catalog. All of this type of information is important to relay to employees to keep them informed and in the loop.

Marketing a New Integrated Library System to Patrons

Just as library employees may have a stressful reaction to a new integrated library system, so may library patrons. The reaction will not be as heartfelt as what employees will experience, but you may see reactions to stress such as seemingly unjustified anger. Patrons may become irritated after the initial installation for different reasons if, for example, they cannot locate the new Web site or the Web site is different and they do not know how to navigate it, or they were not notified of a hold, or they were called too many times by the automated phone system, and so forth.

Marketing the new integrated library system prior to installation can alleviate some of the stress. Library patrons will have an opportunity to casually discuss the forthcoming new system with staff as they check out materials at the circulation desk or ask for assistance at the reference desk. It is important that these frontline employees be knowledgeable about changes and improvements so they can educate borrowers about what to expect.

Press releases to media outlets, the campus newspaper, the parent-teacher association newsletter, local cable outlets, Web-based outlets such as social-networking sites, flyers, and signage are just some of the methods that can be utilized to advertise the forthcoming integrated library system. Use whatever creative methods are appropriate for your facility.

Signage and flyers need a professional appearance. The information should highlight the benefits of the ILS for the borrower.

NEW CUSTOMER FEATURES FOR YOU...

We are changing how we do business to better serve our library users. In a few months we will install new software that will provide the following benefits for our borrowers:

- New Web site loaded with features such as reviews, best seller lists, calendar of events.
- Borrowers can manage their accounts online: renew books and place holds.
- Easy access from home or business to magazine articles, genealogical databases, and other online resources on library's Web site.
- Library contacts borrowers by e-mail or phone regarding holds or overdues.
- Customers who provide an e-mail address will receive a courtesy notice before items are due.

Questions? Ask a library staff member. We are here to serve you.

Flyers with the same information can be available at the desk for the staff to show customers while discussing the upcoming migration to the new system. It is helpful for employees to remember the benefits and have a visual for library patrons to review.

If the library plans to close for a day or two for employee training, begin advertising those dates four weeks in advance. That will give library patrons ample opportunity to be informed about dates the library will not be available. Use this opportunity to once again broadcast the benefits of the new integrated library system for users.

Plan to Thank Funders

It is never too early to plan how to thank funders after the integrated library system has been installed and is operating. Even if the source of funding is internal, such as a capital project funded by the administration, it is important to acknowledge appreciation for improvements made to the library. Not all methods of recognizing funders will work for every type of library. What is appropriate for an academic library may not be applicable for a media center. The following list can generate ideas from which to choose avenues for recognizing donors:

- An eight-foot-by-four-foot banner located in high-traffic area near library. Use wording understandable to the general public, which may not know what "integrated library system" means.

Thank you City of Anywhere for new Circulation/Catalog System

visit us at www.anywherepubliclibrary.org

- Announcements on the library's Web site banner, social-networking site for the library, and the local cable outlet for the school district, college campus, or city. "Thank you Anywhere School District for new circulation/catalog system."
- Press releases with accompanying photographs sent to media outlets announcing the new integrated library system and its funders. "Library Director John Smith announces the installation of new software at the campus library made possible through the generosity of alumnus Peggy Lee."
- Unique and ongoing methods of thanking funders may include pencils, pens, or candies imprinted with a thank-you message.
- Installing an attractive plaque on the wall.
- Poster at the entrance to the library.
- Specially designed screen backgrounds or screen savers on the public computers.

Brainstorm with staff on methods to acknowledge funders. You may receive a unique idea that is sure to capture attention. Planning with staff also helps to spread the word in thanking donors, as employees will pass this information along to library patrons, friends, family members, and other outlets. One of the benefits of early planning for recognition and thanking donors is that it gives ample time to think of a variety of avenues, plan a budget, and not be caught scrambling at the end of the project to develop something. People who show appreciation are in turn appreciated for the time and planning they took to thank funders.

Planning the Appearance of the Library's Web Site

Many ILS vendors provide a Web site as part of the integrated library system package. This is a wonderful benefit, especially for libraries that do not have a staff member to create a Web site. The Web site is the "face" of the library and it is important that the Web site be attractive and easy to navigate. The Web site is also a vehicle for displaying the library's logo, mission statement, or slogan.

Review the templates available from the ILS vendor or the Web sites that the vendor has created for other libraries. Note the features that you find useful and attractive, such as:

- An easy-to-locate search box for searching the online catalog
- Library information, calendar of events, and message from the director
- Online resources
- Best-seller lists, reviews, and featured titles
- Ready-reference Web sites
- Children and teen information
- Staff contact information
- Community information

Work with the vendor on the Web 2.0 technologies that you want to implement for library patrons. These Web tools include blogs, social-networking sites, e-mail or chat reference services, online card registration, and so forth. The Web 2.0 technologies should be part of the library's strategic plan and technology plan in how best to serve its customer base while taking into account staffing levels and the staff's knowledge and abilities.

You will need to submit any photographs of the library that you want to use. If you are featuring people in the photographs, you will need to secure signed permissions—even if using staff members. Photographs with children will need signed permissions from parents or guardians.

In regard to staff contact information, you will need to decide what e-mail address to use for customers submitting general questions via the Web site. You can have the Internet service provider or system administrator create a special e-mail address for this purpose but make sure someone is assigned to check that e-mail address on a regular basis throughout the day and respond to inquiries in a timely fashion.

It is not necessary to post contact information, such as e-mail and phone numbers, for every staff member. This is an internal decision that needs to be made. Staff contact information will be submitted to the ILS vendor for posting on the Web site.

A message from the director can help to set the tone for the organization, especially for a library that is service-oriented. This is an opportunity to market the library's materials, services, and programs. The following is an example by W. Bede Mitchell, Dean of the Library at Georgia Southern University's Zach S. Henderson Library:

Hello and welcome to the web site of Georgia Southern University's Zach S. Henderson Library. I am W. Bede Mitchell, and it is my pleasure to serve as Georgia Southern's Dean of the Library.

Whether you are a student, faculty member, or staff member at Georgia Southern, or an alum or a web surfer interested in investigating our institution, I hope you will examine our web pages and learn more about what we have to offer. Our catalog of library holdings is online and we have information about our wide range of services, collections, and resources on the About the Library page. For some useful tools, I highly recommend that you visit the Using the Library section of our site.

Perhaps you would like to see what we have in our special collections. Georgia Southern University faculty should check out the link entitled Information for Faculty. We hope what you see here will make you want to visit us in person.

As our mission statement says, the Henderson Library is the central repository of recorded information for the university and we are here to serve the students, faculty, and staff of the University as well as members of the general public. The Henderson Library is also the primary focus of the university's links to sources of information at other external sites. These local and external information resources are made available in subjects, formats, and methods consistent with the academic disciplines of the university and with the various needs of the users of the library.

Come see us and take advantage of all our resources!

E-mail the dean of the library.

From *Integrated Library Systems: Planning, Selecting, and Implementing* by Desiree Webber and Andrew Peters. Santa Barbara, CA: Libraries Unlimited. Copyright © 2010.

If staff resources are at a minimum, you will not have a lot of time to update information. Work with the vendor to create a Web site that is usable for your situation. Assign a staff member to update the calendar of events and programming information on a monthly basis. If you post policies, such as a circulation policy, you will need to upload revised editions as they occur. Learning how to update the Web site needs to be part of the training provided by the vendor.

Installation of Hardware and ILS Software

Installers will contact you regarding the installation date for the server(s), ILS software, and client software. The client software is installed on the staff workstations and public-access catalog workstations. The library's network administrator will need to be on-site for the installation of the servers and the client software to ensure that the hardware is communicating on the library's local area network and also with the vendor's servers via the Internet. The installers will load the library's bibliographic and patron records onto the data server and begin testing the software.

Staff Training Sessions

The type of training, along with the length of training, will have been decided in the invoice or contract. If the library opts to provide staff training while keeping the library open, the vendor may provide a training server, either on-site or remotely. A training server contains the ILS software along with the library's data. It allows staff to manipulate patron records and bibliographic records without affecting the actual data. In addition, the library is able to remain open and operating using its existing automation system while the training takes place in the background. Staff will train on the new integrated library system in shifts while keeping the public-service desks operating.

If the library opts to close, then the library director or MIS administrator needs to plan for the following:

- Planning equipment and room for training.
  - Training needs to be held in a room with access to the network or wireless Internet access. The type of access you need depends upon the type of integrated library system you have purchased. If some of the modules, such as the circulation module, are on the library's on-site server, then you will need access to the network. If some of the modules, such as the online public access catalog, are Web based, then you will need access to the Internet, either through the network or via a wireless Internet connection.
  - If you need to access the network, then you will need a hub to connect the "training" laptops or workstations to the network. The hub needs to have enough ports to handle all of the training workstations, along with a port to connect the hub to the network jack. The laptops or workstations will need to have the ILS client software installed on them, so arrange this detail with the trainer. The installer or trainer can load the client software on the training laptops with the understanding that the software will be uninstalled after the training. (The number of client licenses is established in the invoice and contract.)
  - Locate enough patch cables to connect laptops/workstations to the hub.
  - Locate a patch cable to connect the hub to the network jack.
  - Connect bar code scanners/RFID readers and receipt printers to training laptops/workstations.
  - Obtain an LCD projector and screen (or white wall).
  - Check with trainer to see if he is bringing a laptop or if he will use your equipment. His laptop will need to connect to the network unless the modules are all Web based and there is wireless Internet access.
- Stagger due dates so that customers are not returning materials on the first day that the library opens after being closed for a day or two. Give patrons additional days when circulating materials so that everyone does not feel compelled to visit the library the day you open your doors and "go live" with a new integrated library system.
- Manage the book return(s). If you close the library for training sessions, you will need to plan how to handle items returned to the library via the book return(s). Even though your doors may be closed, patrons will still need to be able to return materials. Shelvers or pages, who handle the checking in and shelving of materials, will not be able to check in items until the migration process is complete. Therefore, materials may need to be stored on shelves or carts until they can be checked in and shelved. If the migration process occurs during the first day of training, shelvers can be assigned to scan bar codes (or RFID chips) as soon as workstations and bar code scanners are available. So if training occurs from 8:00 A.M. to 5:00 P.M. and the migration process is successfully completed by noon, staff can start scanning bar codes at 5:00 P.M. and continue shelving through the evening hours.
- Communicate with the vendor when the final migration of data will occur. If the migration process will happen at the end of the circulation training, you will want to plan the circulation training early so that materials can be checked in and shelved.

- Coordinate with trainer regarding the schedule for learning each module. Put the schedule in writing so that the trainer knows when to arrive, how long each session will last, and the number of employees who will attend each session.
- Order delivery of lunch for the staff and trainer. Purchase snacks and drink refreshments for training sessions and breaks.

Migration of Data

Someone has to work with the vendor during the migration process. The migration loads the final version of the library's data (bibliographic records, borrower records, and transaction records) onto the server. This may occur at the same time that the training is proceeding. If you are a small library with limited staff, take into account that the person involved with the migration may miss training sessions.

The staff member responsible for the migration process will work with the vendor to test the scanning of bar codes or RFID chips to ensure that the bar codes are being read by the software. To ensure a successful retrospective conversion and migration, staff members should test several bar codes and check the accuracy of several bibliographic and customer records. Also, check to see if "gap" catalog records migrated correctly. If there are any problems, the vendor will work with the software to resolve the issues. After the productive testing of several bar codes, bibliographic, borrower, and gap records, the vendor may ask the library director to sign a document stating that the migration has been completed to his or her satisfaction.

Do not be in a hurry to sign this document. Allow the training process to proceed and see if any other problems surface.

Going Live

"Going live" is the terminology used for first day the library uses its new integrated library system. Whether or not the trainer is on-site when the library goes live with the new integrated library system depends on arrangements made with the vendor. Whatever the contractual agreement, there are considerations to plan for that will help to make "opening day" a success.

- Schedule additional staff and/or volunteer coverage. If the library has been closed for a day or two, an onslaught of patrons may enter the library on opening day. Additional staff and volunteers can help with managing the larger-than-usual influx of customers. Trained volunteers can help customers navigate the new public access catalog. Additional staff at the circulation desk can help with checking materials in and out, making library cards, placing holds, and answering questions. Extra shelvers can quickly move returned materials to the shelves.
- Selecting the right time of year to "go live" will help to minimize the impact of patron foot traffic on staffing capabilities. A major department store would not schedule a change in its software platform during the busy holiday shopping season. A library should avoid scheduling a migration to a new ILS during its busiest time of the year.

Final Payment to the Vendor

Invoices for software, hardware, training, and services should be paid once you, the customer, are satisfied. It is much easier to obtain satisfaction to a complaint when payment is withheld. Take, for example, a library that has purchased ILS software, a telephone notification system add-on, four bar code scanners, federated searching, and three days of training. Everything is operating to the staff's satisfaction except the federated searching software. It is not functioning as described in the RFP or as demonstrated by the sales consultant. The library would pay the invoice with the exception of the charge for the federated searching software. The staff negotiates with the ILS vendor until a resolution is reached.

A New Level of Service

It has been a lengthy, engaging, and strenuous road in implementing the new integrated library system. Now the library is on a new playing field in the level of service it can provide—and that is stimulating.

Be sure to take the time to thank staff for their assistance and patience. Keep the avenues of communication open so that issues, concerns, and technical problems can be resolved. Anytime new software is installed, there are always questions or minor nuances that must be fine-tuned.

Migrating or installing a new integrated library system is stressful. This is especially true if the library has moved from a simple automation system that just checks materials in and out to a sophisticated ILS that offers many facets of public services, such as a Web site where customers can manage their accounts, automatic e-mail notification, telephone notification, and on and on. One feels as though they have moved to an ILS that is so robust and powerful that it could land a shuttle on the moon—and the learning curve is steep.

Time and experience will resolve these concerns. As the staff uses the new system over the next few weeks and months, they will adjust to the new software, and soon daily operations will become "business as usual." The library director, as the organization's lead person, needs to be encouraging, calming, and diligent in providing staff the information and support they need. Staffers who are savvy with computers will catch on quickly. Ask for their assistance in supporting others who may be struggling.

Again, remind everyone that this is new software, and with time and usage, they will become comfortable and confident. Stress the beneficial aspects of the system, such as, "Remember all the phone calls you had to make to notify patrons that their holds had arrived? Now customers are contacted automatically by e-mail or telephone." Sometimes people have to hear a concept several times before it is ingested and comprehended. Do not be concerned with repeating yourself.

As patrons realize the new benefits of the system, the positive comments and compliments will also encourage any staffers who are struggling. Everyone likes to take pride in their organization, especially when it receives recognition for a job well done.

Take pride yourself for having pursued a project that is a major undertaking. You chose this path for the betterment of the library and those you serve. Only people who have had the responsibility of planning, selecting, and implementing an integrated library system will fully understand all the diligent work you have performed, so, from the authors of this book to you, the reader, congratulations. You are responsible for keeping the library current with technology that provides improved customer service. You are to be commended for your progressive thinking and attitude of service.

Reference

Gordon, Rachel Singer. *The Accidental Systems Librarian*. Medford, NJ: Information Today, Inc., 2003.

Appendix A: ILS Vendors and Features Comparison Grid

	Type of ILS	Hardware/Network Needs	PAC Features	Web Site	Circulation	Offline Circ	E-mail Notification	Cataloging	Z39.50	Reports	Data Conversion	Training	Tech Support	Annual Fees	Third-Party Add-Ons	Similar-Type Libraries as Customers	Price for ILS Software
Company A Sales Consultant:																	
Company B Sales Consultant:																	
Company C Sales Consultant:																	

Appendix B: Long-Range Strategic Plan for the Anywhere Public Library 2011–2021

The Planning Process

The 2011–2021 Long-Range Strategic Plan for the Anywhere Public Library is a culmination of input from the community, a report submitted by consultant Carol Rolfheiser, and recommendations from staff. Bill Edwards was nominated chair of the Long-Range Planning Committee and he led the board and staff through the strategic planning process.

The first step in the planning process was to gather comments from the public. A survey was mailed to residents by the City of Anywhere in its utility bill mailings. In addition, copies of the survey were made available at the library for patrons to complete and a copy of the survey was posted on the library's Web site. Results and comments from the survey were compiled in a final report and used in the preparation of this plan.

A town hall meeting was held to gather comments from the public and to brainstorm what services, programs, equipment, and materials they thought were needed. In addition, copies of the Anywhere Vision 2030 report were distributed to each board member. The latter gave board members a picture of what direction the City of Anywhere was moving in its plans to manage a growing population.

The Friends of the Anywhere Public Library participated in the planning process for the library by providing funds to hire a consultant. A grant from the Temecula City Community Foundation to the Friends of the Anywhere Public Library provided the consultant's fee and travel costs. Carol Rolfheiser, director of the River County Public Library, spent two days observing the operations of the library, reviewing data, and speaking with the library board of trustees, Friends of the Library, and City Manager David Wesson. Ms. Rolfheiser submitted a report entitled "Anywhere Public Library— Service Assessment." Findings and recommendations from this report were utilized in the writing of the strategic plan for the library.

Vision for the Library

The Anywhere Public Library started as a service project by the Girl Scouts of Anywhere under the leadership of Maria Goodnight. The library has grown in its ability to serve the community due to funding from the City of Anywhere, financial assistance from the Friends of the Library, leadership from the library board of trustees, and support from the community at large.

As the City of Anywhere grows, it is the goal of the library board of trustees and library staff to:

✓ Meet the demands for materials, services, and programs.
✓ Provide professional, friendly customer service.
✓ Support lifelong learning.
✓ Promote literacy for all ages.
✓ Continue our proactive role as an essential component of the community.

Values

● An educated, literate people provide a positive influence to the community in which they reside.
● Strive to be a valued department of the City of Anywhere working toward the united goal of serving the community.

- Serve the informational and recreational needs of the entire community.
- Provide a place where cultural, educational, and learning activities thrive.
- Obtain the information requested to the best of our ability.
- Stay current with the technological changes in the delivery and format of information.
- Serve all ages equally and professionally.
- Committed to children and their information needs.
- Be a city department that provides an economic benefit to the community.
- Provide a balanced collection reflecting differing viewpoints.
- Work in cooperation with other departments and be prepared for emergency situations.
- Appreciate involved citizenry who actively participate in improving library services.
- Remain alert to changing constituencies, community needs, and trends.
- Pursue adequate funding to accomplish the library's mission and goals.
- Recruit and retain well-trained staff members who possess the philosophy of quality customer service.
- Recognize the value of staff and appreciate the service they provide to the community.

MISSION STATEMENT

The library is a vital part of the community, providing a broad collection of resources and programs to meet the informational and recreational needs of all ages.

LIBRARY VISION STATEMENT

Provide access to information and programming for personal, business, literacy, recreational, health, and educational pursuits.

LIBRARY SERVICES RESPONSES

To utilize resources properly, the library must choose what services and programs it will administer. A library cannot be all things to all people due to finite finances and staffing. The Anywhere Public Library has identified the following service responses in order to best serve the community with the resources it possesses.

Lifelong Learning: Provide materials and programming to address the desire for self-directed personal growth and education.

Current Topics and Titles: Provide current topics and titles to help fulfill community's interest in popular cultural, social trends, and notable authors.

Business and Career Information: Provide information related to business, careers, work, entrepreneurship, personal finances, and employment opportunities.

General Information: Provide information and answers to questions on a broad array of topics related to work, school, and personal life.

Goal #1: Provide adequate staffing levels to serve the public.

Objectives:

1. By December 2013, hire a professional cataloguer to catalog and process materials.
2. By December 2015, hire two part-time circulation staff to assist with additional traffic at the circulation desk and to work on Sunday afternoons.

3. By December 2019, hire a full-time assistant director to handle technology planning, integrated library system, network and computer workstations, and related hardware and to maintain Web site.
4. By December 2021, hire a librarian to serve preteen and teenage customers.

Outcomes:

1. Patrons receive professional, friendly services that supply needed information and resources.
2. Increased staffing meets the needs and expectations of patrons.
3. The library provides economic benefits to citizens by providing reference materials, programs, and Web-based services that give people the resources and information they need for individual, business, or continuing-education purposes.
4. Staffers develop an informational and interactive Web site.
5. Materials are returned promptly to the shelves for customer use.
6. Staffers deliver a variety of cultural and educational programs for youth and adults that address personal growth and knowledge.
7. Staff provide classes for all ages utilizing the computer training lab.

Budget Impact:

1. Salary for an assistant director with a master's degree in library science will be approximately $XX,XXX per year.
2. Salary for the youth services librarian will be approximately $XX,XXX per year.
3. Salary for two part-time circulation staffers to assist with additional traffic at the circulation desk and to work on Sunday afternoons will be approximately $XX.XX per hour.

Goal #2: Provide outstanding customer service.

Objectives:

1. By December 2015, the library is open on Sunday afternoons.
2. By December 2019, the library installs RFID technology and self-check stations.
3. In 2020, the library board of trustees holds a retreat to explore strategic plans for 2022–2032.
4. In 2020, the library board of trustees hires a consultant who conducts a customer survey and holds focus groups or a town hall meeting.
5. In 2021, the library board of trustees approves the Anywhere Public Library's strategic plan for 2022–2032.

Outcomes:

1. The library provides economic benefits to citizens by providing hours of operation that assist people with full-time jobs and school commitments to have access to the information and resources they need.
2. Patron check out and check in materials themselves.
3. The City of Anywhere is a desirable community with residents enjoying a high quality of life. Patrons use the library for family time on Saturdays and Sundays.
4. The library board of trustees responds to community needs in planning the library's goals and objectives.

Budget Impact:

1. Increase staffing levels to provide additional hours of operations. Refer to Goal #1 for details.
2. Purchase self-checkout stations for $XX,XXX, including cabinetry.

3. Seek funding from Friends of the Library to hire a consultant.
4. Use library fund monies to publish a survey.

Goal #3: Support lifelong learning pursuits for all library users.

Objectives:

1. The library provides economic benefits to citizens by supplying current materials on popular topics for all ages and interests. People have access to the information they need for business, career, and educational pursuits.
2. City of Anywhere is a desirable community with residents enjoying a high quality of life. Residents attend cultural and educational programming.
3. Staffers attend training to remain current with technology and best practices for library operation.
4. Library staff will provide four business-related workshops per year.
5. Provide computer-based classes for all ages to create opportunities for computer literacy for children through seniors.
6. Provide lunch-time programs.
7. Add another lap-time story-time session for babies during the week.
8. Provide tween (ages 9–11) programming for the summer reading program.
9. Provide tween (ages 9–11) programming throughout the year.
10. Provide teen (ages 12–17) programming throughout the year.
11. Add weekly evening programs during the summer reading program for family attendance.
12. Select a diverse collection of print journal titles for all ages and interests.
13. By December 2012, provide outreach programs to senior centers, assisted-living centers, schools, and day care centers.
14. By December 2014, provide access to a variety of electronic resources through the Web site.
15. By December 2015 and 2020, evaluate the need to purchase additional shelving units.

Outcomes:

1. The library provides economic benefits to citizens by supplying patrons with current, relevant materials for informational needs, recreational reading, homework assistance, and lifelong learning. Literate citizenry contribute to their community.
2. Customers access information through a variety of formats, including print, DVDs, CD-ROMs, electronic resources, and downloadable files from the Web site.
3. Young people participate in cultural and educational programming during the summer months, which encourages them to become literate, educated members of the community.
4. Residents enjoy cultural programs each year.
5. Library users attend a variety of educational programs on current topics.
6. Staffers attend a minimum of two workshops each year, one of which will cover skills and knowledge related to technology.
7. Library users access popular books in electronic format, magazine articles, reference books, genealogical resources, and newspaper archives via the Web site.
8. Library staffers encourage early literacy by conducting programs for preschoolers in daycare centers and preschools.
9. Library staffers encourage school-age children to read books and use the library.
10. The library partners with the City of Anywhere senior center to provide educational and cultural programs to seniors.

Budget Impact:

1. Request increases to the materials budget (books, nonprint, periodicals, and electronic) to meet population growth and price increases.

2. Program costs will be $X,XXX per year. This will increase incrementally to $XX,XXX per year by 2021 due to increases in fees demanded by presenters. Matching grants and donations will be sought.
3. Library staff will utilize knowledgeable retirees and other community members to teach classes.
4. Partner with the City of Anywhere Chamber of Commerce on programs.
5. Staffers attend workshops provided by the state library, which are offered free of charge.
6. Shelving unit costs estimated to be $X,XXX per unit. The library will need to change public seating areas to accommodate additional shelving units.

Goal #4: Library patrons utilize current technology to access information.

Objectives:

1. By December 2013, purchase a new integrated library system.
2. By December 2013, replace the Web server and circulation/catalog server for new integrated library system.
3. By December 2013, the Anywhere Public Library Web site is the location people access daily for information.
4. By December 2015, purchase computer reservation management and print-management software for public Internet workstations.
5. Schedule replacement of computer equipment and software on a three-year basis.
6. By December 2015, upgrade Internet access to a T-3 line.
7. By December 2018, replace Wi-Fi equipment in the library and meeting rooms.

Outcomes:

1. The library provides economic benefits to the City of Anywhere by hosting Wi-Fi access to meeting rooms.
2. The library provides economic benefits to citizens by providing computers and Internet access for continuing education and job-seeking purposes.
3. The library users reserve and renew materials online.
4. Patrons receive overdue reminders by e-mail or telephone calls, saving paper, envelopes, and postage.
5. Patrons continue to access the Internet through their own laptops.
6. Internet-based trainings and programs are provided on an ongoing basis by staff.

Budget Impact:

1. The initial cost of an integrated library system is approximately $XX,XXX. This includes the purchase of a Web server and circulation/catalog server equipment. The library will use city capital funds and library funds and seek financial assistance from the Friends of the Library.
2. Approximately $X,XXX per year will be spent on computer equipment replacement. Capital funds, grants, and donations will be utilized for this purpose.
3. Approximately $X,XXX per year will be spent on a software maintenance agreement for the integrated library system. Operating funds will be utilized for this purpose.
4. Computer reservation and print management software will cost approximately $X,XXX.
5. Wi-Fi equipment will cost approximately $X,XXX for antennae and switches.

Goal #5: The physical space of the library serves the community.

Objectives:

1. By June 2012, ask the City of Anywhere to reserve land to the south of the library for future expansion of the Anywhere Public Library. More space is critical with the expanding population and usage of the library.

2. By December 2012, check the carpeting for replacement.
3. By December 2012, check the wooden furniture for refinishing and repair.
4. By December 2012, check the cloth furniture for repair and recovering.
5. In 2015, create a building expansion committee to discuss a building-expansion project. Hire a consultant, plan a budget, and develop architectural sketches.
6. In 2016, hold public meetings and begin a capital campaign for building expansion.
7. In 2017, seek a bond issue for a building-expansion project.
8. By August 2018, start construction of the addition to the library's existing building based on population needs and future growth, enlarge the parking area, and purchase furnishings.

Outcomes:

1. Patrons of all ages participate in programs held in the multipurpose meeting room.
2. Children and parents may utilize the enclosed children's area, which has a staffed reference desk, materials in a variety of formats, and computers with educational software.
3. Teens may utilize a specially designed area that features a staffed reference desk, materials in a variety of formats, and computers with educational software.
4. The City of Anywhere is a desirable community with residents enjoying a high quality of life. Library patrons have the physical space, furnishings, and technology to serve their recreational and informational requests.

Budget Impact:

1. Seek bond funds for the building project and furnishings.
2. $X,XXX to recover seat covers on wood chairs with cloth seats.
3. $X,XXX to refinish wood furniture.

Appendix C: Sample Technology Plan

Anywhere Public Library
Technology Plan
January 2013–December 2018

Rob Payne, Director
Library Board of Trustees, Sandra Smith, Chair
Friends of the Library, Carolyn Klepp, President
David Wesson, City Manager

Library Mission Statement

The library is a vital part of the community, providing a broad collection of resources and programs to meet the informational and recreational needs of all ages.

Library Vision Statement

Library provides access to information and programming for personal, business, literacy, recreation, health, and educational pursuits.

Goals to Improve Library Service via Technology

General statement: All goals, objectives, and evaluations are based on the above mission and vision statements. The Anywhere Public Library strives to provide the best resources and professional services for the community it serves.

1. The library will investigate the purchase of a new integrated library system (ILS) that will better serve the community.
    a) The library will work with the City of Anywhere and outside funding sources to purchase an ILS that meets the needs of future challenges.
        i. Library staff will research ILS software and prices.
        ii. The library director will present this plan to the library board of trustees at its February 2013 meeting.

135

iii. The library director will present this plan to the city manager and the Friends of the Anywhere Public Library to ask for financial assistance at March 2013 meetings.

iv. If needed, outside funding sources will be researched and pursued beginning in July 2013.

Budget Impact: The integrated library system that is purchased will be one that best serves the community and can be operated with little impact on staff time. Systems being considered are ones in which the hardware and software is located on-site and in which the vendor has remote access to troubleshoot the hardware and software. Estimated software costs are $25,000, with $5,000 in annual maintenance fees.

Evaluation: The Anywhere Public Library board of trustees approved the library's long-range strategic plan for 2011–2021. This plan calls for the purchase of a new integrated library system with features to better serve the community, along with modules that save staff time and monies spent on postage and paper supplies. The Anywhere Public Library will be successful in purchasing an ILS that provides excellent customer service and is easily operated and maintained by the library staff. The library will be successful in attaining the necessary funding through the City of Anywhere and the Friends of the Anywhere Public Library.

2. The library will select an integrated library system that will be robust in features but simple in operation and maintenance.

a) The ILS software will be housed on-site.

i. The library will replace the existing data server, which is six years old.

ii. The library will replace the existing Web server, which is four years old.

iii. The uninterrupted power supply will be replaced and upgraded to a better model.

iv. A turnkey ILS will be explored in which the library purchases the hardware and software from the vendor. The vendor loads the software onto the servers before shipping them to the library and handles any server issues with the hardware manufacturer.

v. The library will work with the City's MIS administrator and the ILS vendor to ensure that the ILS can utilize the current network, as the switches, router, and firewall are current and in good working order.

vi. The ILS will utilize the current staff and client workstations as the operating system, processing speed, memory, and other specifications exceed the vendor's requirements.

vii. The latest service packs and browser versions will be installed on each staff and client workstation.

b) A telephone notification system will be purchased so that library patrons are notified of overdue materials and items on hold for them through an automated calling system.

i. The library will purchase the telephone notification system from the ILS vendor to insure compatibility. The ILS vendor will install and maintain the telephone notification system.

ii. The telephone notification system software will be installed on an existing workstation in the staff work area. This workstation is currently on the network, so no additional changes need to be made. The ILS vendor will install software to remotely troubleshoot the notification software.

iii. One dedicated telephone line will be installed at the location of this workstation. The library will work with the phone system company to ensure compatibility with the proposed telephone notification system.

iv. The existing uninterrupted power supply will be utilized for the telephone notification hardware and computer workstation.

c) An automatic e-mail notification system will be purchased so that library patrons receive courtesy notices regarding upcoming due dates, overdue materials, and materials on hold.

       i. The library will select an ILS in which these features do not require staff interaction. E-mails are generated automatically by the ILS software.

      ii. The library staff will work with the MIS administrator and the ILS vendor to ensure that the City's exchange server and its operating system version are compatible with the e-mail notification system.

d) The library will select an ILS vendor who provides a Web site as part of the ILS package.

       i. Borrowers will be able to manage their accounts online: place holds, renew materials, check fine payment history, and so forth.

      ii. Staff will implement Web 2.0 technologies:

         1. The youth services librarian will start and maintain a blog page for teens to discuss books, authors, and programs. A link to the blog will be featured on the library's Web page.

         2. Library staff will create and maintain a social-networking site promoting materials, services, and programs. A link to the social-networking site will be on the library's Web page.

         3. Create a link on the Web site for borrowers to e-mail reference questions. Reference librarians will read and respond to e-mailed inquiries.

         4. Library staff will work with the ILS vendor to implement RSS feed technology.

Budget Impact:

- The library will replace the existing data server and Web server. The library will purchase hardware that allows for future growth in patron records, bibliographic records, and Web traffic. A separate Web server is necessary for the security and integrity of the data server. The library needs to replace the existing firewall in order to protect the Web server from unauthorized access. The estimated cost for both servers is $11,000, and the estimated cost of replacing the firewall component is $2,860.

- The contract MIS administrator for the City of Anywhere will assist the library director in writing the technology portion of the RFP at no additional charge. In addition, the MIS administrator will update any service packs and browser versions at no additional charge to the City of Anywhere or the library.

- The contract MIS administrator will be on-site for the installation of the new data server and Web server plus the installation of the client software on the staff and public workstations. The latter requires turning off the security software on the public workstations to allow for the installation of new software. An estimated $2,400 will be budgeted for the services that fall outside of the City's contract with the MIS administrator.

- The library will budget $1,500 for the purchase of a telephone notification system along with $200 in annual maintenance fees. The ILS vendor will install the notification system at no additional charge. The ILS vendor will maintain the telephone notification system and work directly with the manufacturer in troubleshooting any software and hardware issues without additional costs to the library other than the annual maintenance fees.

- The library will notify the company that manages the City's phone system regarding the installation of a telephone notification system to ensure compatibility plus the access of another dedicated phone line for the library. $100 will be budgeted for the installation of a dedicated telephone line.

- A new uninterrupted power supply (UPS) will be purchased for the equipment closet to handle the larger data server and Web servers needed for the new ILS. The existing UPS will be utilized for the telephone notification system hardware.

Evaluation: The new servers will handle growth in patron records, bibliographic records, and Web traffic over the next four to six years. The new Web site, telephone, and e-mail notification systems will move the library to a new level of service for the community. The library will realize a net growth of 3 percent each year in the number of cardholders along with a growth of 3 percent annually in the circulation of materials. Web site usage will increase by 5 percent each year.

3. Staff training.
   a) The ILS vendor will provide on-site training for all modules and components. Training will be provided to all circulation, reference, and administrative staff; a training day will consist of an eight-hour day.
   b) The ILS vendor will train and advise staff on the daily backup routine for the servers.
   c) The ILS vendor will train staff on any on-site server maintenance that needs to occur.
   d) The ILS vendor will train staff on operation and maintenance of the telephone notification system.

   Budget Impact: Approximately $4,500 will be budgeted for three full days of staff training along with training instructors on-site for "going live" with the new integrated library system. The vendor will also quote follow-up training costs for a 12-month period following the installation of the system in case additional training is needed.

   Evaluation: Staff will receive training that will provide competency in the following areas:
   - Operate daily circulation functions with ease: check-in, checkout, add new patron records, update patron records, place holds, and handle fines and lost-book charges.
   - Ability to perform original cataloging and copy cataloging, use cataloging templates, import MARC records from another server using Z39.50, and import MARC records from vendors. Ability to use authority control functions.
   - Working knowledge of public access catalog, including search strategies, managing patron accounts, and placing holds.
   - Working knowledge of utilizing the library's Web site, including accessing electronic resources and other links. Ability to update Web site information.
   - Staff are able to perform daily backup routines on servers and are able to confirm that backup functions are operating correctly. Staff are able to perform routine maintenance on servers.
   - Vendor will set up telephone notification system, including recording of messages. Staff will have working knowledge of running the notification system for holds and overdues and will be able to run daily reports on results of phone contact and attempted contact.

4. The library will provide the public with a direct, high-speed connection to the Internet.
   a) The library will apply for state telecommunication discounts.
   b) The library will apply for federal E-rate funding each year.
   c) Wireless access to the Internet will be provided in the library at no charge to the public and in the adjoining meeting rooms for programming purposes.
   d) The library director will explore opportunities to increase the amount of bandwidth for Internet access. T-1 technology is becoming outdated, and increased bandwidth is needed by 2015.
   e) The library will provide computer workstations with software and Internet access for the public at no charge:
      i. The library will pursue funding for future replacement costs of computers, keyboards, printers, and supplies.
   f) The public computer and Internet use policy, with safety information for minors and parents of minors, will be updated every three years or as needed.
   g) The library will work with the City of Anywhere to continue the licensing agreement for filtering software.
   h) The library will continue to add online resources to its Web site for public use.

Budget Impact: Upgrading from a T-1 to a bundled T-1 or T-3 line will require the purchase of a new router at an estimated cost of $3,000. In addition, the library will need to pay increased annual Internet access charges at approximately $6,000 per year, including state or federal discounts. Currently, the library budgets $4,000 per year for hardware replacement. An inventory of monitors, keyboards, and computer mice is maintained in storage as workstations are replaced.

Evaluation: The successful completion of this goal will be to replace the T-1 line with either cable, bundled T-1, or T-3. The library will provide access to electronic resources on its Web site. The choice of databases will be determined by patron needs for information. The library will track usage statistics and customer comments regarding the use of online resources.

5. The library will investigate using social-networking sites to market its materials, services, and programs.
   a) Open an account with Facebook and/or MySpace.
   b) Open an account with Twitter.
   c) Designate a staff member to update content on social networks.
   Budget Impact: No budget impact is expected. A current staff member will be assigned this responsibility. No registration fees are paid for the social-networking sites.

   Evaluation: The library board and city manager will approve the plan to utilize social-networking sites to market the library. Staff will meet annually to discuss the outreach effectiveness of these online marketing tools.

6. The library will provide online training opportunities for its customers to help them improve skills needed for the twenty-first century.
   a) The library director and the Friends of the Library will pursue grants to hire a lab instructor on contract basis.
   b) Classes on the library's electronic resources, Microsoft Office software, and other useful topics will be taught in the library's computer-training lab.
   c) Library staff will continue to upgrade and/or replace the wireless antenna, switches, LCD projectors, and laptops needed to support the computer-training lab.
   d) Library staff will market these free classes to the community.
   Budget Impact: Friends of the Library will budget $7,000 annually to provide a lab instructor for the library's computer-training lab. Laptops and LCD projectors will be on a three-year replacement schedule at $22,000 every three years. Fund-raising and grants will be used to fund the computer-training lab.

   Evaluation: Staff will evaluate the effectiveness of this goal by attendance statistics and evaluation feedback from workshop participants. The library will provide training sessions that patrons want and need to improve their computer literacy skills and knowledge.

7. Customers will utilize computer reservation software and print management software to better manage their time and resources.
   a) The library director will pursue funding to purchase the necessary computer reservation and print management software.
   b) Library staff will move children's computers to another location to make available three Internet-accessible workstation areas.
   c) A computer reservation station and receipt printer will be purchased and installed by December 2015.
   d) Two additional public computer workstations will be added over the next one to three years.
   e) The library director will pursue funding to purchase the needed computer equipment, receipt printer, and furniture proposed in b., c., and d.

Budget Impact: An estimated $12,000 will be needed to purchase computer reservation and print-management software, along with a computer reservation workstation and receipt printer. Another $3,200 is allocated for two public workstations, which includes the Microsoft Office Suite and a three-year hardware warranty.

Evaluation: Staff will monitor the use of the computer reservation software and print management software. Equipment purchases will be based on patron demand and need.

8. Library staff will have access to the hardware and software necessary to perform their duties.

   a) The library director will pursue funding to maintain computer workstations, receipt printers, and scanners necessary to provide services to the public.

   b) Library staff will purchase a computer workstation, receipt printer, and desk for the staff work area by December 2016. (The staff work area is a room located behind the circulation desk.) This additional computer workstation will give shelvers a workspace away from the main circulation desk. This, in turn, will free up a computer workstation at the circulation desk.

   Budget Impact: Expenditures listed in (a) are already budgeted for in the $4,500 allocated annually for hardware replacement. Expenditures for (b) are estimated to be $2,300. A network jack and electrical outlet are already in place.

   Evaluation: The library director will monitor the number of people using the library each month, along with the circulation statistics. If patron demand for services and assistance increases at the circulation desk, then a workstation in the staff work area will be required. There are three open network jacks available in the staff work area.

9. The library will explore RFID technology for the circulation desk over the next five years.

   a) RFID increases the speed and ease of checking materials in and out. Instead of a bar code reader scanning each individual bar code on a book, the RFID reader can simultaneously read the RFID tags of an entire stack of books in one scan.

   b) The library director will research cost of equipment and supplies.

   c) If the need arises, library director will justify the expense of RFID technology to meet patron demand in circulating materials.

   d) RFID technology is used in public self-check stations. This option will also be explored when considering this type of technology for the Anywhere Public Library.

   Evaluation: RFID is currently an expensive option for most small and medium-sized libraries. The library director will continue to follow this technology and make recommendations to the board if and when there is a proper time to purchase this software and hardware.

10. The library will provide quality reference and information services to all patrons.

   a) Staff will attend training in-house or through classes provide by the department of libraries, state and national library conferences, and workshops on improving reference and technology knowledge and skills.

   Evaluation: Feedback from staff regarding their knowledge and skills before and after training will give the library director the information he or she needs to pursue additional training.

Professional Development

The City of Anywhere values continuing education as a method to provide outstanding service to the community.

The Anywhere Public Library encourages staff to pursue continuing-education opportunities. The library has an education budget for staff to attend the state and national library conferences and workshops. Information from workshops and conferences keeps staff current on changing library services and resources in the twenty-first century.

Appendix D: Request For Proposal

Writing an RFP is a major, valuable undertaking in creating your list of requirements for an integrated library system and also for creating the basis for the contract to which the vendor must adhere. The following RFP should be utilized as a template illustrating the types of information one may want to present in an RFP.

An RFP asks vendors to respond and verify that the ILS can perform certain, particular functions. If a sales consultant demonstrates a desired software feature, include it in the RFP. Never assume that a demonstrated function comes standard with the product. As mentioned in Chapter 9, one of the benefits of the RFP is that you have in writing from the vendor what the ILS can and cannot do.

Our thanks to the following libraries that shared their RFPs with the authors:

- Pioneer Library System
- Mustang Public Library
- Corvallis-Benton County Public Library
- Chippewa River District Library System
- Mother Whiteside Memorial Library

REQUEST FOR PROPOSAL

FOR AN INTEGRATED LIBRARY SYSTEM

FOR THE ANYWHERE PUBLIC LIBRARY

August 5, 2013

City Clerk
City of Anywhere
1501 N. Anywhere Blvd.
Anywhere, CA 92590

Responses due: September 25, 2013, 3:00 P.M. PT
at the above address

Notice is issued that sealed proposals for the purchase, installation, and maintenance of a turnkey integrated library system for the Anywhere Public Library (hereinafter "Library") will be received at the office of the City Clerk, City of Anywhere, 1501 N. Anywhere Blvd., Anywhere, CA 92590, until 3:00 P.M. Pacific Time, September 25, 2013. Please refer to Chapter 3, Instructions to Vendors, for complete details.

A single proposal will be received for all work to be performed. The selected vendor must serve as the contractor for all functions, modules, features and third-party add-ons contained in their proposals. The Library reserves the right to approve the choice of subcontractor(s) by the vendor stated in the proposal and/or after in the awarding of the contract.

The City of Anywhere (hereinafter "City") reserves the right to reject any or all proposals, to waive any irregularities, and to select the proposal most advantageous to the Anywhere Public Library.

Contact for further information:

For further information, contact project manager Library Director Rob Payne at 951-000-9999 or rpayne@cityofanywhere.org. Inquiries arising from any errors, omissions, or other need for clarification should be submitted in writing either by mail at the above listed address or by e-mail to rpayne@cityofanywhere.org no later than September 25, 2013. The words "Integrated Library System Inquiry" should appear on the envelope or in the subject line of the e-mail. All responses will be distributed to all vendors participating in the RFP process, and the source of an inquiry will not be revealed.

TABLE OF CONTENTS

Chapter 1: General Description

1.1 Statement of Purpose and Objective:

The City of Anywhere is soliciting written proposals for the immediate selection of an integrated library system for the Anywhere Public Library. As stated in its mission statement, "The library is a vital part of the community providing a broad collection of resources and programs to meet the informational and recreational needs of all ages." The Library will select an integrated library system that not only enhances the essential circulation and public-access functions of its existing ILS, but also will move the Library forward in providing new customer-oriented features.

All system components, to include both hardware and software, will reside in a secure equipment room located in the Library. System components will be owned by and remain the sole property of the City of Anywhere.

The selected Vendor will be well established in the design and delivery of integrated library systems. The City is seeking Vendors who employ the latest technological advances in the area of public library services. The City intends to use a request for proposal procurement process, including a technical and financial evaluation, before negotiating and awarding a contract. The contract will not be awarded to the lowest priced proposal. After final evaluations, the award will be made to the Vendor who, in the Library's sole judgment, submits the proposal that is the most cost-effective and advantageous to the Library.

The system to be purchased must be a turnkey system consisting of hardware, software, installation, documentation, supplies, testing, training, migration of all files, and maintenance necessary for ongoing operations. The system must have a proven record of successful operations in public libraries of similar size to that of the Anywhere Public Library.

The Anywhere Public Library serves a diverse population, so the system must contain features for those with visual, hearing, or physical impairments. Screen displays and prompts should be available for persons who read languages other than English.

Vendors are invited to offer alternative solutions in their proposals and to propose enhancements to their existing software to satisfy the Library's requirements.

1.2 Library Overview:

The Anywhere Public Library serves the community of Anywhere with a current population of 17,888. The projected population for 2018 is 25,900. The library also serves those living in adjoining urban and rural areas. The current estimated service population is 38,000. The Anywhere Public Library has a single location with no branches in the foreseeable future.

1.3 System Capacity Requirements for the Anywhere Public Library:

The Anywhere Public Library has an annual materials budget of $XX,XXX. The following table shows the library's current and projected database sizes, transaction loads, and public and staff workstations as of August 2013, along with projections for 2018.

	August 1, 2013	Projected 2018
Bibliographic records (titles)	36,344	48,199
Items records	40,853	49,199
Patron records	22,818	25,099
Annual circulation	163,997	180,397
Concurrent user connections (staff)	7	8
Public Internet workstations	12	15
Public catalog computers	3	4

1.4 Goals of the New Integrated Library System:

- Web-accessible PAC.
- PAC incorporating thesaurus and dictionary entries with metadata in MARC records to provide patrons with spelling alternatives.
- PAC with integrated search results utilizing databases owned by the Library.
- Customers have the ability place holds, renew items, and check and modify patron records online.
- Catalog enrichment features such as book jackets, reviews, and so forth.
- Interactive library Web site.
- Circulation functions.
- Cataloging with Z39.50 access to other catalogs and the ability for other libraries, such at the California Department of Libraries, to access Anywhere's holdings.
- Authority control.
- Ability to contact customers regarding their overdue materials and holds via automated e-mail and telephone contact.
- Reports.
- Ability to add features in the future, such as RFID, self-check stations, computer reservations, and print management.

The Library needs a system that is flexible and that will allow staff to work on a multitude of tasks from various workstations. There are staffers who need to do cataloging, circulation, check item availability, place reserves for patrons, and run statistical reports all on the same workstation. There are currently seven staff workstations.

1.5 Description of the Library's Hardware and Network:

The existing hardware consists of (1) (insert brand name) data server with Windows Server 2003 operating system that serves as both the data server and the domain controller server; (2) (insert brand name) Web server with Windows Server 2003 operating system; (3) (insert brand name and model number) router; (4) (insert brand name and model number) firewall and (insert brand names and model numbers) switches; (5) two wireless antennas for Wi-Fi (one in the library and one for meeting rooms); (6) three (insert brand name and model number) receipt printers; (7) three (insert brand name and model) scanners; (8) 22 staff and public workstations with a Windows XP Professional operating system; (9) one (insert brand name and model number) laser printer for staff and public use; and (10) one (insert brand name and model number) color laser printer for staff and public use. All staff and public desktops are on a four-year replacement cycle.

Servers, router, firewall, and switches are located in a secure equipment room that is air-conditioned and has access to a T-1 connection. All equipment is connected to a UPS.

The Library has a dedicated T-1 connection. Workstations' IP addresses are blocked through the firewall. Wi-Fi is available to patrons.

1.6 Current Integrated Library System:

The Anywhere Public Library currently uses Windows-based (insert name of integrated library system and version).

1.7 Timeline for RFP and Project:

Deadline for submission of questions regarding the RFP	September 15, 2013
City's response to questions sent to vendors	September 18, 2013
Due date for proposals	September 25, 2013
Evaluation of proposals and selection of finalist(s)	September 28–October 1, 2013
Vendor demonstration by finalist(s) (optional on city's part)	October 15–20, 2013
Award bid	October 30, 2013
Project commences	January 2, 2014
Training	April 1, 2014

These dates may be revised if any step takes longer than anticipated or if steps are eliminated. For example, if the evaluation team determines that vendor demonstrations are not necessary, then that step will be dropped. Actual project commencement and completion dates will be determined during contract negotiations. The City reserves the right to postpone the award.

Chapter 2: System Specifications

2.1 Overview of Anticipated System:

The City of Anywhere will select a Vendor who is readily capable of providing an integrated online library system that has working modules immediately available for circulation, cataloging, public catalog, and reports. The selected ILS must have proven capabilities to work with the following added features: acquisitions module, computer reservation and print management software, telephone notification system, and RFID. These added features have a projected implementation over the next one to five years.

The selected Vendor must currently be providing service to a significant number of public libraries. It is preferred that the selected Vendor has experience migrating from the Library's current integrated library system to the Vendor's current system.

The hardware components must be new and off-the-shelf rather than customized for the Library. Given that the City has standardized on Windows platform, strong preference will be granted to this operating system.

All software components must be in current release, thoroughly tested, and must require few or no operating system modifications. The Vendor must discuss cost, availability, and access to future software upgrades. The Vendor's software and hardware must be compatible with existing library workstations, laser printers, routers, hubs, and wireless antennas as discussed in Section 1.5. Equipment design and construction must be consistent with good engineering practices and installed and implemented by experienced, knowledgeable staff. All equipment and materials will be new and not refurbished.

Each item will be of the most current design and manufacture and free of damage, scratches, or other defects.

The proposal must clearly define how the proposed system can satisfy the City of Anywhere's requirements. This RFP states the scope of the requirements and specifies the general rules for preparing the proposal.

2.2 Implementation of System:

The Vendor must provide a detailed description of its implementation plan. The Vendor must agree that the Library and the Vendor will mutually determine the details of the final implementation plan.

2.3 Responses to Functionality

Vendors must respond to every functional, technical, and performance requirement listed in Chapters 5–9 using one of the five response numbers listed in Table 1. Fill in the response number in the blank space that appears before each criterion. Response to this RFP must be completed using a word-processing software or ink.

Table 1 Response Codes

Code	Meaning
1	Operational in at least four public libraries.
2	Available, but not as specified. Vendor must provide description.
3	Feature or service can be demonstrated and is scheduled for a future release.
4	Feature or service is in the early planning stages.
5	Not available.

For items marked "2" in which a description is required, the Vendor must describe in detail the ability of the solution being proposed to meet that item's specifications. If a detailed description is lacking, the response will be considered "5–Not available." If there is no response to a criterion, the library will assume a response code of "5–Not available."

Chapter 3: Instructions to Vendors

3.1 Submission Deadline and Proposal Opening Date:

Sealed proposals must be submitted no later than 3:00 P.M. PT on September 25, 2013, at which time all proposals will be publicly opened and read. Proposals received after the deadline will be returned unopened. The proposal opening will be held at the City of Anywhere City Hall, which is located at 1501 N. Anywhere Blvd. Proposals submitted via fax or e-mail will not be accepted.

3.2 Address for Proposal Submission:

Submit one copy of your proposal in a sealed envelope labeled "Integrated Library System Proposal" to:

City Clerk
City of Anywhere
1501 N. Anywhere Blvd.
Anywhere, USA 92590

3.3 Staff Contact:

The City's staff contact for this RFP is Rob Payne, Library Director. Questions regarding this RFP must be submitted in writing via e-mail to rpayne@cityofany where.org. All questions must be addressed to the City's staff contact. No other staff member will answer questions about this RFP. No informal or oral contacts are permitted.

All prospective consultants may submit written questions about or request written clarifications of the RFP no later than September 15, 2013. Should any errors appear in these RFP documents, consultants should notify the City's contact at the e-mail address above as soon as possible. If it becomes necessary to revise any part of this RFP, an addendum to the RFP will be provided to all Vendors who received this RFP. The City reserves the right to waive nonmaterial errors or omissions in the RFP that do not substantially affect the procurement process or the ability of the Vendors to submit responses. All material answers, clarifications, and responses will be provided by the City via e-mail to everyone who has received a copy of the RFP by September 18, 2013.

3.4 Source Code Maintenance:

The Vendor must place all source codes in escrow by the date the installed system is scheduled to "go live." The Vendor agrees to maintain a current copy of their source code in escrow at all times. The City and the Vendor agree that the escrow agent will hold the source code in confidence as a trade secret of the Vendor and will release the source code to the City only upon the occurrence of the following events:

(a) the Vendor ceases business operations;
(b) the Vendor declares bankruptcy;
(c) the Vendor discontinues to provide maintenance or to provide inadequate maintenance.

3.5 Site Inspection:

The installation site for the system may be inspected by appointment with Library Director Rob Payne.

3.6 Required Proposal Documents:

- **Title Page:** The title page must include the name of the Vendor, address, telephone number, fax number, name of person(s) authorized to represent the Vendor during contracting, and date, along with e-mail address for contact person(s).
- **Corporate background:** Include the date established, type of ownership, and the location of corporate headquarters and major offices.
- **Statement of financial stability:** Adequate financial stability is a prerequisite to the award of a contract regardless of any other considerations. Please include balance sheets and statements of income along with the auditor's reports for your most recently completed fiscal year.
- **Other Information:** Provide names and contact information for public libraries of similar size and needs to the Anywhere Public Library for which the Vendor installed a similar ILS as detailed in this RFP.

3.7 Cost Proposal:

Your proposal must include a statement of all costs that will be associated with the project, including:

(a) Software
(b) Hardware
(c) Data conversion and migration
(d) Site preparation
(e) Installation
(f) Training
(g) Annual software licensing fees
(h) Annual technical/maintenance support charges
(i) Optional system features, including telephone notification system, computer reservation and print-management software, acquisitions module, and so forth.
(j) All other miscellaneous fees/charges/costs not already included in the above list
(k) Total contract price

3.8 Proposal Certificate (Attachment A):

The proposal must be completed and signed by a person authorized to commit the Vendor to provide the good or service. This RFP and all related attachments submitted by the Vendor will become part of the formal contract between the Library and the Vendor. Failure of the successful Vendor to accept these obligations in the contractual agreement may result in the cancellation of the award. Submission of a signed proposal will be interpreted to mean that the Vendor has hereby agreed to all terms and conditions set forth in all of the sheets that make up this RFP. Any deviation or intended deviation from the RFP requirements shall be identified within the proposal at the time it is submitted for consideration. Acceptable deviations will not detract from possible points in the evaluation process.

3.9 List of References (Attachment B):

Provide a list of references who may be contacted regarding the qualifications of your firm. References must, at a minimum, include current clients for whom your firm has provided services similar to those sought in this RFP, including name, mailing address, e-mail address, phone number, fax number, name of contact person, and the amount of the contract.

3.10 Public Records Requirements:

All proposals submitted become the property of the City. The contents of all proposals, correspondence, addenda, financial data, or any other medium that discloses any proprietary aspect of a proposal shall be held in the strictest confidence by the City and Library until the recommendation for award is submitted. After that time, disclosure of the proposals will be in accordance with the public records act and any other applicable laws. Any restrictions on the use of data or information claimed as proprietary information must be clearly marked. This restriction may not apply to cost or price information, which must be open to public inspection.

Chapter 4: Selection and Evaluation

4.1 Selection Process:

The selection of an integrated library system to serve the Anywhere Public Library's needs is an important and complex task. Committee members will evaluate each proposal on the criteria detailed in Section 4.3 of this RFP. The Anywhere Public Library reserves the right to use for evaluation purposes all information gathered during this process, including information gathered from demonstrations, company background, and reference checks.

The evaluation of proposals will occur in three phases:

4.2 Evaluation Phase 1:

The first phase will be to select those proposals that comply with all of the requirements detailed in this RFP. The proposal must be complete and presented in the format as detailed in Chapter 3. This phase will also eliminate nonresponsive and proposals that have not provided answers to all specifications detailed in Chapters 5 through 10. This evaluation phase will be processed on a pass/fail basis. Vendors that pass Phase 1 will continue to Phase 2.

4.3 Evaluation Phase 2:

The Anywhere Public Library shall be the final judge of the capability and performance of the products proposed. The Anywhere Public Library will also be the final judge of product support and future ability to upgrade the system proposed. Prior to awarding the contract, the Library reserves the right to request a demonstration of the proposed system before the selection of a finalist or finalists has been completed. Failure to demonstrate the system may forfeit the proposal.

Each of the general evaluation criterion below fall under one of the following categories (the priority given to each category is also provided for your reference):

Weighted Value for Each Category

A.	Financial history of company and its customer base	10 percent
B.	Project management and references from similar-type libraries	15 percent
C.	Cost of integrated library system	25 percent
D.	Ability to meet specifications in the RFP and Support	50 percent

Evaluation Criteria

1. The ability to meet or exceed the functions specified in the RFP. (D)
2. The ILS is able to use the library's existing network and infrastructure. (C and D)
3. The Vendor's ability to implement the hardware and software, provide technical assistance in a timely manner, and support the add-ons detailed in the RFP. (B, C and D)
4. The ability of the ILS to meet future growth in materials and borrowers and remain current with technological innovations. (D)
5. Total costs in procuring the system along with hardware and software maintenance and support for five years. (C)
6. The Vendor's experience in successfully implementing integrated library systems that communicate with current suppliers, interlibrary loan consortium, and so forth. (B and D)

7. The number of implemented systems similar to our type of library and the ability to provide patron references for similar type libraries and systems. (A and B)
8. The financial stability and history of the Vendor. (A)

Finalists for the award of this RFP may be invited to respond to specific questions or provide further information in person or in writing during the evaluation process, including an on-site demonstration of all or parts of the proposed system. Failure to provide additional information, if requested, may disqualify a proposal from further consideration.

The City of Anywhere does not assume any liability or responsibility for costs incurred by vendors in responding to this RFP or requests for interviews, additional data, or other information with respect to the selection process.

Chapter 5: Basic System Requirements

5.1 Basic System Requirements:

5.1.1 Vendors must be able to quote costs and provide all of the following products and services required for successful system implementation and operation:

————	a.	Hardware
————	b.	Software (both operating and application)
————	c.	Hardware and software installation
————	d.	Hardware and software maintenance
————	e.	Data conversion/migration
————	f.	Database loading
————	g.	Training
————	h.	Additional training, if requested by the library
————	i.	Documentation

5.1.2 The system modules/functions listed below must be fully developed, operational, and in current use at multiple current customer sites:

————	a.	Circulation with the ability to add RFID
————	b.	Cataloging and item entry
————	c.	MARC bibliographic and authority record import/export
————	d.	Authority control
————	e.	Public access catalog
————	g.	Library's Web site created and maintained by Vendor
————	h.	Reports
————	i.	System administration
————	k.	Z39.50 server
————	l.	Z39.50 client
————	m.	Z39.50 copy cataloging client

———— 5.1.3 The system must be fully integrated, using a single, common catalog database for all operations and across all modules or functions.

———— 5.1.4 The system must allow the Library to load and index records from any bibliographic utility or database chosen by the Library, without the need for Vendor intervention or additional cost, provided the records are in standard USMARC format.

—————— 5.1.5 The system must allow records to be created "on the fly" by any staff member with as little as one field of information.

—————— 5.1.6 The system must allow staff to access any and all system functions for which they are authorized from any workstation.

—————— 5.1.7 The system should accommodate devices designed for handicapped access.

—————— 5.1.8 The system must require no additional purchases or local programming in order to become operational.

—————— 5.1.9 The Library will own its own data and be able to easily export that data at no additional charge. **Description required.**

—————— 5.1.10 Vendors must describe the proposed hardware, software, and process for storing and retrieving bibliographic and patron data. **Description required.**

—————— 5.1.11 Vendors must describe the minimum hardware and software requirements of servers and clients to support the system software. **Description required.**

—————— 5.1.12 The system must be scalable. The Vendor will describe the ability to add modules or functions, clients, and other servers over time. **Description required.**

—————— 5.1.13 The system must support the use of hardware that provides for system redundancy to provide continuous operation. The Vendor will describe the redundancy capabilities of the system. **Description required.**

—————— 5.1.14 Vendor-supplied hardware must be installed by the Vendor's employees or approved subcontractors.

—————— 5.1.15 The system must be an open-architecture system and provide maximum flexibility and compatibility regarding data import and export and integration with other systems.

—————— 5.1.16 The system must be fully Z39.50 (latest version) compliant for client and server.

—————— 5.1.17 The Vendor will supply a stand-alone, client-based version of the software that will allow circulation to continue in the event of a system, power, or communications failure.

—————— 5.1.18 The system must have the ability to concurrently run all application modules or functions on the same hardware configuration.

—————— 5.1.19 The system must allow access to all modules or functions from any workstation with one staff logon.

—————— 5.1.20 Servers should communicate over the network at a minimum (insert speed).

5.2 Hardware and Software Standards:

—————— 5.2.1 The system server hardware must not be proprietary and run on (name operating system).

—————— 5.2.2 The system clients must run on (name operating system).

—————— 5.2.3 The system must accept input from devices such as bar code scanners or RFID technology.

—————— 5.2.4 The system must have the capability to export any part of the patron or bibliographic database in a format that can be imported into common database and spreadsheet software.

5.3 System Security:

—————— 5.3.1 The system must accommodate three levels of security: network level, database level, and application level.

—————— 5.3.2 The system must allow the restriction of specific functions to specific users.

———— 5.3.4   The system must allow restriction of access to local or remote databases based upon the:

        ———— a.   IP address of the user

        ———— b.   user's log-in ID

5.4 Patron Authentication:

———— 5.4.1   The system must be able to authenticate cardholders by SIP (or other designated protocol).

———— 5.4.2   The system must retain a cardholder's authorization as he or she navigates among databases.

5.5 System Administration:

———— 5.5.1   Staff must be able manage system without Vendor intervention.

———— 5.5.2   Staff must be able to shut down and restart the system without Vendor intervention.

———— 5.5.3   The system must check the integrity of the entire file system during each restart of the system.

———— 5.5.4   The server(s) must log all system errors by date and time.

5.6 Training and Documentation:

———— 5.6.1   The Vendor must describe and provide a copy of its training plan along with all related costs to support this project. **Description required.**

———— 5.6.2   The Vendor must provide on-site training for Library staff.

———— 5.6.3   The Vendor must provide a minimum of two eight-hour, consecutive days of on-site training in the use of the system modules, features, and administration.

———— 5.6.4   The Vendor must provide a minimum of one eight-hour day of on-site assistance when the library goes live with the new system.

———— 5.6.5   The Vendor must quote costs for additional training requested by the Library within one year of installation.

———— 5.6.6   The Vendor will provide all necessary instructional materials required for training in the effective use of the system.

———— 5.6.7   The Vendor must train Library and system administration staff to manage and operate the system on a day-to-day basis:

        ———— a.   start up and shut down the system

        ———— b.   monitor system performance and perform routine system-management tasks

        ———— c.   handle emergencies

        ———— d.   troubleshoot and resolve routine problems

        ———— e.   load records from cataloging utilities or other databases

        ———— f.   run file backup operations

        ———— g.   perform recommended preventive maintenance and security measures

———— 5.6.8   The Vendor must include a complete description of the documentation package available with the system.

———— 5.6.9   The Vendor must provide documentation updates and release notes electronically.

5.7 Technical Support, Warranties, and Migration of Data:

———— 5.7.1 The vendor must give a written description of the system support provided during and after installation. **Description required.**

———— 5.7.2 The Vendor must affirm that the system software to be installed is the latest released version available and that the software is not in a product-testing phase.

———— 5.7.3 The Vendor must provide a software-maintenance program that includes all future software updates. **Description required.**

———— 5.7.4 The Vendor must have the ability to connect to the system remotely so that the Vendor's support staff can perform maintenance and software updates.

———— 5.7.5 The Vendor must agree to place required service calls to subcontractors if necessary.

———— 5.7.6 Software maintenance and upgrades must be provided at no additional costs during the first 12 months of operation.

———— 5.7.7 The Vendor must provide maintenance of system software on an annually renewable contract.

———— 5.7.8 The Vendor must agree to license the software for perpetual use for a fixed fee without additional royalties or service fees, except for fees for annual software maintenance.

———— 5.7.9 The Vendor must be able to provide technical support from 9:00 A.M. to 9:00 P.M. Pacific Time six days per week (Monday through Saturday).

———— 5.7.10 The Vendor must agree to accept non-emergency requests for technical support through a toll-free phone number and e-mail address.

———— 5.7.11 The Vendor must describe any routine or preventive maintenance activities and how often these activities may occur and if there is downtime. **Description required.**

———— 5.7.12 The Vendor will describe all hardware and software proposed for the project. **Description required.**

———— 5.7.13 All hardware purchased from the Vendor will be free from defects and conform to the specifications supplied by the Vendor.

———— 5.7.14 All Vendor-supplied hardware and equipment must be unmodified and off-the-shelf. All manufacturers' literature will be provided to the Library.

———— 5.7.15 Vendor-supplied server/workstation hardware must carry a minimum three-year warranty, under which equipment maintenance will be provided without additional costs.

———— 5.7.16 Vendor-supplied server/workstation hardware must carry an on-site, next-business-day guarantee. Furthermore, the Vendor will guarantee that only new replacement parts will be installed.

———— 5.7.17 The Vendor will load all of the Library's current borrower records into the system.

———— 5.7.18 The Vendor will load and index all bibliographic records and items in standard USMARC format provided by the Library.

———— 5.7.19 The Vendor must load and index, without added cost, at least one added "gap" file containing additional records created by the Library during the interval between the initial data transfer and completion of system installation and training.

Chapter 6: Circulation Module

6.1 General Functions:

—————— 6.1.1 The system must read the Library's current bar codes. Samples of the Library's material and patron bar codes are given in Attachment D. Please describe if any additional costs are involved in using the current material and patron bar codes. **Description required.**

—————— 6.1.2 The following, at a minimum must be displayed in each patron's record:

—————— a. Name
—————— b. Complete mailing address, including county
—————— c. Alternate address
—————— d. Telephone number
—————— e. E-mail address
—————— f. Borrowing category
—————— g. Lending status (restricted or not)
—————— h. Driver's license number
—————— i. All material on loan and in order by date
—————— j. Reserves ready and reserves pending
—————— k. Number of claims returned and items claimed returned
—————— l. Comment field

(Describe length restrictions.)

—————— 6.1.3 The system must allow the library to determine circulation rules.

—————— 6.1.4 The circulation module must allow authorized staff to restrict borrower accounts as needed.

—————— 6.1.5 The circulation module must allow the Library to set expiration dates on patron accounts.

—————— 6.1.6 The circulation module must allow entry of the patron and item identification bar codes using both a laser scanner and keyboard.

—————— 6.1.7 The circulation module must not confuse patron bar code numbers with material bar code numbers.

—————— 6.1.8 The circulation module must produce receipts for all patron-related transactions and staff must be able to print receipts on demand only.

—————— 6.1.9 The system must update item status information in the public catalog immediately as it changes during check-in and checkout.

—————— 6.1.10 The system must keep statistical records of all transactions.

—————— 6.1.11 There must be an offline circulation feature in case of server or network failure.

6.2 Checkout:

—————— 6.2.1 The system must be able to check out items when the borrower's bar code card is not presented.

—————— 6.2.2 The system must alert staff if no record exists for the patron entered.

—————— 6.2.3 The system must be able to create temporary item records and permit circulation of Library materials that are not yet in the bibliographic database.

—————— 6.2.4 The system must automatically display at least the following information on the checkout screen:

———— a. patron name

———— b. borrowing category

———— c. patron bar code number

———— d. lending status (restricted or not)

———— e. item identification number

———— e. short title

———— f. call number

———— g. due date

———— h. outstanding blocks (if any)

———— i. comment field on patron's record

———— 6.2.5 The system must alert staff if an item being checked out is already checked out to another patron and allow them to override the alert and checkout the item.

———— 6.2.6 The system must verify that the correct patron is checking out material at time of the loan.

———— 6.2.7 The system must check all items for outstanding holds, charges, and circulation restrictions before allowing them to be checked out.

———— 6.2.8 The system must detect items that have not been checked in, allowing for a checkout function.

———— 6.2.9 The system must treat each checkout as a separate transaction, but be able to list all checkouts for each person on one receipt.

———— 6.2.10 The system must support RFID technology and self-check systems.

———— 6.2.11 New patrons must be able to charge materials immediately after registration.

———— 6.2.12 The system must allow convenient renewal of all or selected items checked out.

6.3 Check-in:

———— 6.3.1 The circulation module must allow staff to change the check-in date for managing the book drop.

———— 6.3.2 Staff must be able to check in items by bar code, ISBN, or title.

———— 6.3.4 The circulation module must be capable of displaying the following information at check-in:

———— a. patron name

———— b. patron bar code

———— c. title and due date of item

———— d. overdue alert

———— 6.3.5 The circulation module must alert staff at check-in if an item is on hold and offer the option for staff to print a hold slip.

———— 6.3.6 During check-in, the module must accommodate transactions such as "claimed returned," "damaged," or other related status comments.

6.4 Blocks:

———— 6.4.1 The system must provide automatic restriction of borrower privileges for Library-defined criteria.

———— 6.4.2 The circulation module must allow the option for all blocks to be overridden by staff.

———— 6.4.3 The circulation module must alert staff to blocks by audio and/or visual alarms.

6.4.5   Staff must be able to easily pay fines and clear delinquencies from within the same window.

6.4.6   The system must block patrons with expired accounts, overdue materials, and unpaid fines from placing holds, borrowing, or renewing items.

6.5 Holds and Renewals:

6.5.1   The circulation module must generate an automatic e-mail notification of received holds for patrons who have an e-mail address in their account.

6.5.2   The circulation module must generate a report for calling customers through a third-party telephone notification system regarding received holds.

6.5.3   The system must block the placing of holds on lost or missing items or non-circulating items.

6.5.4   The system must allow staff to view and alter the sequence of holds within a queue.

6.5.5   The system must automatically activate the next hold in the queue when a hold is removed and generate a hold notice to the next patron in the queue.

6.5.6   The system must monitor the length of time items sit on a hold shelf.

6.5.7   The system must automatically print hold slips when items on hold are checked in.

6.5.8   The system must allow the patrons to renew items online, by telephone, or in person.

6.5.9   The system must allow staff to renew overdue items with the request of payment or no payment.

6.5.10 The system must allow the Library to restrict the number of renewals.

6.6 Fines and Overdues:

6.6.1   The circulation module must generate an automatic e-mail notification of overdue notices for patrons who have an e-mail address in their account.

6.6.2   The circulation module must generate a report for calling customers through a third-party telephone notification system regarding received overdue notices.

6.6.3   The system must allow the Library to set the parameters for issuing overdue notices and bill notices.

6.6.4   The circulation module must calculate and display fines at time of checkout, check-in, or renewal.

6.6.5   The system must allow full or partial payment of fines and print receipts on demand.

6.6.6   Staff must have the option to exempt fees and fines as individual cases arise.

6.6.7   The system must automatically cancel the lost status when lost books are returned.

6.6.8   The system must keep a history of patron fines and fees payments.

6.7 Notices and Other Functions:

6.7.1   The system must call or e-mail patrons regarding materials on hold. Vendors must describe what third-party telephone notification system their system supports.

——— 6.7.2   The system must generate an e-mail message when a patron's hold has expired. Vendors must describe if the e-mail notification system and whether or not a third-party company will be used.

——— 6.7.3   The system must generate calls, e-mails, and print notices according to schedules that are linked to the Library's calendar.

——— 6.7.4   The system must call, e-mail, and/or print (on demand) billing notices for patrons' overdues.

——— 6.7.5   The system must, on demand, call, e-mail, or print overdue notices of all materials overdue since the last notification.

——— 6.7.6   The system must prepare/print bill notices on demand that include replacement charges.

——— 6.7.7   The system must automatically print notices in a style that can be inserted in a #10 window envelope.

——— 6.7.8   The system must support telephone notification of overdues, fines, holds, and so forth.

——— 6.7.9   The system must support e-mail notification of overdues, fines, holds, and so forth.

——— 6.7.10 The system must record the date for each notice sent.

——— 6.7.11 The system must be able to generate and print a list of items tagged as lost after a specified period of time.

——— 6.7.12 The system must record the date upon which any item is assigned a special status on the item.

——— 6.7.13 The system must be compatible with electronic inventory control systems in both offline and online mode.

Chapter 7: Cataloging Module

7.1 General Functions:

——— 7.1.1   The catalog module must support cataloging records that are updated in real time and are shared among all other modules or subsystems.

——— 7.1.2   The catalog module must store records for all types of media for which there is a defined USMARC record.

——— 7.1.3   The catalog module must be able to retrieve, at a minimum, items by bar code number, title, author, ISBN, and ISSN.

——— 7.1.4   The catalog module must support item records which contain, but must not be limited to, the following fields:

    ——— a.   bar code number
    ——— b.   current loan status
    ——— c.   statistical category
    ——— d.   last activity date and frequency of circulation
    ——— e.   call number, including prefix
    ——— f.   price
    ——— g.   date entered into system
    ——— h.   note field (indicate character restriction)
    ——— i.   publication date

——— 7.1.5   The catalog module must accommodate library-defined MARC tags.

——— 7.1.6   The system must not delete items with the status of checked out and must inform staff before deleting an item with a patron hold.

——— 7.1.7   The system must print spine labels.

———— 7.1.8 Password access with one security level for authorized staff to make changes, deletions, and additions.

7.2 Standards:

———— 7.2.1 The catalog module must be capable of creating and maintaining a bibliographic database with full USMARC records and utilizing appropriate data from those files in other modules.

———— 7.2.2 The system must fully support all MARC bibliographic and authority record formats.

———— 7.2.3 The system must support bibliographic records that contain, but are not be limited to, the following fields:

    ———— a.   title
    ———— b.   author
    ———— c.   call number
    ———— d.   format
    ———— e.   place of publication
    ———— f.   publisher
    ———— g.   publication date
    ———— h.   call number, including prefix
    ———— i.   edition
    ———— j.   LCCN
    ———— k.   ISBN
    ———— l.   ISSN
    ———— m.   subject headings
    ———— n.   series
    ———— o.   content notes
    ———— p.   subject(s)
    ———— q.   variant title
    ———— r.   added entries
    ———— s.   date added or modified

———— 7.2.4 The catalog module must be both ISBN 10- and 13-digit complaint.

7.3 Creating and Editing:

———— 7.3.1 The catalog module must provide full-screen MARC editing.

———— 7.3.2 The catalog module must supply cataloging templates in MARC format containing required and recommended bibliographic fields.

———— 7.3.3 The catalog module must provide a simplified interface that allows staff members unfamiliar with MARC to catalog bibliographic records. The data from this interface must be stored in MARC format, allowing it to be retrieved, indexed, and searched the same as full MARC records.

———— 7.3.4 The catalog module must perform data validation during the input of bibliographic information.

———— 7.3.5 The catalog module must enable fields to be added, modified, or removed during record modification.

———— 7.3.6 The catalog module must automatically transfer bibliographic information to the item records.

—————— 7.3.7 The catalog module must support the creation of brief records that can be utilized in the circulation module.

—————— 7.3.8 The catalog module must check for errors in bibliographic and authority records when importing and saving records and alert staff to these errors.

7.4 Importing and Exporting Records:

—————— 7.4.1 The system must enable MARC records to be imported or exported to and from diskette, e-mail, or other storage/communication device.

—————— 7.4.2 The system must be able to search any Z39.50 database, import MARC bibliographic and authority records into an editor, and save these records to the database.

—————— 7.4.3 The system must be capable of overlaying bibliographic records over matching "on order" records.

—————— 7.4.4 The system must alert staff of duplicate records.

—————— 7.4.5 The system must automatically match on field(s) to facilitate overlay of duplicate authority records.

—————— 7.4.6 The system must be able to import records at any time.

—————— 7.4.7 The system must have the ability to export bibliographic, item, and authority records from the system in appropriate MARC formats.

7.5 Authority Control:

—————— 7.5.1 The system must automatically check authority headings.

—————— 7.5.2 Staff must be able to replace incorrect headings in bibliographic records with authorized headings.

—————— 7.5.3 A detailed alert must appear when entry of bibliographic data does not match an authority record.

—————— 7.5.4 The system must display the results of an authority file search from which staff may select the appropriate entry.

—————— 7.5.5 The system must provide real-time support for Library of Congress subject headings and name authorities.

—————— 7.5.6 The system must store authority records in conformance with the MARC formats for authority records.

—————— 7.5.7 Staff must have the ability to create new authority records if no existing records are in the system.

—————— 7.5.8 The system must be capable of incorporating changes in the MARC authority format as new national standards are developed.

—————— 7.5.9 The system must enable staff to perform global edits and updates to authority records.

Chapter 8: Public Access Catalog (PAC)

8.1 General Functions:

—————— 8.1.1 Patrons must be able to choose what type of search strategy they want to use.

—————— 8.1.2 Patrons must be able to limit search by format, language, call number (including prefixes), publication date, and date added to the collection.

—————— 8.1.3 The system must ensure that the PAC interacts with the circulation system in real time.

—————— 8.1.4 Staff are able to define aspects of how the PAC displays information, including help screen information.

—————— 8.1.5 The PAC provides search results that utilize databases owned by the Library. **Please describe**.

—————— 8.1.6 Catalog enrichment features such as book jackets and reviews are available. **Please describe**.

—————— 8.1.7 The PAC must include Web portal features such as licensed databases, library information, recommended title lists, sets of recommended Web sites, library information, maps, news, weather, and calendar.

—————— 8.1.8 The Web portal must allow authenticated patron to access licensed databases from locations outside the library. Please state if there is an additional cost for the remote patron authentication feature.

—————— 8.1.9 The Vendor must create and maintain the Web site.

—————— 8.1.10 Library staff can perform routine Web site maintenance.

—————— 8.1.11 The PAC must provide Spanish and other language versions.

—————— 8.1.12 The system must provide an option for a children's PAC interface.

8.2 Hardware and Software Standards:

—————— 8.2.1 The system must be able to function on a standard keyboard.

—————— 8.2.2 The system must be fully compliant with the USMARC and Z39.50 standards.

—————— 8.2.3 The system should be able to search any Z39.50-compliant database or server.

—————— 8.2.4 The system's public catalog interface must be accessible from any type of client running a Web browser.

8.3 Searching:

—————— 8.3.1 The PAC must be graphical and have easy-to-follow prompts.

—————— 8.3.2 The PAC must allow keyword, browse, and exact-match searching.

—————— 8.3.3 The system must perform full text searching of all bibliographic fields when doing keyword searching.

—————— 8.3.4 The PAC must allow implicit Boolean searches.

—————— 8.3.5 The PAC must support implicit and explicit right-hand truncation keyword searching.

—————— 8.3.6 The system must allow the patron to move forward and backward in a search without having reenter search terms.

—————— 8.3.7 The system must be able to search both local and Z39.50 external databases simultaneously.

8.4 Display

—————— 8.4.1 The PAC must display for the user the total number of records found along with brief bibliographic information.

—————— 8.4.2 The PAC must provide both brief and full record display options with a single keystroke or mouse click.

———— 8.4.3 The system must allow the Library to define the default sort order for each type of display.

———— 8.4.4 The system allows the Library to customize what formats appear first in a listing.

———— 8.4.5 The PAC must be capable of displaying circulation status and due date in both brief and full display.

———— 8.4.6 The full record display should provide an option to view the MARC record.

———— 8.4.7 The system must allow the library to choose the wording for status messages.

———— 8.4.8 The PAC must have hyperlinked author and subject fields.

———— 8.4.9 The PAC should be able to display Web sites that are cataloged in item's bibliographic record.

———— 8.4.10 The PAC must include "see" and "see also" references.

8.5 Borrower Accounts:

———— 8.5.1 The Library's PAC/Web site must clearly display access to patron account information.

———— 8.5.2 Borrowers must be able to log in and review their account that displays items checked out, items on hold, and fines owed.

———— 8.5.3 Borrowers must have the option to keep a history of their checkouts.

———— 8.5.4 Borrowers must have the ability to place and cancel their own holds.

———— 8.5.5 Borrowers must have the ability to renew their own materials.

Chapter 9: Reports Module

9.1 In addition to responding to the specific criteria in this chapter, the Vendor must describe and provide samples of reports that can be produced by the system. **Description required.**

———— 9.1.2 The system must be able to run all reports in a variety of formats, including PDF, HTML, XML, CSV, and Excel.

———— 9.1.2 The system must allow staff to run the report module at any time.

———— 9.1.3 The report module must allow reports to be scheduled to run at a specified time or on a periodic basis.

———— 9.1.4 Reports must display on screen before printing.

———— 9.1.5 Reports can be sorted by any field in the generated report.

———— 9.1.6 The system must be able to generate patron statistical reports based on any specific field or a combination of fields in the patron record.

———— 9.1.7 The system must be able to track circulation statistics for all of the following transactions:
———— a. check-ins
———— b. checkouts
———— c. renewals
———— d. library cards issued
———— e. holds
———— f. notices generated by type

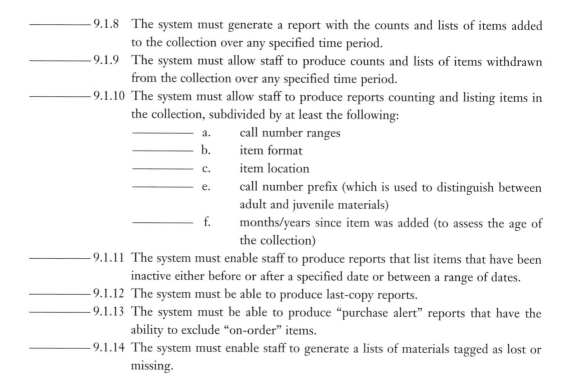

——————— 9.1.8 The system must generate a report with the counts and lists of items added to the collection over any specified time period.

——————— 9.1.9 The system must allow staff to produce counts and lists of items withdrawn from the collection over any specified time period.

——————— 9.1.10 The system must allow staff to produce reports counting and listing items in the collection, subdivided by at least the following:

——————— a. call number ranges

——————— b. item format

——————— c. item location

——————— e. call number prefix (which is used to distinguish between adult and juvenile materials)

——————— f. months/years since item was added (to assess the age of the collection)

——————— 9.1.11 The system must enable staff to produce reports that list items that have been inactive either before or after a specified date or between a range of dates.

——————— 9.1.12 The system must be able to produce last-copy reports.

——————— 9.1.13 The system must be able to produce "purchase alert" reports that have the ability to exclude "on-order" items.

——————— 9.1.14 The system must enable staff to generate a lists of materials tagged as lost or missing.

Chapter 10: Added Features

Over the next five years, the Library plans to purchase additional features and modules for the selected integrated library system. The proposed added features include an acquisitions module, computer reservation software, print management software, a children's public access catalog interface, and RFID technology. Vendors must describe what add-ons, including third-party companies, their system supports.

Chapter 11: Project Management, Installation, and Final Testing

The library director will serve as the project manager for the Anywhere Public Library. The Vendor will also provide a project manager. The project managers will be responsible for negotiating the contract, scheduling benchmarks toward a successful implementation, and monitoring the progress of the benchmarks and deadlines.

A project schedule will be established at the beginning. The schedule will include deadlines specifying what must be accomplished, submitted, or delivered by each party. The library director and the Vendor's project manager will maintain weekly contact to measure progress toward completion of the project.

The Library's project manager will test and certify as operational all Vendor-installed hardware and software. All hardware installations must meet manufacturers' installation standards, along with all applicable state and federal safety standards. The installation must not cause interference in the operation of any other equipment or systems in the facility.

ATTACHMENT A:
AGREEMENT TO TERMS AND CONDITIONS OF THE
REQUEST FOR PROPOSAL

The proposal must be completed and signed by a person authorized to commit the Vendor to the goods or services detailed in this request for proposal. This RFP and all related attachments submitted by the Vendor will become part of the formal contract between the Library and the Vendor. Failure of the successful Vendor to accept these obligations in the contractual agreement may result in the cancellation of the award. By signing this proposal, the Vendor hereby agrees to all terms and conditions set forth in all of the pages of this RFP, unless listed below as an exception.

Company Name:

Authorized Representative:

Signature:

Contact Information:

Please list all exceptions to the requirements specified in the attached pages of this request for proposal. Exceptions must be numbered and listed on this sheet. Attach additional sheets if necessary.

ATTACHMENT B:
REFERENCES

Please provide contact information for three public library references that are similar to the Anywhere Public Library in population served, collection size, and/or circulation transactions. Installation of integrated library system must have occurred in the past four years.

Reference #1:

Library Name:
Contact Person:
Address:
Telephone:
E-mail:
Date of installation:

Reference #2:

Library Name:
Contact Person:
Address:
Telephone:
E-mail:
Date of installation:

Reference #3:

Library Name:
Contact Person:
Address:
Telephone:
E-mail:
Date of installation:

ATTACHMENT C:
SAMPLE MATERIAL AND PATRON BAR CODES

MATERIAL BAR CODES

PATRON BAR CODE

Glossary

24/7/365 – 24 hours /7 days a week /365 days

AACR2 – Anglo-American Cataloging Rules, version 2. The standard used in the English speaking world for material used in an online catalog.

AASL – American Association of School Librarians; http://www.aasl.org

ACRL – Association of College and Research Libraries; http://www.acrl.org

Add-on / Added-feature – in this book we refer to software features and modules that are not part of a basic Integrated Library System that are purchased separately and interact with the system to enhance functionality, but are not necessarily fully integrated into the system itself.

Authority record – standardized forms for names, titles, and subjects. See also MARC Authority Records.

Bandwidth – the rate of data transfer measured in bits/sec that helps describe the capacity of the delivery of Internet services. For example a fiber optic line has very high bandwidth that delivers text, graphics, video and audio files, much faster than a copper telephone line.

Bar code – a series of vertical lines printed in a sequence that translates into a unique number when read by a bar code scanner. Bar codes are attached to item records and patron records.

Bar code scanner or reader – a peripheral device attached to a computer that emits a laser light that reads bar codes and inputs the coded numbers into the computer.

Bibliographic records – records that describe the nature of materials held in a library.

Bibliographic utility – a company or organization that provides bibliographic records as a service. OCLC, the Online Computer Library Center, is an example of an organization in which member libraries can access its bibliographic database (http://www.oclc.org).

Cat-5 cabling – Category 5 (now superseded by 5e) is the specification designated for twisted pair copper wiring that is guaranteed to handle frequencies up to 100 Mhz. Category 5 is able to transmit data up to 100 Mbits/sec (Megabits per second). Cat-5e, while still specified for 100 Mhz frequencies, is capable of gigabit (1000Mbits/sec) networks. Category 6 cabling is rated to guarantee 250 Mhz frequencies.

CD/ROM – compact disc read-only memory, is a disc to which data is written by laser technology. Such discs can be read-only, meaning they can only be written to once; read-once write many, meaning the discs can be written to repeatedly as long as there are unwritten sections of the disc available; read-write (CD-RW), meaning the discs can be written to repeatedly and the data can be overwritten. Popular as a form of data storage because the discs are relatively inexpensive, simple to use, and hold from 500–700 MB of data.

Client – a computer workstation that communicates with the server.

Client-Server Architecture – a computer network design characterized by a server ("host") that serves data and software functions to one or more client computer workstations. The structure differs from server to terminal structures in that the clients do some of the processing.

Cloud computing – a general term for services that are hosted through the Internet. Providers of the services manage the software, data, and maintenance of the system and then provide access to users on the basis of time accessed and amount of services used.

Collection agency – a module added on to Integrated Library Systems that allows a third-party agency to help retrieve delinquent materials with the added incentive of impacting credit reports when items remain unreturned or unpaid.

Courtesy notices – notification sent to the borrower that his/her materials are close to or beyond the due date or that materials they have requested are ready to be picked up at the library.

CPU (Central Processing Unit) – the part of a computer that executes the instructions in a software program.

Data server – In an Integrated Library System, the data server is the main hardware component from which the library tracks circulation and other transactions.

Data verifying software – software that helps libraries migrate their data from one system to another.

DMZ – "de-militarized zone", network ports that are designed to be accessible to the public on the outside of the firewall so the internal network remains more protected.

Dual core and Quad core – Core in this sense refers to the CPU (Central Processing Unit) of the computer, with dual core meaning there are two processors and quad meaning there are four.

DVD (Digital Video Disc) – an optical media format similar to CD-ROM, but is capable of storing up to ten times the amount of data. Like CD-ROM, discs are written by laser technology and can be either read-only or read-write.

E-commerce – functionality developed by "third party providers," which is added on to Integrated Library Systems that allow borrowers to pay for fines and fees, usually online, using a credit card.

Federated Searching – a system of multiple databases searching where a single search input retrieves and displays results from several discrete databases simultaneously.

Firewall – a networking hardware unit that scans and filters data and other transmissions coming into a network that insures greater network security. The firewall is capable of blocking designated kinds of traffic.

Focus groups – individuals brought together in a group to ascertain their opinions and comments about library services, materials, policies, long range plans, and so forth.

Gap file – the file of bibliographic records that is created between the time that records have been extracted for retrospective conversion and before the library "goes live" with the new Integrated Library System software.

Going Live – the term used for the first day in which the library utilizes the newly installed Integrated Library System software.

Holds – Materials that are reserved by library users to check out when the materials are returned by other borrowers or retrieved from the shelves by library staff.

Hosted – a type of arrangement with the ILS vendor in which the library purchases the automation software but the vendor hosts the software on its servers.

Integrated Library System – a software system that brings together all the library functions surrounding the creation and use of the borrower, item, and bibliographic databases. The various elements of the system work together to manage library processes and provide access to the resulting data through a unified interface.

Inventory – a process of a circulation system that creates a report of the library's holdings that tracks what should be on the shelf, what is known to be checked out, what can be otherwise accounted for, and what is missing.

ISBN – International Standard Book Number.

Justification statement – a succinctly worded statement that accompanies the budget. The statement clarifies the basis for the budget request.

LAN (Local Area Network) – a computer network that operates within a small enough geographic area that the services of telecommunication utilities are not needed.

Long Range Strategic Plan – a written plan of action that directs the library in accomplishing stated goals and outcomes over a specified length of time such a five, ten or more years.

MARC – MAchine Readable Record. The standard for describing materials developed for catalog records by the Library of Congress.

MARC21 – a standard further developed from the original MARC format that is followed by catalogers and vendors in the creation of bibliographic records.

Migration – the process of selecting a new ILS and then transferring library data from one ILS to another.

MIS Administrator – Management of Information Systems Administrator, the person responsible for overseeing all information systems, usually computer-based, in an organization.

Modules – elements of an Integrated Library System that automate specific library functions, such as circulation or cataloging.

MP3 – a patented format for encoding audio signals digitally. MP3 files are saved on computer storage devices.

Online Public Access Catalog (OPAC) – Library catalogs that are accessible through the Internet, or other networked system.

Open-Source Software – a participative network of software authors who openly share the creation of software so that the source code is freely available.

Operating System (OS) – is the foundation of all system software on the computer. It controls input and output devices, controls memory, manages files, and prioritizes commands.

Partitioned Router – a network device through which two or more networks can operate while being kept securely separate.

Patron database – a computerized collection of borrower information such as name, address, telephone number, e-mail address, date of birth, items checked out, fines, and so forth.

PC Reservation software – personal computer reservation software. This software allows library users to reserve time on the library's public computers.

Peripheral – a device that is externally attached to a computer workstation or server to perform specific input, output, storage or other functions, such as a printer, scanner, RFID antenna, camera, and so forth.

PLA – Public Library Association; http://www.pla.org

Print management software – software than manages print requests made by individuals using the library's public computers so that payment is made before print jobs are released.

RAID – Redundant Array of Independent Disks, a stack of multiple hard drives that allow data to be duplicated and backed up automatically to reduce data loss.

RAM – Random Access Memory, the array of switches in a computer within which software programs operate and information is processed in real time before being transmitted to storage devices.

Receipt printer – a printer attached to circulation computers that print a receipt for the borrower listing items checked out and the date those items are due.

Remote access – utilizing the library's Web-based or other resources outside of the library's physical building or space.

Request for Proposal – a document sent to companies notifying them of the library's interest in their products/services. Also known as an "RFP," the document gives detailed requirements to which the company responds. In most organizations, the RFP process follows specific, strict administrative procedures.

Reservation System – a software system that enables time management of public computers in libraries by authenticating users and timing their computer use in sessions.

Retrospective Conversion – the process of transferring one format of data into another format that will be used by a newer computer implementation.

RFID – Radio Frequency Identification, a system of tags that broadcast specified information such as bar codes that are received by antennas as input into an Integrated Library System.

RFP – see Request for Proposal.

Router – a network devices that manages network traffic, insuring that all the data packets are transmitted to the correct location.

SaaS – Software as a Service, an arrangement made with Integrated Library System vendors where the vendor hosts the library's data on their equipment to save the library hardware costs. The library uses their database through the Internet.

Self-Check – hardware and software provided for library customers so they can check out and/or check-in their own items.

SIP2 – Standard Interchange Protocol, version 2, a standardized method of authenticating users so that designated database elements can be accessed.

SLA – Special Libraries Association; http://www.sla.org

Stand-alone – a type of arrangement made between a library and Integrated Library System vendor where the library owns and operates the hardware necessary to run the ILS software.

Strategic Plan – see Long Range Strategic Plan.

Switch – a network device that connects servers, workstations, or other stations using cabling.

System Administrator – the library staff member responsible for operating and maintaining the ILS, who is also the library's liaison with the ILS vendor.

System capacity requirements – the hardware and software requirements for the Integrated Library System in order to properly manage and operate the library's patron database, bibliographic records, transactions and add-ons without any performance degradation or errors.

Technology Plan – a written plan covering goals and outcomes for technology-based services, hardware and software implementations, and employee training. This plan covers a limited span of time, normally only three to five years.

Telephone Notification System – a module added on to an Integrated Library System that enables library customers to be notified by telephone when their items are overdue or when items they have requested are available.

Thin Clients – a device with minimal computing capacity through which a user accesses software functions from a centralized host.

Third Party Software Providers – software developers who provide needed capabilities that are not part of the basic ILS software. Purchase of the third-party software may be made through the ILS vendor or by direct purchase from the third-party providers themselves.

Turnkey – a type of arrangement made between a library and an Integrated Library System vendor where the library owns the hardware necessary to run the ILS software, and the vendor provides sufficient support to minimize the computer expertise needed by the library.

UPC – Universal Product Code, the bar code number on dvds, music cd-roms, magazines, and other products used for commercial sale purposes.

UPS (Uninterrupted Power Supply) – a battery system to which computers and other devices are connected to insure consistent power to the computer. A UPS not only suppresses electrical surges, but also provides power to attached devices during power outages, allowing time for computers to be shut down more slowly with no crash, so that data is not corrupted.

USMARC – United States MARC standards, see MARC.

Vendor implementation plan – detailed project timeline with responsibilities, tasks, and deadlines for the successful installation of the Integrated Library System.

Virtual Machine – a server that can be partitioned so multiple discrete software systems and processes, including operating systems, can be operated independently through a single hardware unit.

Web 2.0 – Web-based tools that invite the user to interact with library's Web site and other library users, such as blogs, reviews, catalog tagging, and social network sites.

Web server – a computer from which an organization's Web site is operational.

Webinar – presentations or demonstrations that are conducted via the Internet and viewed on a workstation monitor or LCD projector.

WAN (Wide Area Network) – a geographically wide-spread network that requires telecommunications utilities or providers to transmit data among the servers and workstations.

Z39.50 – a standardized query language that is used to simultaneously search multiple different databases.

Selected Bibliography

Integrated Library Systems

Books

Bilal, Dania. *Automating Media Centers and Small Libraries: A Microcomputer-Based Approach*. Greenwood Village, CO: Libraries Unlimited, 2002.

Bolan, Kimberly. *Technology Made Simple*. Chicago: American Libraries Association, 2007.

Burke, John. *The Neal-Schuman Library Technology Companion*. New York: Neal-Schuman, 2006.

Cibbarelli, Pamela, ed. *Directory of Library Automation Software, Systems, and Services 2006–2007*. Medford, NJ: Information Today, Inc., 2006.

Cohn, John M., Ann L. Kelsey, and Keith Michael Fiels. *Planning for Integrated Systems and Technologies: A How-to-Do-It Manual for Librarians*. New York: Neal-Schuman Publishers, Inc., 2001.

Gordon, Rachel Singer. *The Accidental Systems Librarian*. Medford, NJ: Information Today, Inc., 2002.

Matthews, Joseph. *Library Information Systems: From Library to Distributed Information Access Solutions*. Englewood, CO: Libraries Unlimited, 2002.

Schultz-Jones, Barbara. *An Automation Primer for School Library Media Centers and Small Libraries*. Worthington, OH: Linworth Publishing, Inc., 2006.

Wilson, Katie. *Computers in Libraries: An Introduction for Library Technicians*. Binghamton, NY: Haworth Information Press, 2006.

Articles

Abram, Stephen. "It's about a respectful discussion." http://stephenslighthouse.com/?p=2745. Accessed October 30, 2009.

Breeding, Marshall. "Library Automation in a Difficult Economy." *Computers in Libraries*, March 2009, Vol. 29, Issue 3, pp. 22–24.

———. "Next Generation Library Automation: Its Impact on the Serials Community." *Serials Librarian*, January–June 2009, Vol. 56, Issues 1–4, pp. 55–64.

———. "The Elusive Cost of Library Software." *Computers in Libraries*, September 2009, Vol. 29, Issue 8, pp. 28–30.

———. "Opening Up Library Automation Software." *Computers in Libraries*, February 2009, Vol. 29, Issue 2, pp. 25–27.

————. "The Viability of Open Source ILS." *Bulletin of the American Society for Information Science & Technology*, December 2008, Vol. 35, Issue 2, pp. 20–25.

Dougherty, William C. "Managing Technology: Integrated Library Systems: Where Are They Going? Where Are We Going?" *Journal of Academic Librarianship*, September 2009, Vol. 35, Issue 5, pp. 482–485.

Hadro, Josh, ed. "OLE Project Gains Support of Kuali Foundation." *Library Journal*, December 15, 2009, Vol. 134, No. 20, p. 21. (Open-source alternative for research libraries.)

Kinner, Laura. "The Integrated Library System: From Daring to Dinosaur?" *Journal of Library Administration*, June 2009, Vol. 49, Issue 4, pp. 401–417.

Molyneux, Robert E. "Evergreen in Context." *Bulletin of the American Society for Information Science and Technology*, December 2008/January 2009, Vol. 35, No. 2.

O'Brien, Lynne. "Mellon Foundation Awards $2.3 Million for OLE Development." http://oleproject.org/2010/01/11/mellon-foundation-awards-2-3-million-for-ole-development. Accessed January 11, 2010.

Pace, Andrew. "OCLC Web-based Service Challenges ILS Vendors." *American Libraries*, June/July 2009, p. 38.

Pace, Andrew. "21st Century Library Systems." *Journal of Library Administration*, August 2009, Vol. 49, Issue 6, pp. 641–650.

Zhonghong, Wang. "Integrated Library System (ILS) Challenges and Opportunities: A Survey of U.S. Academic Libraries with Migration Projects." *Journal of Academic Librarianship*, May 2009, Vol. 35, Issue 3, pp. 207–220.

Strategic Planning

Books

Matthews, Joseph. *Scorecards for Results: A Guide for Developing a Library Balanced Scorecard.* Westport, CT: Libraries Unlimited, 2008.

————. *Strategic Planning and Management for Library Managers.* Westport, CT: Libraries Unlimited, 2005.

Nelson, Sandra. *Implementing for Results: Your Strategic Plan in Action.* Chicago: American Library Association, 2008.

Nelson, Sandra, for the Public Library Association. *Strategic Planning for Results.* Chicago: American Library Association, 2008.

Technology

Books

Bolan, Kimberly, and Robert Cullin. *Technology Made Simple: An Improvement Guide for Small and Medium Libraries.* Chicago: American Library Association, 2007.

Burke, John J. *Neal-Schuman Library Technology Companion: A Basic Guide for Library Staff, 3rd edition.* New York: Neal-Schuman Publishers, Inc., 2009.

Lowe, Doug. *Networking for Dummies.* Hoboken, NJ: Wiley Publishing, 2010.

Wilson, Kate. *Computers in Libraries: An Introduction for Library Technicians.* Binghampton, NY: Haworth Information Press, 2006.

Technology Planning

Books

Bolan, Kimberly, and Robert Cullin. *Technology Made Simple: An Improvement Guide for Small and Medium Libraries.* Chicago: American Library Association, 2007.

Gordon, Rachel Singer. *The Accidental Systems Librarian*. Medford, NJ: Information Today, Inc., 2002.

Matthews, Joseph R. *Technology Planning: Preparing and Updating a Library Technology Plan*. Westport, CT: Libraries Unlimited, 2004.

Web Sites

New Jersey State Library, Library Development Bureau, http://www.njstatelib.org/LDB/E-Rate/utechpln.php. Several links on technology planning and sample technology plans.

North Central Regional Education Laboratory, http://www.ncrel.org/sdrs/areas/issues/methods/technlgy/te300.htm. Web page on technology plans for public schools.

Techsoup.org, http://www.techsoup.org/learningcenter/techplan/index.cfm. Web page with article links on technology planning for nonprofits.

WebJunction, http://www.webjunction.org/techplan. Web page with links on creating and writing a technology plan.

Related Topics

Books

Anderson, Rick. *Buying and Contracting for Resources and Services: A How-to-Do-It Manual for Librarians*. New York: Neal-Schuman, 2004.

Articles

Abram, Stephen. "What is Cloud Computing?" http://stephenslighthouse.com/?p=2707. Accessed October 14, 2009.

Anderson, Rick, Jane White, and David Burke. "How to be a Good Customer: Building and Maintaining Productive Relationships with Vendors." *The Serials Librarian*, 2005, Vol. 48, Issue 3/4, pp. 321–326.

Bertot, John Carlo. "Public Access Technologies in Public Libraries: Effects and Implications." *Information Technology and Libraries*, June 2009, pp. 81–92.

Brevig, Armand. "Getting Value from Vendor Relationships." *Searcher*, October 2008, Vol. 16, Issue 9, pp. 28–34.

Brooks, Sam. "Introduction: The Importance of Open Communication Between Libraries and Vendors." *Library/Vendor Relationships*, 2006, Vol. 44, Issue 3/4, pp. 1–4.

Coe, George. "Managing Customer Relationships: A Book Vendor Point-of-View." *Library/Vendor Relationships*, 2006, Vol. 44, Issue 3/4, pp. 43–55.

Gagnon, Ronald A. "Library/Vendor Relations from a Public Library Perspective." *Library/Vendor Relationships*, 2006, Vol. 44, Issue 3/4, pp. 95–111.

Kantor-Horning, Susan. "Self-Service People." *Library Journal*, August 1, 2009, Vol. 134, Issue 13, pp. 16–19.

Robkin, Shai. "Managing Multivendor RFID Rollouts." *American Libraries*, November 2009, Vol. 40, Issue 11, pp. 44–47.

Shadle, Steve. "Electronic Resources in a Next-Generation Catalog: The Case of WorldCat Local." *Journal of Electronic Resources Librarianship*, 2009, Vol. 21, Issue 3/4, pp. 192–199.

Stanison, Christine. "What They Never Told You about Vendors in Library School." January–June 2009, Vol. 56, Issue 1–4, pp. 139–145.

Wakimoto, Jina Choi. "Scope of the Library Catalog in Times of Transition." *Cataloging & Classification Quarterly*, 2009, Vol. 47, Issue 5, pp. 409–426.

Web Sites

ALA TechSource. http://www.alatechsource.org. Contains information about current trends and discussions in library technology.

Boss, Richard W. "Negotiating Contracts with Integrated Library System Vendors." http://www. ala.org/ala/mgrps/divs/pla/plapublications/platechnotes/negotiatingils.cfm. Accessed November 24, 2009.

Library of Congress. "Understand MARC Bibliographic: Machine-Readable Cataloging." http:// www.loc.gov/marc/umb. Accessed November 9, 2009.

National Institute of Technology and Standards. "NITS Definition of Cloud Computing v.15." http://csrc.nist.gov/groups/SNS/cloud-computing/index.html. Accessed October 7, 2009.

Index

About the Authors

DESIREE WEBBER, MLIS, has worked in special, public, and state libraries. While employed with the Oklahoma Department of Libraries (ODL), she coauthored a library services and technology grant and assisted public and institution libraries in automating for the first time. She also consulted with libraries in writing their long-range plans and technology plans and was co-coordinator of the ODL computer-training lab. She is currently the director of the Mustang Public Library in Mustang, Oklahoma, where she manages the library's integrated library system.

ANDREW PETERS, MLS, has worked in academic and public libraries. He is the associate director for technology at the Pioneer Library System (PLS), a multicounty library system headquartered in Norman, Oklahoma. He has been the technology director for 25 years at PLS and has installed three generations of integrated library systems.